Around the World in Eighty Years

With Nothing By Chance

The international odyssey of an American doctor

Edwin W. Brown, M.D., M.P.H.

Proleptikos Press

Indianapolis, Indiana
proleptikos@aol.com

Copyright 2007 Edwin W. Brown

No part of this book may be reproduced, stored in a retrieval system, or transmitted by any means without the written permission of the author.

ISBN: 978-0-9794841-0-0 (hc)
ISBN: 978-0-9794841-1-7 (sc)

Cover illustration: Victoria and the Peak
A painting of Hong Kong in 1850 by an unknown artist
Used by permission of the Hong Kong Museum of Art

Printed in the United States of America

Dedication

To Pat, the wife of my youth -- still hanging in there 55 years later; sons Ted and Jack; daughter Wende; their spouses Carrie, Jan, and Jeff; grandchildren Andy, Kiersten, Kayla, Liz, Matt, and Stephen; and a host of friends world-wide – all of whom have brought so much joy to my life.

AROUND THE WORLD IN EIGHTY YEARS
....with nothing by chance

CONTENTS

Chapter:
1 - It must be in the genes p.8
2 - An early beginning and an early tragedy p.11
3 - When "fundamentalist" was an acceptable word in our society p.14
4 - Dennis the Menace p.17
5 - A rapid ascent on the academic ladder p.22
6 - Not your typical prep school p.26
7 - Three colleges and Army basic training -- all in less than a year p.29
8 - The winds of war – by now not much more than a breeze p.33
9 - Chasing the "front lines" p.37
10 - To the victor belongs the spoils p.41
11 - Battling boredom p.44
12 - 'Tis better to have loved and lost than never to have loved at all p.47
13 - Caring for a little lamb – who became a wolf in sheep's clothing p.50
14 - Flying on a wing and prayer p.52
15 - A mystery revealed p.56
16 - A short-lived beginning p.59
17 - Taking the cure p.62
18 - What fools these mortals be! p.65
19 - Reality check p.69
20 - Patience -- a virtue yet to be learned p.72
21 - Young Doctor Kildare p.75
22 - "The best-laid schemes o' mice and men..." p.79
23 - From southern Virginia to northern Greenland p.83
24 - Following the ghost of Robert E. Peary p.88
25 - Nanook of the North p.91
26 - Land of the midnight sun p.95
27 - "Westward, ho!" p.99
28 - Opportunity knocks – but which door to open? p.102
29 - Decisions, decisions again p.106
30 - "From Greenland's icy mountains to India's coral strands..." p.110
31 - India's coral strands? p.114
32 - Britain's jewel in the crown p.117
33 - A unique opportunity to exercise diplomatic privilege p.121
34 - A pleasant side-trip and further activities in India p.125
35 - Lo, the mighty hunter p.129   -

36 - 'merica, and a new career   p.133
37 - Afghanistan beckons   p.136
38 - The incautious ambassador   p.140
39 - Life in the fast lane – with a call from the White House   p.144
40 - Inside the Beltway and an interesting friendship   p.146
41 - Alice in Hoosierland   p.151
42 - The end of the gypsy life, with a sigh of relief from all   p.154
43 - A dream now to be realized   p.158
44 - Wheeling and dealing   p.162
45 - "And my God will meet all your needs ...."   p.168
46 - An ill omen   p.172
47 - The World Health Organization   p.176
48 - "Apocalypse Now"   p.179
49 - A temporary detour   p.183
50 - When prisoners take prisoners   p.187
51 - The search for David Zook   p.191
52 - In the footsteps of Lawrence of Arabia   p.194
53 - Hazards at home and on the road   p.198
54 - Life under the Saudi version of *shariah*   p.201
55 - A delinquent dean, a welcome change, and a strange interlude   p.204
56 - Rank hath its privilege   p.208
57 - "Vanity of vanities, saith the Preacher; all is vanity."   p.211
58 - Unorthodox use of official privilege   p.216
59 - Dealing with the Communists again   p.219
60 - The fall of the Wall and a fresh breeze from Moscow   p.223
61 - The CIA disconnection   p.227
62 - Extracurricular pursuits   p.230
63 - Into "retirement"   p.234
64 - The National Prayer Breakfast fellowship   p.239
65 - An unanticipated humanitarian adventure   p.242
66 - The Sudanese experience   p.246
67 - Another African assignment – with embarrassing results   p.249
68 - A further introduction to Eastern Europe   p.253
69 - Our family acquires another extension   p.257
70 - A change of focus   p.260
71 - New friends in Serb-occupied Bosnia-Herzogovina   p.264
72 - Thrilling developments in China   p.267
73 - Romania revisited – with God's marvelous provision   p.271
74 - A hobby that grew like Topsy   p.274
75 - Serendipity, thy name is golden   p.279
76 - And the beat goes on.....   p.283
77 - Quo vadis?   p.286

PREFACE

Why would other than friends and family want to read an autobiography of someone of whom they've never heard – and, moreover, what would lead such a person to suppose that a publisher might be interested in it? Only the reader can answer the first question, and the answer to the second is deprived of practical significance by reason of your now holding this book in your hands – and if you're in a bookstore at this moment and haven't yet purchased it, please do so. The publisher will sleep better when a few copies have been sold.

I confess that the first question long deterred me from putting pen to paper until I responded to Proverbs 19:13b* and decided to turn off the tap. Seriously, my longsuffering wife, Pat, and many friends for whom my tales had not yet become repetitious have long encouraged me to share my experiences with a larger audience. After much thought, it did seem useful to let others see how the vagaries of such a convoluted life's journey could have but one explanation—the quiet, persistent intervention of the One to whom life had been committed at an early age. And Pat already had a title for the book—*Not By Chance*. Just after my 80th birthday, however, I was blessed with the thought of a title that might better catch the viewer's attention – with apologies to Jules Verne.

(*..a nagging spouse is like a leaky faucet. [*The Message*])

As any motivational speaker will assert, "goals and objectives" are the *sine qua non* of a successful, rewarding life. Yet I cannot remember until very recently a time at which I personally gave any serious thought to setting goals and objectives for my life. Perhaps my mother's untimely death when I was eight years old had something to do with it, given all the uncertainties attendant upon such a tragedy. In any case, whatever personality quirk may have been responsible for this failure, my life has essentially been that of taking each day as it came – and, when an appealing opportunity presented itself, being quick to seize it. As the account herein reveals, my life has been one of constant flux – a continual moving on from one situation to another. (Could this be a form of what physicists call "Brownian motion"?).

I am not proud of the lack of purpose demonstrated in much of my life, but I am deeply grateful to my Lord and Savior, Jesus Christ, for the astonishing way in which he has carried me along in spite of my many shortcomings. June 2003 marked the 50th reunion of my Harvard Medical School class. One of my classmates had become dean of the school, and many others had held positions of distinction on its faculty and in other medical schools. Mine had been a much less illustrious career, but one that had carried me all over the world, in a variety of interesting and exciting pursuits. I share my life's journey with you in the hope that you, too, have experienced the joy that comes from a personal relationship with a loving Heavenly Father, whatever may be or have been your calling in life, made possible by the grace he freely offers to all who will accept it.

1 -- It must be in the genes

I'm convinced that the urge to travel to distant lands, however influenced by one's immediate circumstances, is genetically determined. Some of us are just born with it. And like other genetic traits, it may or may not skip one or more generations—nor is it necessarily common to all siblings in a given generation. My younger brother Dick, for example, has for virtually all of his 79 years resided in the same county where he was born. Except for a two-year Army tour that took him to Japan after World War II, he has been content to confine his travel to North America.

The earliest traceable beginnings of the Brown wanderlust are to be found in the history of great-great-great-great grandfather Henry Brown. Born in Ireland in 1733, he left the *auld sod* for the New World sometime prior to the American Revolution, settling in New York City. Potato famines having been a recurring factor in Irish emigrations in past centuries, perhaps it was the lure of magnificent spuds swimming in a great pot of Irish stew at the end of the rainbow that caused him to pack up and set sail for the Colonies. Whatever the reason, I am indebted to him for setting the pace.

With the onset of the American Revolution, he joined the Connecticut irregulars, serving for the entire seven years of the war. He then bought a farm in upstate New York and in 1803 sold it and headed west for greener pastures, homesteading in the Western Reserve of Connecticut near what is now Akron, Ohio. The annals of Ohio history record little of Henry, who died quietly in 1837 at the age of 104. However, these pastures proved green indeed for his two sons, James and Daniel, whose exploits are duly recorded in *Fifty Years and Over of Akron and Summit County*, by Ex-Sheriff Samuel A. Lane, published in 1892.

A highly successful business started by Jim in his early twenties and carried on with him as CEO for more than 40 years took the brothers as far west as California—and they came very close to expanding their business interests to the Far East in a remarkable venture that could have left their heirs on easy street for generations to come. They were, as fate would have it, the only ones in succeeding generations of Browns who were adept at making money – which, as the good ex-sheriff describes in considerable detail, was exactly what they did. His chapter on the Brown brothers is entitled, "The Counterfeiters of the Cuyahoga".

One's imagination runs rampant in contemplation of what might have been! Acquiring a large sailing vessel in the Port of New Orleans in 1837, Jim, his brother Dan, and several of the key executives of the firm equipped it with the tools of their trade, the output of which would enable them to purchase vast quantities of jade, silk, and other exotic goods in China, Japan, and India for resale at handsome profits in Europe and America. Indeed, given the relatively modest cost of producing the wherewithal with which they would purchase these Oriental treasures, their profit margin would have been enormous. (Had the venture succeeded, it would have provided an interesting contrast to the "Made in Japan" epithet that was to characterize shoddy pre-war Japanese goods sold in America a hundred years later – the Japanese might have used "Made in America" to describe the shoddy American currency with which they found themselves.)

Unfortunately, this magnificent scheme came to naught—and the two brothers found themselves in the local lockup on the very morning they were to set sail. Their free-spending celebration in a harbor tavern on the eve of departure had caught the attention of the local gendarmerie. Suspecting either piracy or smuggling (two of the more profitable pursuits of the day) as the source of their largesse, the authorities boarded the ship in the wee hours, just before it was to have sailed on the outgoing tide.

To their surprise, instead of evidence of engagement in such commonplace pursuits, they found $1.5 million in freshly-printed currency—and enough printing equipment, paper and ink (as well as a passenger list including master printers and engravers) to enable the lads to cope with the boredom of the long outward voyage by adding another $2 million to their hoard of cash. Having already gained some twenty years' experience in reproducing the coinage and currency of some of the best banks in the country prior to the Federal government getting into the money-printing business, great-x-3 grandfather Jim Brown and uncle Dan were highly-qualified to undertake their venture of a lifetime—and were it not for that foolish indiscretion they would doubtless have succeeded.

But all's well that ends even not so well, and the perpetrators were released when the counterfeit plates to have been used in evidence against them mysteriously disappeared from the sheriff's office the night before the trial was to begin. The urge to travel remained strong, however, and in 1850 they joined the westward migration to California to seek their fortunes in the newly-discovered gold fields — not by digging for the stuff, but by offering freshly-printed currency for gold dust and nuggets. They were thus well-received, for at that time no paper money was in circulation in the area, and large quantities of coins received in payment for gold were too heavy to carry about and too difficult to conceal from predators. And lest they encounter fellow Buckeyes who might associate the name Brown with the counterfeiters of the Cuyahoga, they assumed the ingenuous surname West.

When their customers sent some of the bogus Brown bills home to their families in the east, however, the fraud came to light, and the brothers had to beat a hasty retreat. The only immediate means of transport was a ship bound for South America, which they summarily boarded, loot in hand. (They seem not to have learned that ocean voyages could be hazardous to one's health.) Pursued by a posse of vigilantes aboard another vessel, they abandoned ship when it reached the Isthmus of Panama, and headed for the Atlantic coast. Sadly, their journey through the jungles of Panama proved deadly for brother Dan, who contracted yellow fever and died shortly after reaching home. Jim, however, made it back in good health, but what happened to all that gold remains a mystery to this day. Certainly the proceeds never filtered down to later generations of the Brown family.

Jim lived to the ripe old age of 75, literally dying with his boots on when he slipped and fell while leaping from one boat to another on the old Ohio canal while being pursued by Federal agents. (He still hadn't got it in his head that traveling by sea was to be avoided.) His was a long and inglorious career – over 50 years devoted to perfecting the art of money making. Yet he did have one claim to fame of a far more respectable kind– a presidential pardon for humanitarian services rendered during an early period of imprisonment.

In 1846, Jim Brown was sentenced to 10 years in the Federal prison at Chillicothe, Ohio, for counterfeiting U.S. coinage. His conduct in prison was exemplary, and he was eventually put in charge of the prison hospital. When cholera broke out in the prison in 1849, his extraordinary efforts in mobilizing his fellow convicts in the care of the afflicted prisoners, many of whom thus survived the epidemic, won him a pardon from President Zachary Taylor (the original of which is to be seen in the National Archives, and a photocopy of which hangs over my desk). But as we've seen, he again succumbed to the urge to travel, heading for California only a year later.

2 -- An early beginning and an early tragedy

The travels of Jim and Dan Brown were a hard act to follow, and with the exception of grandfather Brown's military service in Cuba in the Spanish-American war, three generations were to pass before fate decreed that I should take up the gauntlet. My own travels began with what is my earliest memory—a train trip in 1927 from my Youngstown, Ohio, birthplace to my father's new place of employment in Buffalo, New York. As I was only a year old at the time, the memory is sketchy but distinct. For the next sixteen years, however, my travel was to be limited to the annual summer excursion from our home in the Buffalo, New York, suburb of Williamsville to my grandparents' home in Akron, Ohio.

Visiting grandfather Brown was the highlight of the year. He was a master story-teller, who regaled us with the exploits of those memorable forbears who forever earned a place in the annals of Ohio history. He himself left his mark on the history of Akron, Ohio. Nothing as dramatic as the earlier Brown brothers, to be sure – but Daniel Webster Brown (known as "Web" in his adult years) was, to use the appellation made famous by *Readers Digest*, "the most unforgettable character I've ever met".

At 18, he was the youngest Sergeant Major in the Ohio militia, with whom he fought in Cuba in the Spanish-American war. He later became advertising manager for the Republic Rubber Company of Youngstown, Ohio, from where his interest in drawing then took him to Akron, where he served as political cartoonist for the *Akron Beacon-Journal* for 46 years. Retiring at the age of 75, he took up painting, in the genre of the Grandma Moses school, and died quietly at the age of 99.

On one such holiday, however, real tragedy befell our family. In the early summer of 1934, while vacationing at grandfather's home, our young mother Doris slipped on the front porch stairs while dashing out of the house to retrieve 2-year-old brother David from a mud puddle in which he was wallowing. Though painful, the severe abrasion she sustained on her leg did not keep her from traveling home a few days later. Soon thereafter, however, the wound became infected, and within a week of this seemingly minor injury, our beloved mother died of septicemia at the age of 32, leaving a young father of 34 and his 3 small boys, ages 2, 6, and 8.

Unable to care for three small boys on his own, Dad accepted his in-laws' invitation to have Dick and me live with them in Buffalo – to my delight, for I adored my maternal grandmother. One of the church families had already taken in David, so Dad sold the house and moved in with us.

Pearl Washburn McClellan was the epitome of a loving grandmother, idolized by her grandchildren. Harrison Benjamin McClellan, on the other hand, was pretty much the antithesis of Grandma. Not a mean old codger by any means, but generally a grump – although it was not until many years later that I was to learn the cause of his chronic complaints. (I never found out why his parents reversed the names of the president after whom he was named – but I always thought it was cool to have two grandfathers named after famous Americans.)

Harry was an unforgettable character in his own right – but he never talked about himself or his family, so it was not until reading his obituary in 1947 that I learned that he had played with John Philip Sousa's band, and was distantly related to the Civil War general, George B. McClellan. His other claims to fame, modest though they were, were two. One, the McClellan Music House, founded in 1910, was the foremost purveyor of band and orchestra instruments in Buffalo, New York, for the first half of the 20th century – and the reason my father and mother moved from Youngstown, Ohio, in 1927, when her father offered my father a job as salesman. Selmer and Conn were the two great makers of woodwinds and brass in those days, but with the wartime shortage of brass resulting in cessation of production of most musical instruments during that period, the family business was sold off soon after the war.

His other claim to fame – of which I learned many years later while in medical school—was having been a victim of the 1933 Chicago World's Fair outbreak of amoebic dysentery, with 1700 cases and 98 deaths, the result of defective plumbing in one hotel where many of the visitors stayed, which permitted sewage to contaminate the drinking water supply.

Grandpa's amoebic infection was never cured, and eventually ended up as a liver abscess that finally led to his demise. The operative word around the McClellan household was Grandpa's "bowels", and on the kitchen counter his stock of therapeutic pills, powders, and potions were lined up like soldiers at the ready. I was particularly fascinated by his favorite standby, *Serutan*, a laxative favored in those days. I discovered (being then and yet today a great reader of labels, cereal boxes, and other such erudite examples of American literature) that this was "Nature's" spelled backwards (less, of course, the possessive apostrophe, which the genius who came up with that trademark couldn't quite fit into it).

Grandpa spent a lot of time in that kitchen at 83 Frontenac Avenue in Buffalo, not only to be within ready reach of any medicament he might require, but also because it was the only place in the house in which Grandma would allow him to indulge himself in his favorite snack – Limburger cheese. One doesn't see much Limburger cheese among the vast offerings of today's supermarkets, but back in the '20s and '30s of my recollection, he had no difficulty finding it – possibly because he was the only customer for the smelly stuff, of which one merchant in town kept a supply on hand just for him. In any case, when we would return from shopping (that wonderful weekly excursion to retail establishments offering a panoply of delights for a young lad), the ritual consumption of that fetid foodstuff would begin with Grandma shooing us kids out of the kitchen and closing all doors leading thereto, as Grandpa sat down at the kitchen table and began to unwrap his treasure.

Grandma loved to cook, and her pies were the highlight of any meal – although she was unable to enjoy them because she was a diabetic. One can never forget the ultimate compliment that Grandpa routinely paid her for her culinary artistry. It was always the same routine: "Well, Harry, how do you like the pie?" And then those endearing words: "I'm eatin' it, aren't I?"

Grandpa was an ardent Republican, and with Roosevelt in office during those halcyon days with our grandparents, there was always plenty of grist for the mill from whence came a steady commentary on the deplorable state of the union. Of course, this was also the height of the Great Depression, which had a none-too-salutary effect on both his business and his bowels. As for the news reporting of the day, cynicism was Grandpa's stock in trade. Among my fondest memories was being invited in 1937 (by which time my father had remarried) to accompany these grandparents and their unmarried (from time to time) daughter (who for years served as their chauffeur) on a trip to North Carolina – the first of my major travel adventures. One morning while there, the blaring headlines of the paper delivered to our guesthouse in Weaverville declared: AMELIA EARHART MISSING OVER PACIFIC. Without bothering to read the article, Grandpa immediately assessed the matter: "Damned publicity stunt!" I'm not sure he ever accepted the fact that she had really gone missing.

3 – When "fundamentalist" was an acceptable word in our society

Regrettably, life at their house was not to last long. Taking in a young widower and his three small boys was a generous act indeed, and in spite of the somewhat crowded conditions, we all got along famously – or so I thought. What escaped my young eyes and ears was the play that my mother's younger sister, Margaret, was making toward my father. It was, however, an unrequited love, for my father had no interest in her whatever. She had been married at 16, divorced at 17, and at the time had a series of male friends of questionable character.

As I was to learn later, he had discussed the matter with the pastor of our church in Williamsville (which we continued to attend faithfully after my mother died), and a plan was worked out to offer refuge if and when the situation became intolerable for him. That day arrived in February 1935, when he came home from work as usual, got into an argument with Margaret, and abruptly ordered us to grab our pajamas and toothbrushes and get into the car. Totally bewildered, we were driven to Williamsville, where Dick and I were deposited at the parsonage. With baby brother David at the Lechners, and our dad having been offered a spare bedroom by church friends, the Fidingers, we were again together in Williamsville.

Needless to say, this was a rude dislocation as far as I was concerned, for I found myself no longer under the daytime authority of a grandmother who spoiled me rotten, but under the oft cold discipline of a fundamentalist Baptist preacher's wife, who had three kids of her own to manage as well. I became the bedfellow of their older son Milburn (two years older than I), and Dick the bedfellow of the younger son Ralph (a year younger than he). Their daughter Marian, who was about my age, had a room of her own. (Although I had already developed a considerable affection for a succession of young ladies in the first, second, and third grades, this one was not among them, so I had no objection to sharing the bedroom of the older son rather than that of his younger sister.)

My parents, like their parents, were not regular churchgoers, so when my mother accepted the invitation of a neighbor, Faye Hilgeman, to visit her church in Williamsville (the Helen M. Randall Memorial Baptist Church) when I was five, this was a unique experience for us – a church home that was to be mine for the next 12 years, until I joined the Army in 1943, and for my brother Dick for a lifetime!

Like so many people in this world of ours, my parents were fine, loving, moral human beings attempting to bring up their children to be fine, moral, loving human beings. They lacked only one thing – a personal relationship with Jesus Christ. Soon after beginning to attend the Baptist church, they were invited to a Keswick conference in nearby Canada – a gathering of Christians and those seeking to know more about Christianity, modeled after the famous conferences held each summer in the town of Keswick in the Lake District of England. Here they committed their lives to Christ as their Lord and Savior.

Returning home, they tried to explain this vital change in their lives to their five-year-old. I doubt that much of it sunk in, but I did notice one significant change. My favorite time of day was about 6:00 each evening, when I was always at the front window awaiting my father's return from work. Few things delighted me more than to see him drive in, derby hat on his head and smoking a cigar. Then something changed radically – the derby was still there but the cigar had disappeared. (However one might regard the Baptist proscription of such things as movies, dancing, card playing, the use of alcohol, and smoking, the prohibition of smoking was eventually vindicated by medical science.)

I would be terribly remiss if I failed to mention the outpouring of love that Baptist congregation showed to that young widower and two motherless boys – a love that continued long after my father married a schoolteacher in the congregation some three years after my mother's death. I am deeply indebted to such men as Howard Lindow, Harry Brooks, and my father, who taught our Sunday School class at various times; and to others such as Aubrey Noble, an Englishman who constantly reminded me to "throw my shoulders back and stand straight"; Harris Harvey, whose depth of knowledge of the Bible was always an inspiration; Florence and Louise Lindow, at whose home we were always welcome when we wandered down the street from the parsonage; and the many others who showed how much they cared for me, my brothers, and our father.

I have many other fond memories of those early years – and of that particular house at 142 Garrison Road in Williamsville, New York, where we were living when I was five. The most notable was the day I decided to play postman. I was intrigued by a box uncovered one day in the front closet, behind the hanging coats. It was full of bundles of envelopes, wrapped in ribbons, each one bearing the black Special Delivery stamp used in those days. On that notable day, I took one of these bundles and set forth down the street, carefully placing one of the letters in each of the mail slots in the front doors of the houses along our block. Proud of my work, I returned home, soon thereafter to be questioned by my lovely young mother as to where I had wandered when she had come looking for me. I was disappointed that she appeared less than thrilled – apoplectic would probably be a more suitable descriptive – when I told her of my delightful adventure. I never knew how many of those letters were read by their recipients before she was able to retrieve them.

I noted earlier my interest in a succession of certain young ladies in my early years. One of these was a lovely creature with the equally lovely name of Natalie, with whom I fell madly in love in the second grade. We had by that time moved to one of the many different houses in which we lived in Williamsville during those years (the reason for which I shall mention shortly), and were now at number 96 Highland Drive, next door to my good friend, Bobby Senior. One afternoon I overheard a conversation between my mother and Bobby's which devastated me. I was not aware that Natalie had been an overnight visitor at the Seniors until this over-the-back-fence *tête-à-tête* revealed the awful truth. Would that I could have known such bliss.

The following year, now at 44 Rinewalt Street, having only had the pleasure of Natalie's presence while at school, I decided one day to seek her out at home. I consulted the phone book, finding two listings under the name "Fretts". One was on a street I didn't recognize, but the other was on Main Street, which I could access only two blocks from our house. For reason unknown I grabbed my little red wagon, went up to Main Street, found that the number at our corner was much higher than that in the phone book, and headed downstream. It must have been close to a mile when I at last came to the desired number – only to find to my dismay that it was the office of her father's surveying company. It was a long and lonely walk home.

Some time later, however, fate smiled upon me. I was seated on a rock across the street from our school, watching two boys playing marbles. To my utter amazement and joy, who should wander by and sit down on the adjoining rock but my beloved! Croaking out a weak, "Hi!", I pondered long the situation, but at last made my move. I leaned over, kissed her on the cheek – and hightailed it out of there, lest she respond with something less than affection. When it came to establishing a meaningful relationship with a girl, I was a sniveling, weak-livered coward.

4 -- Dennis the Menace

Under the careful instruction of the pastor and several Sunday School teachers, I made a firm profession of faith in Jesus Christ at age 12 – a faith that has continued to sustain me. But living in the parsonage with the preacher was not one of the happiest periods of my life. We were loved, to be sure, but somehow their own children always seemed to be somewhat more privileged than were we two foster children.

Given the restrictions imposed in a Fundamental Baptist preacher's home, it was difficult to avoid getting into trouble. I had no particular problem with such forbidden pursuits as movies (having no spending money anyway) and dancing (only high school kids went to dances in those days), but the Baptist prohibition against card games using those evil spade-club-heart-diamond gambling tools was my downfall. (Card games such as Rook were okay – Baptist bridge, some called it.) Soon after our arrival at the parsonage, I found that one of my prized possessions had gone missing. In the early 1930s, card collecting was limited to playing cards, the bubble gum people having not yet introduced the baseball and other card craze that was soon to sweep the country. Collecting playing cards involved getting ones with as many different pictures or designs on their backs as one could trade for. Grandma McClellan's favorite pastime was solitaire, and she kept several different decks of cards on hand. Favored by a gift of just one of these decks, I had an instant trading capacity of 54 cards (including the jokers). By the time we moved to the parsonage, I had an impressive collection, which soon went missing.

Arriving home from school one cold day in February, I was solemnly greeted by Mrs. Keen, who summoned me upstairs, and withdrew from the drawer of her sewing table my beautiful collection. Ecstatic with joy, I exclaimed, "Oh, you found my cards!" Instead of "Yes, dear!", and pressing them into my hot little hands, her response was a stern "Come with me!" I was led down the stairs, into the living room, and up to the fireplace, its logs ablaze. One by one she handed me the cards to toss into the flames. I don't think I ever forgave her for such excruciating torture.

I was often confined to my room after school for various and sundry infractions of the rules. On one such occasion, observing a neighbor girl for whom I had a particular dislike walking by below, I quietly raised the window, poked the barrel of my trusty BB gun through one of the three ventilation holes in the storm sash, and fired off a round. It was a perfect shot – right at her little *derrière*. The abrupt yelp was music to my ears, and she hadn't a clue as to what bit her.

The BB gun was a Christmas present from my father, who unfortunately failed to include with it a lecture on gun safety – an inappropriate gift for a 9-year-old in any event. I nearly lost an eye soon thereafter when I fired at an old bass drum at the other end of the basement and instantly felt the sting of the ricocheted pellet against the bony edge of my eye socket. Some time later, while visiting the Lechners at the other end of the village, who had taken in my infant brother, I made a more serious error in judgment. Their 10-year-old daughter Norma had often referred to the neighbor two doors down the street as a mean old man, and so on this occasion I brought the gun with me, having conceived a plan of retribution. From the confines of the Lechner chicken coop I had a direct line of sight to the window in the door of that neighbor's chicken coop. It was a no-brainer shot, but unaware that the owner was in his chicken coop at the moment, I was spotted running back into the house. It was several years before I was again allowed to have a BB gun.

But life in those days was not without its memorable pleasures. I had now abruptly moved from P.S. 66 in Buffalo to the third grade of the Williamsville Elementary School, but the trauma of the move was decidedly mitigated some months later, when I entered the fourth grade – and learned that my father had for some time been "courting" Harriet Trago, a member of our church and the older sister of my teacher, Annette Trago. The special position I occupied in the life of the lovely Annette (whose beauty I fully appreciated even at the tender age of nine) flowered (from my perspective, at least) when at midyear she became my aunt. Sad to say, I confess to having taken advantage in numerous ways of that special relationship – but somehow she put up with me with considerable grace, and it was overall a happy experience for both of us. I adored my Aunt Annette.

Life in a Baptist preacher's household was interesting, to say the least. The Reverend Clarence M. Keen was an imposing man – and, as I look back on it – an impressive preacher. One of the more memorable dinner-table conversations included some of his observations on the deplorable state of undress exhibited in those days on the public beaches. (Bear in mind that this was 1935.) Taking in hand a box of kitchen matches, he lamented, "It won't be long before you could put a woman's bathing suit in this box. Why, the way they're going, they'll be wearing nothing but a jock strap one of these days!" (Later that evening I had to ask Milburn, that older source of all knowledge and wisdom, what a jock strap was – and found the idea rather intriguing. Pastor Keen didn't live long enough, however, to see how accurate were both his predictions. I doubt that he could have truly envisaged the string bikinis of Ipanema Beach in Rio or the topless beaches now to be found over much of the world.)

The village of Williamsville has inevitably changed from what it was when we first moved there from Buffalo in 1930, but most of the Williamsville I knew is still remarkably the same. For reasons not entirely clear to me, but certainly having something to do with the depression (although my father had a steady job in my grandfather's music store), we moved frequently from house to house in the village during the 1930s. All those houses are still there today, and all of them were (and still are) rather decent homes, occupied by solid middle-class families. For us, however, they were always rental houses, so I must assume that problems with the landlords accounted for the frequent moves -- six different houses in less than seven years, all within not much more than a quarter of a mile of each other. The only reference I can recall to displeasure with a landlord occurred when I was about seven, when I heard my father say to my mother, "That landlord is nothing but a big windbag!" I pondered that comment long and hard, picturing an inflated paper bag and wondering what a landlord was.

When I was in kindergarten, we met in a commercial building in the center of the village (later a supermarket and more recently a funeral home). Midway during the year, however, the teacher informed us that we would be moving to a brand new elementary school at the other end of the village. This was such an exciting prospect that I insisted my father take me to the new school on that glorious morning before anyone else would arrive, so that I could be the first one in the new kindergarten room. I had already become the favorite of my teacher, Miss Meugel, and I deemed it essential to be waiting eagerly at the door when she arrived to unlock it – and I was. Prior to falling hopelessly in love with my Aunt Annette in the fourth grade, I had gone through the same idyllic phase with regard to Iris Meugle.

Calling on her in Williamsville recently when I learned she was still alive, I introduced myself as Buster Brown who was once her pupil (a nickname acquired at birth and by which I am still known – thankfully – only in Williamsville.) "Of course, I remember you!", she replied – and for the next half hour we had a most delightful conversation, including a startling revelation: "I remember when you came up to me one day and asked, 'Do you know why I ask so many questions, Miss Muegel?' " "No, Buster – why do you ask me so many questions?" "Miss Muegel, it's because I want to know everything about everything!" How far the would-be mighty inquirer has fallen!

Following my father's remarriage in the summer of 1937, we moved into the first home of our own, no longer subject to the vagaries of discontented landlords. It was (for us boys) a grand house, on a large lot in a new residential community in open country four miles east of Williamsville, called Harris Hill Gardens. (I used to wonder where it got that name, there being nothing but flatlands all around, and no gardens apparent.) There we were to remain until I went off to college six years later.

As noted earlier, my father sold band instruments for my grandfather. In order to attract customers, the latter had developed an extensive rental business through high school music departments – the only such in the whole of western New York state. For a modest rental fee the students could try out any instrument until they were sure of their choice before investing in a purchase. Dad was thus on the road much of the time, traveling from school to school with his wares. My greatest delight was being allowed to accompany him from time to time, particularly to band contests that drew bands from surrounding high schools. There he would set up a display, which included the sale of enameled pins—replicas of the various instruments— the sale of which I was allowed to handle.

I particularly cherished these times with my father. My stepmother Harriet had taken on an enormous responsibility in assuming the care of three little boys, the oldest of whom frequently tried her patience, as did the youngest, David, who always sought to emulate his oldest brother. Dick, the middle one, played it cool by being less obvious in his derelictions and thus usually escaped punishment. (He was such a *good* boy!) Being just a little fellow, Dave got off easily, but as the one who "should have known how to behave", I was frequently banished to my room or made to stand in the corner facing the wall – a form of punishment used by Harriet during her many years as a second-grade teacher. I thus always looked forward to my father's homecoming in the evening, as I had as a little boy, and when he would phone to say that he had gone farther away than planned that morning and would be staying overnight, it was always sad news.

Halloween was a major event in those days, with seemingly harmless pranks (which today would not seem so harmless) such as marking windows with bars of soap (or, worse, using a piece of wax), sticking pins in doorbells to keep them ringing, and generally making a nuisance of oneself. One Halloween was particularly eventful, resulting in a near tragedy. Dick and I had run across the main highway with a bunch of our fellow miscreants to soap the windows of the gas station, and as we darted back across the street in front of an oncoming car there was a screech of brakes. The man and wife leaped out of the car, the woman screaming as they ran not toward us but toward what appeared to be a bundle of rags on the road in front of the car. It was not rags, however, but little brother Dick who had apparently lagged behind and was now lying in pain in the road. Fortunately, there was a phone booth at the gas station, and an ambulance soon arrived, leaving me to run home and tell our parents what had happened while the driver of the car followed the ambulance to the hospital in the city. The next few hours were tense ones, but aside from some nasty bruises and a broken collar bone, he survived what could have been major injuries or death.

Younger brother Dave had also had a narrow escape from serious injury when left in my care one day while Mom, Dad, and baby Paul were in town, and Dick was at a friend's house. I decided (unwisely) that he could be left alone and went off to see my friend Wayland Johnson, who lived about a mile away. Upon my return I was shocked to see the local fire truck just leaving, and a neighbor consoling the crying little boy with minor burns on his hands. Finding a can of paint remover in the garage, he had decided to test it for flammability – by pouring a large puddle of it in the middle of the garage and lighting it with a match. How he escaped being seriously burned as the stuff became a roaring inferno I knew not, but the evidence of the intensity of the blaze could clearly be seen in the blackened rafters of the garage and the smoke throughout the upper level of the house.

The neighbor had heard his screams, phoned the fire department, and then used our garden hose to douse as much of the flames as he could before the firemen arrived. Our parents arrived shortly after I did, and I immediately told them what had happened. As Mom looked at the charred timbers I was appalled to hear her shout to Dad, "Oh, Ed, look what that boy has done!" Only then did she turn her attention to the poor little kid and minister to his wounds. Needless to say, I was aware that I was the real culprit.

5 – A rapid ascent on the academic ladder

The Harris Hill School was a two-room schoolhouse, with four grades in each room. My fifth grade class was a single row of 7 or 8 desks along the window, with three rows of equal length to the right for the other three grades. Stella Steinhoff, who was both teacher and principal, would begin each day instructing the fifth grade for 45 minutes or so, give us a great pile of "homework" intended to more than occupy us for the next 3 hours, and then move on to the sixth grade row. With recess and lunch hour intervening, she thus covered each grade twice a day.

The homework assignment seemed to be geared to the abilities of the least capable, so I invariably finished mine in short order, devoted the remainder of the time to "art work", using drawing paper supplied for art classes. (I have no memory, however, of our ever having had art as a subject.) The comic strip most favored by us lads was "Buck Rogers – 25th Century A.D.", and my great friend Wayland Johnson and I competed vigorously to see who could design the finest space fleet. I don't recall that any of our vessels or rocketry resembled what was to go into space less than 50 years later, but Wayland (who had shared with me the secret that this was his middle name, his first being Homer and an embarrassment to him) was clearly the better artist. Recently retired from a lifelong career on the faculty of the Pennsylvania Academy of Art in Philadelphia, Homer W. Johnson made his mark in the art world, while my later artistic efforts were limited to drawing a salary.

Of course, this prolific output of artwork eventually made its way home, to the increasing annoyance of my ex-school teacher stepmother. Appalled that I should be thus wasting so much of my time in school, she went to Mrs. Steinhoff in midyear and asked that I be put in the sixth grade, so as not to have all that time to waste. Mrs. Steinhoff concurred, and the next day I moved to the next row.

It's difficult, of course, to completely ignore what's going on in the next row even when one is engrossed in doing his homework and designing his space fleet, so sixth grade proved not much more demanding than fifth grade. Though my artistic efforts were temporarily curtailed by my advanced placement, by the end of the year the output of artwork had regained its former level of production. Again, my stepmother complained to the principal, who in turn suggested that I skip the seventh grade and go directly into the eighth grade that September. Fearing that I would not fit well into the cultural milieu of kids that age, Mom declined the offer, and my rapid rise on the academic ladder came to an abrupt halt.

With continuing expansion of the local community, the Harris Hill School underwent a radical change in the fall of 1938, when the two basement rooms were turned into classrooms, and two new teachers were added to the staff. The new teacher for the eighth grade, Howard McLernon (a young Irish-American who quickly demonstrated his Irish temper) was also named principal. At the first session, he announced that he would take roll by calling out our last names, to which we would respond with our first names – the immediate repercussion of which was to make me wish my parents had been more thoughtful. When he came to "Brown", I dutifully replied, "Buster". At this, his face flushed, and his voice rose to about 100 decibels. Shaking his finger at me, he shouted, "I've heard about you, you smart aleck! Don't you ever answer me again like that!" My classmates were as dumbfounded as I, and one in the front row quickly responded feebly with "But that's his name, Mr. McLernon!"

Many years later, while visiting the Buffalo area, I called upon Howard McLernon, now the principal of a large high school in an adjoining city. Not only did he receive me with great warmth, but astounded me with his knowledge of my achievements in the previous 20 years. I must not have been such a rotten kid as he at first supposed me to be—but, as I've noted, they still call me Buster in those parts.

Graduation from the Harris Hill School in 1939 was to be, I dreamed, a memorable event for quite a different reason. My father, who had promised me a new suit for the occasion, took me to Bieber-Isaacs, next door to Grandfather's music store in Buffalo, where the large sign in the window proclaimed the offering of such attire "from $4.95 up". When he magnanimously decided to spring for a $5.95 model with two pair of pants, I was elated. At this stage in my life, many of my classmates of the male persuasion were wearing long trousers, whereas I, the youngest kid in the class, was still in knickers. (Should any of my British friends be reading this, knickers were male outer leg wear that fastened just below the knee – not female undergarments!) At last, I was to graduate into (and in) long pants! You can imagine the shock when I learned that the $5.95 two-pants suit comprised a pair of short pants and a pair of knickers. Not until I entered high school that fall did I acquire my first pair of long pants.

Parker High School was four miles from our house, in the village of Clarence, New York. Williamsville High School was four miles in the other direction. My preference was clearly for the latter, which was much larger and attended by my best buddy in our church in Williamsville, Don Weimer. However, Harris Hill Gardens was just inside the Clarence school district, so Parker High School became my academic home. Here there were 50 in my class, compared to less than one-third that number in grade school.

Don was always a storehouse of information about our church and its members, gleaned from overhearing conversations between his mother and others – including such choice tidbits as the fact that the full head of hair sported by old Mr. Fry, who was sitting in front of us one day, was in fact not his own. Thereafter, I always made it a point to sit behind Mr. Fry whenever possible, that I might more carefully study that fascinating bit of hirsute splendor. It seems that this bit of intelligence was acquired by Mrs. Weimer when she called upon the Frys one day and caught him with his hair down.

It was a long walk from our house to the main highway where we were picked up and dropped off by the school bus, and from time to time I missed the bus. Hitching a ride from a passing motorist was then the only way to get to school, but on one very cold day no ride was forthcoming, walking was out of the question, and I was forced to return home – with ice-coated ears. With mother's gentle ministrations, the ears were slowly warmed, and I was allowed to remain home, but to this day my ears are unduly sensitive to cold.

On less threatening days, a missed bus often required considerable walking between rides, most of the motorists of that day seeming oblivious to the pressing need of a young lad to get to school. Getting rides in late afternoon was even more difficult, for which reason I rarely participated in after-school activities. Sports were the primary of these, and skinny little kid that I was, I could never compete anyhow. I did, however, manage to acquire a "letter" in one intervarsity sport during my senior year, thus vindicating myself in that area of academic accomplishment. It was in tennis, but the only reason I made the team is that the coach desperately needed two more players to complete the team, and Wayland Johnson and I were the only remaining applicants. I recall participating in only one match with another school, and it was a total disaster, Wayland being as inept at the game as I.

My greatest frustration in high school was girls – and my inability to invite one on a date because of lack of transportation. None of my friends had a car of his own, and in any case, my strict Baptist upbringing prevented my attending either of the two usual venues – movies and school dances. Our church attempted to provide alternatives, but this was of little help to me, having no romantic inclinations toward any of the lasses at our church – and it was four miles in the other direction to boot. Once a day a Greyhound bus ran between Harris Hill Gardens and Williamsville, but it was rarely available at needed times. Hitch-hiking was the only alternative to visiting friends in Williamsville, and rides were as scarce as those in the other direction. I vowed that when I eventually acquired a car I would never pass up a hitch-hiker – and until our society changed to the point that picking up strangers except under very special circumstances became foolhardy, I kept that vow.

Winter was the worst time to be hitch-hiking, when the cold winds blew eastward off Lake Erie, inundating the greater Buffalo area with snow that turned the landscape into a model of Siberia. It was not unusual to walk through alleys of snow made by the stuff having been shoveled higher than one's head. On the other hand, with the stuff lying about most of the winter, the streets in our neighborhood were great for sledding, and we thought nothing of sneaking up behind a slow-moving car and grabbing hold of the rear bumper for a joy ride – and being tossed off violently when the car picked up speed and turned a corner.

Summer brought its own hazards as well – especially on the Fourth of July. There were no restrictions on the sale of fireworks, and we kids would blow every cent we had on cherry bombs, penny rockets, and giant crackers. When blowing empty tin cans sky high became boring, we would see how long we could hold a fire cracker in our hand after lighting it before tossing it away. On one occasion I recall having used the wrong hand to make the toss – tossing the match in my right hand and looking with paralyzed horror at my left hand as the cracker exploded. Fortunately, it was a small one and the only damage was some temporary numbness. How we escaped serious injury was a mystery.

6 – Not your typical prep school

High school was not much of a challenge, and when I found myself a Junior in a Senior civics class – and two years younger than the other kids – I felt the necessity of distinguishing myself by being the class clown. One memorable day I was reading a comic book shielded by my textbook while the teacher discussed the forthcoming presidential election, the race for which had just been entered by Wendell Wilkie. Noting that he was known as a "dark horse candidate", she asked, "What's a dark horse candidate----Edwin?" (None of that "Buster" nonsense with the Parker High School teachers!) Not anticipating the question, and ignorant of the answer, I looked up blankly and replied, "A black one?"

Coming hard upon another inane stunt fifteen minutes earlier and not worth describing here, this moronic response was more than she could take, so it was off to the study hall for me – the standard punishment for misbehavior. As she was writing out the pass required to go there, I meekly asked, "Could you make that the library instead?" There I could find something to while away the time, having already done my homework for the next day at the beginning of history class. (I rarely took homework home, much preferring to spend the evenings listening to such radio programs as Jack Armstrong, Renfrew of the Mounted, The Shadow, Amos and Andy, and such. Instead, I would routinely do the homework for each class in the preceding class. Some education!) Little did I dream that this sudden change in venue, from study hall to library, was to have a most profound effect on the direction in which I would eventually go.

The librarian, Miss Carnahan, was also the high school guidance director. Having taken no occasion to offer me any guidance in the preceding three years, she looked up from a pile of mail she was opening and seized the opportunity to practice her guidance counseling by interrupting my study of the latest issue of *The Saturday Evening Post* and summoning me to her desk. (Little did I dream that I would some day write for that noble publication.) "Would you be interested in attending the Carnegie Institute of Technology next year, Edwin?" "Where's that?" I replied (as if that were in any way relevant to the question). Looking at the papers in her hand, she noted that it was in Pittsburgh – a metropolis of whose existence I was only vaguely aware and which could have been just east of Timbuctu for all I knew. She then added, "Here's an application form for the college, and for a scholarship. Take it home and show it to your parents."

At that point in my life I hadn't the foggiest notion of what I might do after high school, beyond "going to college"—although my parents were in no position to fund my further education. The thought of a scholarship was appealing, so I dutifully did as directed, assuming this would be just the first of other such offers to come through her office in the next twelve months or so. Such was not to be the case, however.

Graduation from high school in those days required successful completion of examinations given by the New York State Board of Regents in the various required subjects. All senior male students were urged to take the Regents examinations in January 1943, with the hope they would pass them before being drafted into the armed services prior to June graduation. Although I was only 16, with no fear of the draft, I took them – and was the only person in my class who passed them. When I learned shortly thereafter that the State of New York had just lowered the age limit for factory employment from 18 to 16 to meet the increasing demands of the war effort, I saw this as a way to earn money for college and decided to leave school.

When I informed the principal of my intent, he told me I couldn't do that, on the basis that "it had never been done". I immediately hitch-hiked to the office of the superintendent of schools in Williamsville and presented my case. He agreed that it had never been done, but saw no reason why it could not be done and informed the principal accordingly. I then went to the Curtiss-Wright factory in Williamsville, where I was given a few basic lessons in riveting and assigned to rivet engine nacelles on C-46 aircraft. Being small of frame, I was selected to crawl into the wings to apply a "bucking bar" against the rivets my partner inserted from below and hammered home. With several other teams riveting elsewhere on the wings, the decibel level undoubtedly reached damaging levels which probably contributed to my present need for hearing aids. Nonetheless, I was often so sleepy from the 48-hour week that I frequently fell asleep on the job, only to have my partner awaken me by shouting at me from the access opening to the wing. Somehow I even managed to compose my graduation speech on the job, and in June I joined my class again for that happy event

My father was fortunate to have a steady job during the depression, and although it paid a living wage, there was never any surplus cash in our household. At one point he gave Dick and me a weekly allowance of 25 cents each, and I was exceedingly frugal in spending mine – so much so that I had several dollars in reserve, when for some reason my father needed a quick loan and asked if he could borrow it. He did, but somehow he never got around to repaying it, and that was the end of our allowance.

I tried numerous ways of earning money, first as a caddy at the Buffalo Country Club. This required hitch-hiking four miles in each direction and sitting around the caddy shack, sometimes the entire day, waiting to be assigned to a member. It was here that I learned that far too many men apparently obtained their wealthy status by underpaying their employees, judging from the fees I was paid for carrying an enormous bag of clubs – many of which were never used – for four tiring hours.

I also tried selling magazines door-to-door, and eventually selling Fuller brushes in the same manner. I hated it, embarrassed trying to persuade someone to buy something they probably didn't need, or couldn't afford in the neighborhood to which I was assigned. I worked on Saturdays as a bagger and stock boy in the A&P in Williamsville for a time, for 25 cents an hour. But hitch-hiking there early in the morning and being driven home by my parents when they finished grocery shopping at 9:00 at night became a drag. So when I learned that Western Union in Buffalo was hiring messenger boys for 35 cents an hour, I jumped at the chance.

This required riding my bicycle ten miles into the city each Sunday evening and riding it home on Saturday morning, living with my grandmother during the week. She always prepared a delicious bag lunch for me, and proudly dressed in my Western Union uniform, I would set out each morning in anticipation of what the day would hold. It was a great job, the only drawback of which was the all-too-frequent telegram having a red star stamped on its envelope. America was now at war, and there were apparently simply too many casualties to be able to send an officer to the home when such occurred. So telegrams were used, with one red star denoting that the loved one was wounded or missing in action, and two for killed in action. I would simply hand the telegram to whomever came to the door, feigning ignorance of its contents, and leave as quickly as possible. What a brutal way to send such news!

7 – Three colleges and Army basic training – all in less than a year

Admitted to Carnegie Tech with a full tuition award, I was off to Pittsburgh in the late summer of 1943 to begin my college education. A job in the athletic department, with the impressive title of assistant manager of the basketball team (i.e., in charge of all the dirty laundry), paid for some of my meals, and a wealthy old bachelor gave me a bedroom in his palatial home in return for services as part-time caretaker. An occasional gift from home was sufficient to meet my other financial needs.

Pittsburgh was often a grim place in those days, with smog sometimes so thick that the street lights had to be turned on at noon. As the end of the term approached, I decided to transfer to Houghton College, a small Christian institution about 50 miles from home. The reason, however, had nothing to do with Pittsburgh's air pollution. I had a difficult time getting acquainted with girls in an institution where female students were few in number. With civilian males greatly outnumbered by men from the armed services assigned to the school, I yearned to be in a college where the competition was less formidable.

The first trimester of the accelerated wartime program at Carnegie Tech ended in October, and I headed home. My father, who knew Stephen Paine, the president of Houghton, drove me to the school and presented me at the president's office. When asked by Dr. Paine what major I had in mind, given the fact that Houghton did not offer an engineering program, I responded with, "Gosh, I don't know. What would you suggest, sir?" Somewhat taken aback by this profound reply, he noted that they had a large percentage of pre-seminary students, and when I declared that not to be my calling, he then said the next largest group was that of premedical students. "Good! I'll be premedical!" – and thus after such depth of thought and planning I chose my professional career.

Given my reason for leaving Carnegie Tech, Houghton should have been a splendid choice, with about three girls to every guy at Houghton as the result of the draft, for which I was still much too young. Although many of them were of the long-skirt, no-lipstick, tight-hairdo variety favored in that ultraconservative Wesleyan Methodist culture, I did near the end of the term finally manage a date with a cute little blonde from Holland, Michigan, by the name of Joyce Valkema. No sooner had the romance begun, however, than fate was to abruptly part us.

Having by now totally depleted my funds in spite of a small scholarship from Houghton, I talked my father into giving me the required written approval to enlist in the Army at age seventeen. The inducement was the promise of at least one semester at another college, under Army auspices, before turning eighteen and having to go on active duty. On that fateful evening when I arrived home from my first date with Joyce, I received a phone call from my father telling me that a telegram had arrived from the Army, ordering me to report to Amherst College in Amherst, Massachusetts, less than two days hence. A bus ride home early the next morning and a train that afternoon brought me to Amherst at 9:00 a.m. the following day. I was now enrolled in the third institution of higher education in less than six months.

Having never been in New England, I was enthralled by the charm of that western Massachusetts town and its Ivy League college. It was a heady experience for a country boy from western New York, and I enjoyed every minute of it – until my education was rudely interrupted four weeks later when I was quarantined in the college infirmary with scarlet fever for the entire middle month of the 3-month term. Too ill at first to crack the books and too lazy thereafter, I decided to abort that phase of my education, quit the program, and go on active duty, having now turned 18. When I so informed my professors upon my release from the infirmary, I ran into a solid brick wall. Not one was willing to let me leave, and each tutored me in his spare time to bring me up to speed on the work I had missed – and I left with five A's on my grade report as the result of their magnanimity. I was thus to learn how the commitment of dedicated faculty members made so many of our American colleges and universities so great.

Army service was one of the most rewarding experiences of my young life. Assigned to a special branch of the field artillery for basic training at Ft. Sill, Oklahoma, I found myself facing physical challenges that would surely result in my discharge as being unfit for duty – and I wanted nothing more than to make the grade. It was the summer of 1944, and the tide had turned in the war, so we were all anxious to get into it before it ended. I was now a tall, skinny kid of 18 (6-foot-3 inches, and 133 pounds dripping wet), and when I applied for Officer Candidate School midway in my training, the review board must have had difficulty keeping from laughing during the interview. Needless to say, they politely turned me down.

The obstacle course was sure to be my downfall. There was absolutely no way I would be able to scale the 8-foot wall (or whatever its height), and traversing an enormous mud puddle on a rope overhead was clearly an impossibility. It was hard enough to use my bony arms to do pushups during PT, and the drill sergeant didn't take kindly to my faking it by using my knees to improve the leverage. However, my guardian angel came to the rescue, and I managed to complete the program. The final event was the 25-mile hike in full battle gear under a scorching Oklahoma summer sun, but by now I was reasonably sure that I was going to make it. I did – and was particularly proud of myself when I managed to carry the gear of Sol Stein, an elderly (at least 40, I would guess) draftee who was on the verge of collapse during the last few miles.

Upon the completion of the 4-month basic training, we were assigned to the 617th Field Artillery Observation Battalion at Ft. Bragg, North Carolina – and by now I had found the love of my life, Betty Seligman, a beautiful 18-year-old blonde high school student whom I met at a church party in Williamsville while home on my first furlough. At the time she was the "steady" of my friend Jack McInnes, who magnanimously concurred (much to his later regret) in her request to correspond with me. Her patriotic gesture was much appreciated (by me), and on my next furlough prior to going overseas five months later, it became obvious that we were God's gift to each other – and I was the envy of my barracks mates when she sent me her lovingly-inscribed senior class photo to hang at the head of my bunk.

Life at Fort Bragg was a cut above Fort Sill, and the continued training was a relief from the rigors of basic training. I did manage to get myself in serious trouble at one point, however, for accidentally discharging my carbine on my shoulder (and nearly blowing off my head) while on guard duty one night. Called before the battalion commander, I was offered the choice of a "summary court martial or punishment under the 104th Article of War". The former sounded particularly grim, so I opted for the latter, which involved merely punishment meted out by one's battery commander. Fortunately, I was still a private, so he couldn't demote me, and my punishment was but a week of KP (kitchen police – that delightful Army euphemism for peeling potatoes and doing general scut work in the mess hall). My captain must have felt sorry for me, for not long thereafter I was promoted to corporal.

Fort Bragg was also the home of the 82nd Airborne Division, which used both parachutes and gliders to put troops on the ground. The gliders were ungainly wooden machines, towed by C-47 troop transports which would hook on to them on the ground and then release them over the drop zone – hoping they would land without disintegrating. Having never flown in an airplane, I decided one evening that this would be a novel experience, so I went out to the airfield to see if I could bum a ride in one of the C-47s. As it turned out, the last one of the day was just beginning to taxi out to the runway, so I ran out to where the pilot could see me and stuck out my thumb in my best hitch-hiking pose. To my surprise, he brought the big plane to a halt and motioned me to the passenger door on the other side, where a crewman reached down, dragged me on board, and told me to put on a parachute and sit on the metal bench seat along the side. He then disappeared into the flight deck, leaving me alone as the only person in the passenger section of the plane. We taxied out, picked up our glider, and were airborne. After some time the pilot released the glider, returned to the base, and the sergeant reappeared to help me down to the ground. It had been a great evening!

Basic training at Ft. Sill had exposed us to the different functions performed by an artillery observation battalion, whose function was to direct the fire of our artillery units from the ground (as opposed to direction from the air) by sight and sound, as well as to detect the location of enemy artillery. The specific function of our unit was to record the moment of the flash of an exploding shell as viewed by colleagues with binoculars and calculate the time for the sound to reach a series of microphones embedded in the ground. The information thus obtained from each of the microphones then enabled the triangulation of the exact position of the explosion. My particular function was to do the actual triangulation – not a particularly glamorous one but certainly essential to the success of the artillery fire. One always hoped, of course, that the shells heard flying overhead would continue on their way to their intended destination – and that they had come from our guns and not theirs.

While still at Ft. Bragg, we bid farewell to the 285th Field Artillery Observation Battalion, which had been organized long before ours and was therefore ordered to Europe many months before we were. Sadly, it was this unit that was captured by the Germans during the Battle of the Bulge, with more than 100 of its member massacred at Malmedy.

8 – The winds of war – by now not much more than a breeze

By the time the Washington brass decided we were ready for combat, the war was fast running down. Our unit was transferred to the Hampton Roads, Virginia, staging area in February 1945, and two days before we were to embark I was admitted to the hospital with a strep throat. The attending physician wanted me to remain in bed for a week, but I pled with him to discharge me so that I could leave with my unit. Duly impressed with my loyalty to my unit, he agreed to give me a supply of sulfa drugs and let me go. I hadn't the nerve to tell him I was afraid I might be assigned to an infantry unit if left behind.

Arriving at the dock in March 1945, it immediately became clear that I wasn't going overseas unless they hauled me aboard in a freight sling. Loaded down with rifle, backpack, and a considerable additional load of contraband intended to ease the strain of the impending ocean cruise, I took one look at what appeared to be a mile-long gangway by which we were to board. I was already staggering under the excess weight, and ascending that formidable incline was out of the question. But once again – and probably with some reluctance this time – my guardian angel came to the rescue, and I made it aboard. The USS Wakefield was a converted passenger liner, formerly the SS Manhattan, of dubious pedigree, and the conditions on board left much to be desired. Crammed into bunks six-high, I at least had the presence of mind to take the upper one. It took some effort to climb into it, but when a bunkmate gets seasick, it pays to be top dog.

In keeping with military security, we hadn't a clue of where we were headed until it became apparent that we were eastbound, and not headed south toward the Panama Canal and the Pacific. Now informed that our destination was Naples, Italy, we were given some exciting tourist literature intended to make us behave like gentlemen toward the natives. With the surrender of Italy the previous year, the Italians were now our allies, and our government was not keen about our forgetting that, lest we might shoot some poor civilian whom we mistakenly assumed to be the enemy.

Naples harbor looked like the graveyard of the Italian and German navies combined by that late stage of the war. Disembarking and herded into trucks that would take us to shelter for the night, we were besieged by street urchins offering to trade their virgin sisters for a pack of cigarettes or gum. Our billet was a 3-story building of unknown original purpose, and after a meal of questionable content, my squad was assigned to the third floor, with wooden bunks that felt as if they had been carved by Michelangelo from a solid block of marble. Although I had avoided *mal-de-mer* on the voyage, it caught up with me in the middle of that night, and I was barely able to make it to a window to rid myself of my stomach's contents. As I thus relieved myself, I barely observed a couple in fond embrace three stories below my window but had no desire to shout a warning lest they mark the window and come up and annihilate me. Whether they were targeted or no, I know not, and the rudimentary Italian learned from the manuals passed out at sea was insufficient to comprehend the meaning of the shouts below.

The next day found us aboard the *Sestriere*, an Italian freighter that somehow managed to stay afloat on the dreadful journey to Livorno, up the coast. Again, time has graciously allowed me to blot out the memory of that unseemly cruise ship, except for one unforgettable feature – the toilet facilities. Try to imagine an old-fashioned "outhouse", 20 or 30 holes wide, suspended over the side of the ship and open below. Fortunately, the weather favored us, and no sudden windstorm arose that might have created updrafts.

From Livorno we were transported inland to a tent site on the outskirts of Pisa, to await our trucks and equipment, which presumably were given more favorable treatment than we were. We remained in this tourist resort for about a week, which gave us a weekend for sight-seeing. On that Sunday afternoon I found myself atop the Leaning Tower of Pisa, watching hundreds of American bombers pass overhead and could hear their ordnance being dropped on the city of Bologna. Again, I yearned to soar in the bright blue yonder, so I bummed a ride over to the nearby airbase and asked if I might hitch a ride on the next bombing run. Protocol here was somewhat different from that back at Fort Bragg, and I was told that I would have to have written permission from my battery commander. I headed back to camp to see if I could hit up the old man, but found that we were packing up to head off to the war the next day – and thus we became a tiny part in what the history books were later to call the Po Valley Campaign.

To my regret, we never did really catch up with the war. Technically, we were in a combat zone, so we drove at night and camped during the day, so as to be able to spot any enemy troops that might be on the attack. The only enemy troops we saw were in long lines of German trucks, cars, personnel carriers, and whatever else could be filled with German soldiers, all heading south to prison camps, herded along by a lone American soldier in a jeep at the back of the convoy. My best buddy, Bill Slocum, had a more interesting encounter with the enemy, however. Bill was the driver of our truck (being in the field artillery we rode, not walked, wherever we went), and when we stopped for the day on the second day out, he related the events of the night before. "That stupid lieutenant of ours got us lost during the night, so the idiot told us to turn on our headlights so he could figure out where we were." (Army vehicles had tail-lights with four tiny apertures, designed to keep the vehicle behind at the correct distance while driving with headlights off. If the driver could see the light in all four openings, he was too close. If the tail-light appeared to have only two of these lights showing, the distance was correct. If it appeared to be only a single light, you were too far behind.) "So there we were, cruising down the highway with lights ablaze, when we came upon long lines of tanks on either side of the road. We waved at them, and they waved at us. By the time we had passed them, it dawned on me that American tank-jockeys don't wear black uniforms!" We had driven right through a German tank column, which was as confused as we were.

The reason none of us in the back of our truck had been able to witness the only "action" we were to encounter in that illustrious military campaign was the result of my demand for comfort, war or no war. Back in our camp near Pisa, I was appalled to find that our wooden bunks had no mattresses. Although no such convenience was to be found, my fertile brain conceived the idea that a hammock would do nicely in lieu of a pine slab – but where to find material for a hammock. Unfortunately there were no empty tents from which one might have surreptitiously removed a few yards of fabric, but further investigation revealed a reasonably satisfactory substitute not far away, in the storage yard of a company of engineers who were building bridges over a nearby river whose bridges had been blown up by retreating Germans. Under cover of darkness, I sneaked into their grounds and made off with some rolls of chicken-wire fencing, strong enough to hold one's weight but supple enough to provide a modicum of comfort.

The next day was given to replacing the bottom of the bunks in our tent with this more satisfactory substitute, and we had a lovely night's rest. This was not to last for long, however. Some craven wretch in our company, doubtless out of sheer jealousy, ratted on us, and I was forced to replace the boards and ignominiously return the stolen goods.

But there was more to be done as we faced the long and tedious journey that lay before us in reaching the front lines (which were moving northward at a rapid pace). Each of our trucks carried twelve of us, on bench seats along each side. Contemplating a long, bumpy ride each night on the road was not pleasant, so I again gave serious brain time to dealing with the problem of how to get enough sleep under those conditions. One possible solution was to have 2 or 3 of us take turns sleeping on the floor of the truck – but who wants to be awakened from a sound sleep to give way to the next guy? No, the only workable solution was to provide adequate sleeping space for 12 bodies – and the only way in which this could be one was to create a two-tier arrangement. No problem! There were plenty of wooden boards stashed nearby, left over from building floors and bunks for the tents, so I found a saw and proceeded to fashion boards to be placed with ends on the benches across the width of the truck bed. Before starting our journey each night, six of us would bed down for the night, lying side by side cross-wise on the floor. The other six would put the boards in place cross-wise over the bench seats, and they would then bed down on top of us. I presented the plan to my truck mates.

Oh, such doubting Thomases in our vehicle! "Okay, Brown, it's your idea, so you can have the honor of sleeping downstairs – and if the boards break, it's your tough luck." I suspect that Thomas Edison was laughed out of the room when he first suggested that the gas light might one day be replaced by some device powered by electricity. So, volunteering to be the first one in for the night, I stripped down to my underwear, stashed my rifle, helmet, and outer garments between my back and the cab of the truck, and crawled into my sleeping bag. Five other hearty volunteers joined me, and we were then sealed in for the night by the six above. As artillerymen, we weren't particularly adept in the use of small arms, so in any case the only prudent thing to do in the event of an encounter with the enemy would have been to surrender. The sleeping arrangement worked out surprisingly well, and we were the only members of our company who managed to get a decent night's sleep on that northward journey.

9 -- Chasing the "front lines"

At one of our daytime stops, an artillery spotting plane was making practice landings in a nearby field. These were little single-engine Piper Cubs, whose very brave pilots put themselves in constant danger by flying over enemy lines to direct artillery fire. Not only were they subject to being shot at from the ground, but when the Germans still had an air force, they were fair game for enemy fighter pilots. One such artillery spotter had actually managed to record a "kill" of an enemy fighter, although these planes were obviously not equipped with fire-power. Luring the enemy fighter too close to the ground while attacking him, the pilot suddenly executed an evasive maneuver, and the fighter pilot, unable to pull out of his dive in time, slammed into the ground.

Having nothing better to do, and frustrated in my previous effort to become airborne in Pisa, I walked over to the adjacent field in the hope of getting a ride. It wasn't a nice, big B-17, but at least it was a flying machine, so the next time the pilot made a landing, I hailed him. He taxied over, and I asked if I might join him, which he obligingly permitted. The next half hour was the wildest of my life. He proudly showed me all the maneuvers he knew to avoid being shot at from the ground or the air, and by the time he landed, I had had all the flying I wanted for some time to come.

One of our last stops on the road to victory was outside Milano, where we stayed overnight, this time in a luxurious, abandoned villa. Although the marble floors were not overly comfortable on which to sleep, it was a nice change. That evening, an excited Italian civilian approached us, shouting, "Benito finito!" The one Italian-speaker in our company learned that Benito Mussolini, his mistress Claire Petacci, and two other Fascist leaders had been captured in the mountains along the Swiss border while trying to escape to Germany, had been executed by Partisans, and were now hanging by their heels in a gasoline station in downtown Milano.

The end of the road for us in the Po Valley Campaign, as the last engagement of the war in Italy became known, was the small town of Saronno, northwest of Milano. The Germans had evacuated the town the day before, and we rolled in mild fanfare – nothing like the liberation of Paris however! It was obvious to all that the war was over, and for the Italians there was little to celebrate. They had joined the wrong side at the outset, and now they felt like defeated enemies – albeit very friendly ones. The Italian Partisans had gone after the Germans after the surrender of

Italy to the Allies, and it was they who had tracked down and executed Mussolini. The good folks of Saronno had not been particularly fond of the Partisans, who were Communists, so perhaps this was why our entry into town failed to evoke any celebration. As an unofficial part of their battle dress, American GIs wore scarves under their shirts, the color of which designated their type of unit – light blue for infantry, yellow for cavalry, and red for field artillery. Our neckware was thus a source of curiosity to the locals, who would come up to us on the street, point to our scarves, and ask, "Communista?". The reply, "Non! Artilleria!" would invariably bring a sigh of relief.

Some 50 years later, I had the opportunity to visit Saronno for a weekend. My Italian lady-friend, about whom I shall speak later, took me to a concert sponsored by the Rotary Club of Saronno, and having some banners from my own club in Indianapolis, I presented one to the president of their club, Paolo Lazzaroni, head of D. Lazzaroni & Co., biscotti makers whose delicacies have been sold worldwide since 1758. He expressed his appreciation and then shared a story with me, one he said he had told very few people. "When I was a little boy of eight, the Americans came to our town. I was playing in front of my house, and when I saw their trucks coming down the street, I then did something strange, which is why I've rarely told this story to others. I ran into the house, found a piece of red cloth my mother was using for some purpose or other, and wrapped it around my neck—and I don't know now why I did that. I ran out of the house, and was lifted into one of the trucks by one of the American soldiers. He gave me some chocolate, and when they reached the school not far away, he said goodbye to me. I fell in love with America that day, and determined that I would go there some day. Now, of course, we have offices in New York, and I get there frequently."

Having not yet mentioned that I had been in Saronno at the end of the war, I replied, "You say you don't know why you put a piece of red cloth around your neck? I can tell you why you did that!", which evoked a look of amazement. "It was because we were wearing red cloth around our necks that day!" I later received a long, handwritten letter from him, expressing his thanks for being able to share that memory with me, and the startling revelation it produced.

We were billeted in a large school, where we stayed for several weeks. Not long after arrival, the church bells all over town began to ring, and we received the news that the Germans forces in Italy had surrendered – some five days before the German surrender in the rest of Europe. The only German soldier we saw arrived in the school yard a day or so later, escorted by several Partisans who wanted to turn him over to us rather than shoot him. We, of course, hadn't the foggiest idea of what to do with him, but he was escorted to our battalion commander, who was housed elsewhere, and who presumably figured out how to deal with the problem. The pathetic German was very unhappy, however, that we failed to retrieve the watch that he loudly complained was taken away from him by the Partisans!

War or no war, the Army always had something for us to do, so I found myself one day standing in front of the entrance to the school, rifle on my shoulder, doing a stint of "guard duty". Three little girls, about 12 or 13, shyly approached and hesitatingly said, "Good morning!" in broken English, and then, as is customary with little girls, giggled at each other. They then added, "You speak English?" "Yes," I said, to which they replied, "We speak English!" Thus was established a friendship with Bianca Zerbi and her two friends that was to last, through correspondence, for five or six years after the war until it gradually dwindled away as we all became involved in other aspects of our lives.

In 1961, while driving through Italy with my wife and three little ones, we were hurtling down the *autostrada* between the Swiss border and Milano, when I spotted a small sign at the side of the road, "Saronno – 2 km". I slammed on the brakes (as did several irate drivers behind me), and swerved off the road with my wife screaming, "What's the matter!!!!" "You've got to see Saronno, where I ended up the war." "I don't want to see Saronno! It's getting late, and we've got to find a hotel room in Milan." "There's plenty of time for that, dear." (Why do married men and woman always add "dear" when they're determined to have their own way?)

Saronno had grown considerably since 1945, but I eventually found the center of town, and the narrow street leading therefrom on which Bianca's parents had their bookshop. But there was no longer a bookshop there. "Good! Let's get out of here," rejoiced the memsahib. "No, I've got to find her!", and left our enormous American station wagon filled with stuff and family to seek my former friend. (We were on our way to India, having come by ship from New York to France with our car, which had to be delivered to the American consulate in Naples before we could fly on from Rome.) I went into a nearby business establishment of some size, hoping to find someone who might have known the Bianca family.

Resurrecting the remnants of the limited Italian learned sixteen years earlier, I explained to the manager that I had been in Saronno sixteen years before as an American soldier, and was hoping to find a friend named Bianca Zerbi. After asking around if anyone knew her, he motioned to me to follow him, and headed down the street. After stopping at several residences in the neighborhood, without obvious success, he proceeded to a small apartment building several blocks away – despite my protests that it was not important to pursue the chase. By now I knew it was hopeless, and that my wife, sitting there in the car on a narrow street in the hot sun with our three whining urchins, would arrange for a contract on my life as soon as she could locate a member of the local mafia.

I was leaning in despair on the railing of the stairwell, looking down four flights of stairs, when he knocked at a door across the hallway. An attractive young blonde about 30 years of age opened the door, and he explained the nature of his mission, not knowing my name, only that I had been an American soldier in Saronno in 1945. She stared at me in amazement, and in a rich Italian accent, said, "Edwin?"

I nearly fell down the stairwell. We greeted warmly – and I learned that she had forgotten most of her English. But her brother would be home at any moment, and he would translate for us. Returning to the car (I refrain from describing the scene), I managed to convince my wife that we should drive over to the apartment for a brief visit. This we did, exchanged addresses with the now Bianca Zerbi Cova, and then proceeded in haste to Milan in stony silence.

Many years later Pat and I again had opportunity to visit Saronno, where we were royally entertained. Bianca had contacted her other two childhood friends in nearby cities, one of whom spoke excellent English as we enjoyed bringing each other up-to-date in the intervening fifty years. Paolo had arranged for us to be guests of honor at the weekly Rotary Club meeting, covered by the local newspapers and televison as he waxed eloquent about my having told him why he put a piece of red cloth around his neck that day long ago – and the mayor had dug photos out of the city's archives showing our trucks rolling into the city after the Germans fled.

10 — To the victor belongs the spoils

Until then, through college and the Army, I had experienced no problem in avoiding any consumption of alcoholic beverages, in keeping with my strict Baptist upbringing. This made me particularly popular with my buddies, who, when the weekly ration of free beer and cigarettes provided by the Army overseas was handed out, were only too delighted to trade Coke and candy bars for my fags and brew. I had a close call in Saronno, however. Our mess sergeant, a Southern Baptist lad, had made the acquaintance of a Protestant family (a rarity, of course, in Italy) and invited me to join him for a Sunday afternoon visit. Upon being seated in their living room, we were offered small glasses of a clear liquid, to the nature of which I was oblivious until I took a sip. I somehow managed to control my choking, but my throat burned as if I had swallowed molten lead, my eyes watered profusely, and I was on the verge of panic. How to avoid having to consume the rest of the dreadful potion without insulting my hosts? Just then the doorbell rang, and as they all got up to greet the visitor, my eyes flew frantically about the room and came to rest on a large potted plant just within arm's reach. I hastily emptied the glass into the pot, sat back in sweet relief – and surreptitiously kept watch on the plant the remainder of the visit, expecting it at any moment to suddenly keel over.

The only other episode of note during our pleasant 1945 stay in Saronno was a bicycle excursion to Lake Como on a Sunday afternoon, Bianca's parents having generously offered the loan of their bicycles to me and another friend, Ray Volk. It was a delightful experience, for the war had stopped short of the Italian lake region, and the town of Como was sublime. The German surrender had not yet been announced, and we had no idea whether we would summarily be ordered out on the road again. So when I saw a road sign near Como that showed the Swiss border to be only a few kilometers down the road, I had a splendid idea. "Let's just pedal down there, Ray, and see if we can get into Switzerland. Then the Swiss will have to intern us for the duration of the war, and we could have a great time there." Mind you, I had no qualms about taking up arms against the enemies of my beloved country, but thus far they had been few and far between, and there was every evidence that the gap had widened beyond recovery. I was definitely not going to have the opportunity to be a war hero. Somewhat dubious, Ray reluctantly agreed to give it a try. But fate, in the form of an uncooperative Swiss border guard, thwarted our plans, and we rejoined our battalion at the end of a thoroughly pleasant day.

The war ended without my having to fire a shot in anger – or even hear one fired, for that matter, unless one counts the bombs dropped on Bologna. Soon we were ordered to deploy ourselves southward while awaiting further orders from Fifth Army headquarters, so we soon found ourselves camped out on a bombed-out airfield near the spa town of Montecatini Terme.

Rumors were rife regarding our future. Would we be shipped directly to the Pacific, where the war still raged, or might we go home first? We were soon boarded into railway freight cars, all our vehicles and heavy equipment being turned over to unknown Army personnel, and began a long train journey through the length of Italy, terminating in the port city of Bari on the Adriatic Sea. The railway cars were what were known as "40-and-8s" in the first World War, which these relics had apparently survived, for each was thus marked in faded French: *quarante hommes at huit chevaux* (forty men or eight horses). Fortunately, we had no horses, and only a dozen or so of us were consigned to each car. It was a slow but scenic trip – so slow at times that I got out and walked alongside the moving train. After one meal-stop (our ever-present cooks and Army food never deserted us), I climbed on the engine and rode for miles with the grimy Italian train driver. He seemed to be a decent chap, who delighted in blowing the whistle at every road crossing. At one point I gestured a request to blow the whistle as we approached a crossing, and instead of a single long toot, I did a "shave-and-a-haircut – two bits" (five short rhythmic toots, a pause, and two more short toots) for the benefit of my buddies riding behind. The poor train driver almost had a convulsion – not from laughing, but because I had scared the wits out of him and probably signaled the rail personnel downstream that some horrible disaster had occurred.

In Bari we were quickly put aboard an American liberty ship freighter, and then learned to our utter ecstasy that we were homeward bound! What a difference from the outbound journey! Our bunks were only four-high, situated around the perimeter of the cargo hold, where we were able to watch movies from bed; the food was out of this world; and it was the greatest cruise I could ever have hoped to be on. Back in Williamsville for a 3-week furlough, I was reunited with my family and the beautiful Betty, during which time the Japanese surrendered and we knew we were home free.

My original enlistment papers read that I was joining the Army for "the duration of the war plus six months". However, with millions of men being demobilized, it turned out to be eight months. I was ordered to report to North Camp Hood, outside Gatesville, Texas, which proved to be an even longer train ride than the original one to Fort Sill, Oklahoma. This was the home of an armored division, so there was little for an artillery battalion to do, and life was disgustingly boring.

Gatesville had a small airport, so I decided to broaden my flying experience by taking a flying lesson. A shortage of funds brought that pursuit to a rapid halt, and I never took up the past-time again. Many years later, while visiting friends in Zell am See, Austria, I was given a spectacular glider flight over the Alps with an instructor, and was encouraged to come back and get a glider pilot license, which could be done in as short a time as three weeks with several flights a day. I planned to do it the following summer, but became so involved with other summer travel plans that I forgot about the glider lessons – until one Sunday morning during a church service on a steep mountain side in Switzerland, when I glanced out the window just in time to see two gliders sail by no more than a hundred yards away. By then, sadly, it was too late in the year to take up that pursuit, and as the years passed I gave up the idea of becoming airborne by my own two hands.

I considered asking for a transfer to the tank corps, but after bumming a ride in one of those monsters and taking a whirl at trying to drive the thing, I opted out of that possibility. The Protestant chaplain for our outfit was a former Salvation Army officer, and a great friend, so I volunteered to be his chaplain's assistant – and when I learned that some of our guys were being transferred to Fort Sill, I prevailed upon him to pull strings for me and get me on the list. This he did – and shortly thereafter I found myself not only back in the Field Artillery Training Center where I had taken basic training, but in the same wooden hut in which I had lived in those days.

11 – Battling boredom

Although we were supposed to be training recruits, none arrived to be trained, so out of sheer boredom I volunteered to be the company clerk, having taken a course in typing in high school. This also gave me the singular opportunity to ask our captain if I could add my name to the list when the colonel asked for names for promotion, and I thus became a sergeant. So anxious was I to show off my three new stripes to my one and only back home, I worked out a shrewd plan over the Thanksgiving day weekend. Finagling a 3-day pass from the captain, I got my first sergeant to cover for me at the regular Friday morning dress parade, and on the Wednesday evening before Thanksgiving Day I took off for home, stretching a four-day weekend, and a three-day pass into a 7-day furlough. Hitchhiking to Oklahoma City during the night, I arrived at Tinker Air Base early in the morning, and bummed a ride on a military transport to Cleveland, from where I hitchhiked home by road.

My strategy was to use half my time to get home, and the other half to get back, so two days later I sadly bid farewell to family and would-be fiancée, had my father drive me to the Buffalo airport, and waited until a military plane might come in on which I could bum a ride. Soon an A-26 attack bomber pulled in for fuel, and when the pilot entered the waiting room, I asked where he was headed. "Fort Benning, Georgia," he said. Well, that wasn't exactly westbound, but figuring that anywhere was better than Buffalo, I asked for a lift. Unfortunately, he had already offered his only spare seat up front to another GI, but I was free to ride in the rear gunner's compartment, behind the bomb bay. The only problem was that it was unheated, and I was wearing only an Army field jacket. However, the other passenger offered me one of his "long johns", so we went into the men's room, where I donned his warm underwear – and we were off. The pilot had instructed me to put on a parachute, and that if it became necessary for him to ditch the plane, he would call on the intercom and open the bomb bay doors, at which point I was to unzip the canvas door in front of me and dive through the bomb bay to safety.

We were not long into flight, with freezing air whipping through the cracks around the bomb bay doors and into my uninsulated compartment, when I came to the obvious conclusion. I had never been so cold in my life, and looking down on the snow-covered Pennsylvania mountains through the rear gunner's window, I knew there was no point in even thinking about using the parachute. I would simply go down with the ship. Fortunately, we made it to Andrew's Air Base in Washington, D.C., where we stopped for refueling and a hot meal – and where the other passenger got off. Reboarding, I was now comfortably ensconsed in the front of the plane, behind the pilot. The radio operator pulled down and latched the twin canopy doors over our heads, and we were off – and so were the canopy doors, with a resounding crash, which also sent my cap into orbit. The radio operator managed to pull them back down, but now freezing air poured through a large hole in one of them. The pilot took one look at me, minus my cap and the warm underwear I had returned to its owner at Andrews, and made a rapid return to the field, since there was no possibility of my continuing on that flight.

Not until late the next day was I able to get a ride on a C-47 Army transport plane headed for Topeka, Kansas, and I had now lost a day. Nor was there anything headed south from Topeka by air, so I was back on the road again – now wearing a sailor's cap kindly given me by a Navy passenger on the C-47. Rides were few and far between, and I reached Fort Sill after dark and one day late—and eligible for a court martial for being AWOL. My first sergeant again covered for me, however, but he made it abundantly clear that he was not very happy about it.

Although official duties were essentially a bore, off-duty hours offered the opportunity to become in a more rewarding activity during the last few months at Fort Sill. I became part of a group of GIs, under the leadership of an artillery officer, First Lieutenant Stan Block, (who later became a professor at the Illinois Institute of Technology) and Master Sergeant Bob White, helping the local Salvation Army officer, Major Ezra Miles, with his Saturday night street meetings in Lawton, the nearest town to the base. The major had compromised with our group by agreeing to omit the base drum and tambourines favored by the SA, and we supposedly added a greater degree of credibility in the eyes of the passing GIs, with our uniforms joined with those of the Salvation Army personnel in singing, praying, and offering testimony to what Jesus Christ meant to us.

When Bob White was demobilized, and Stan was about to be, I was asked by Stan to take over the leadership. Once a month, we also put on a program for teenagers in the local high school under what we called Voice of Christian Youth, inviting in outside speakers for the occasion. One such was a Kansas City physician, Dr. Walter Wilson, a well-known Christian author in those days. For a 19-year-old, it was a great privilege for me to become acquainted with this interesting man. But at last the "duration-plus-six", which had extended to plus-eight, came to a close, and after being sent to Fort Dix, New Jersey, for demobilization, my Army days were essentially over. I remained in the Army Reserve, however, and some five years later was able to supplement my income while in medical school by going on active duty for the summer in Buffalo, assigned to the Army Reserve office in our city.

The demobilization process at Ft. Dix was fairly brief, with a medical exam to determine that one was at least relatively fit, followed by a brief ceremony during which we received that beautiful piece of paper bearing the words the words, *...is hereby Honorably Discharged from the military service of the United States of America. This certificate is awarded as a testimonial of Honest and Faithful Service to this country.*

We were provided with bus service into New York City, where I found lodging for the night at a Manhattan church offering such accommodation to servicemen, before I was to catch a train to Buffalo the next day. I had dinner at a Japanese restaurant (my first such) and returned to the church a couple of hours later to bed down for the night. While taking a bedtime shower, I began to itch under my arms, then over my chest, and soon my entire body, which had broken out in red welts. Panic-stricken, I went to the man in charge of the facility, who phoned an Army dispensary in the city, only to be told that the Veterans Administration was now responsible for my medical care.

He then phoned the nearest VA hospital, which was many miles away in the Bronx, and was told that I should come to their emergency department. I wiggled uncomfortably on the long subway ride, and waited some time at the hospital until the doctor on duty was able to see me. He was unimpressed. "It's only the hives. You must have eaten something to which you're allergic. Here's some calomine lotion to put on it. You should be okay again by morning."

By now it was well after midnight and I was the only passenger in my car on the subway back. I tried to smear the miserable stuff all over myself, but soon gave up and succumbed to sleep. As he had predicted, it was gone by morning – and thus I first learned of my allergy to shellfish, as I was able to determine many years later while in medical school.

The trip home was uneventful, and I was joyously greeted by my family when they picked me up at the train station.

12 – 'Tis better to have loved and lost than never to have loved at all

Arriving back in Williamsville in April 1946, I did what any red-blooded American boy would do under the circumstances – made up for lost time. Lost time in my case was a boyhood sadly deprived of boy-girl relationships. Although the primeval urge had overcome me as early as the second grade, for the next decade shyness restricted me to a good-old-Charlie-Brown fantasy world in which there was another little red-headed girl (or blonde, or brunette, it mattered not) across the aisle in my classroom each year. In high school, with the lack of available girls and sources of entertainment within 4 miles of our home, and no access to transportation other than hitch-hiking (which seemed a somewhat inappropriate means of transporting a date), my fantasy world continued until I went to college.

But now the love of my life was but a few blocks from home, and I made up for those lost years. No sooner had dinner ended at our house than this pathetic, love-starved lad was hurrying to her house, returning some 6 or 7 hours later. This went on for over a month, seven nights a week, all day Saturday, and most of Sunday, until her father figured that the only way he was going to get me out of the house at a respectable hour was to offer me a job in his factory. Having now to arise at 6:00 a.m. instead of noon put a severe crimp in this teenage romance, and, as I was soon to find, allowed the unthinkable to happen.

Having not yet been able to afford a car, and being able to borrow that of my father or hers only on occasion, our scope of entertainment had been severely limited. Still immersed in my Baptist culture, I neither danced nor went to movies – both of which Betty enjoyed, and which her Methodist upbringing did not proscribe. She had started taking classes at the University of Buffalo, and, as I was to learn later, there she met some worthless Lothario who had a model A Ford and asked her to a dance one evening (probably a draft-dodger who got rich working in a war plant). When I phoned her earlier that evening to determine at what time we might meet, she informed me that she was tied up that evening, which seemed a bit curious. Walking disconsolately down the main street of the village an hour or so later, I was horrified to see her drive by with this reprehensible creature. Words cannot describe the agony of that moment.

Such breaks occurred with increasing frequency in the routine that had characterized our relationship until that dreadful moment, and by midsummer I decided it was time to begin thinking about picking up the threads of my university education again—or entering a monastery. One of my older friends, John Sheffer, who had just graduated from medical school at the University of Buffalo told me he was going to teach a late summer class in biology at Houghton College and suggested I drown my sorrows by signing up for his class, as well as a sophomore English class that his wife, Shirley, was scheduled to teach. This I did, and at the end of summer, with two weeks free before the beginning of fall semester, I suggested to my roommate, Bob Kalle, that we hitchhike to some remote place. For some unknown reason, Nova Scotia struck me as being about as remote as one could get, not having the foggiest idea of where it was, other than "up north somewhere". So we went to the library, found an atlas, and Nova Scotia appeared to be just the ticket.

Though my father thought us mad, he drove us to the nearest highway the morning of our departure, inquiring when we might expect to return. Having mapped out a trip of some 2500 miles in ten days, I made a hasty mental calculation, based on averaging 250 miles a day, and glibly responded with, "Oh, I should think we'll be back a week from Thursday—probably late in the afternoon." Amazingly, we made 500 miles that day, arriving in Boston by evening, thence onward through New Brunswick to Prince Edward Island, and barely across the border to Amherst, Nova Scotia, before heading back toward Quebec City, Montreal, Toronto, and home. At 4:00 p.m. on that predicted Thursday, I came sauntering up the driveway, where my dad was perched high on a ladder, painting the house. "Hi, Dad! I'm home." He was barely able to keep from falling off the ladder, having probably never expected to see me again.

I returned to Houghton the following week, now entering what was to be the third semester of a college education that had already involved me in three different educational institutions for the first two semesters. Not to worry, however. Just get through this next year, and I was off to medical school – or so I thought. My sole knowledge of the medical education process was limited to what I had been told back in the middle of World War II, when doctors were urgently needed for military service – one takes two years of premed, and then three years in medical school and *voila!* – you're an M.D. It was thus time to begin applying to medical schools.

Having not the foggiest notion of where to apply, I began sending postcard requests for application forms to whatever university came to mind, saying that I was completing my second year of premed studies – and invariably received back postcard replies informing me that a minimum of three or four years of premed studies was required. Impossible! I could never survive the boredom of another two years after my current one – or even one more year. Moreover, I hadn't the funds to put in that much more time. Even the newly enacted GI Bill would provide barely enough to get me through medical school if I began the following year. But I still had the year at Houghton to finish in any case, so I continued my studies in a half-hearted manner while contemplating the possibilities of going into some other area of study.

Faced with such uncertainty, I concentrated on "enjoying college". The war was over, the pressure was off, and it behooved me to make the most of my college experience. But how does one manage without a car in a tiny rural village whose sole off-campus attraction was a general store? And how does one buy a car with what was left after paying tuition, room and board from one's meager summer earnings? So much for that thought! But standing on the steps of the college library one warm October afternoon, I was taken by the sight of one of my classmates putt-putting by in a 1928 Model T Ford he had recently acquired from a nearby farmer.

As he slowed down in front of me, I jokingly shouted, "How much will you take for that thing?" He replied, jokingly of course, "How much have you got? By an odd coincidence I had just come from the post office, where I had received the last of my unemployment compensation checks after quitting my factory job that summer. I reached in my pocket, pulled out the check, and said, "Twenty bucks!" "It's yours!", said he, and with a grand flourish I endorsed the check to him, and he took me for a driving lesson.

Unfortunately, I never got to drive the buggy off the campus, for a few days later, while tooling up the hill to my dormitory, there was a loud "clunk" in the transmission, and thus ended the life of my first automobile. I pushed it off the road, where it lay for several weeks until a workman at a nearby construction project offered me $30 for it, as is. Flushed with pride at my skill in making such an enormous profit on the sale, I quickly accepted his offer – only to learn later that any Ford dealer in Buffalo would have gladly paid me $100 for it, just to display it in his showroom when the new 1947 models came out. I never was a shrewd businessman.

13 –Caring for a little lamb – who became a wolf in sheep's clothing

About that same time, I received a postcard from my brother Dick, who had graduated from high school several months earlier. He said he had enlisted in the Army in order to be able to attend college under the veterans benefits program upon completion of his tour of duty, and had just arrived in Fort Knox, Kentucky. This came as quite a blow to me. The lad was only 18 and had never been away from home before. He was so innocent—how would he ever cope with Army life?

I had always been very protective of my little brother. Although he was only two years my junior, that was to me an enormous gap in age and maturity. It was my role in life to look after him, a responsibility I took very seriously. He was the quiet one; I had to be his spokesman.

I had no choice but to leave school the next day, make my way to Kentucky, and see what I could do to ease him into the rigors of Army life. I immediately informed each of my professors that I had to deal with a family emergency that would take me away for at least the rest of the week, and hit the road. A local farmer carried me as far as Buffalo, where I went to a large truck depot and sought a ride to Ohio. By the following evening I arrived in Fort Knox, where Dick introduced me to his platoon sergeant as a WWII veteran, and I was in. He offered me the room of his number two, who was away for the weekend, and introduced me to the mess sergeant. Free transportation, and now free room and board – can life get any better than that?

It was clear that my first task was to make him look more like a soldier before he actually started his basic training program, thus to impress the drill sergeant with his ready adaptability to military life. New recruits invariably wear their cap incorrectly and don't know how to deliver a proper salute to an officer. An hour's practice before me and a mirror, some lectures on how to deal with one's superiors, and I had transformed him into the image of a real fighting man. It was a worthwhile weekend. I was convinced that he would be able to handle himself, and left him with the old Army dictum: "Keep your eyes open, your nose clean, and never volunteer" – unless, of course, it was clear that the assignment for which you were volunteering was guaranteed to get you out of more odious tasks. I cited, for example, one bitterly cold morning at Fort Bragg when our platoon was lined up preparatory to a forced march exercise. As we were about to head out, the first sergeant asked if there was anyone in the ranks who was skilled in replacing window glass, since there a number of panes in the barracks that needed work. Sensing that this would essentially be inside work, I immediately shot up my hand. He gratefully directed me to the supply sergeant, who would supply me with the necessary materials. Of course, I had never replaced a window pane in my life, but the supply sergeant kindly offered a few pointers, and I spent a lovely warm day indoors.

As fate would have it, my concern for his welfare proved to be completely unfounded. While on duty in Japan some months later, his unit was asked to send two men to a tennis tournament in Osaka. He and his buddy immediately volunteered and were soon comfortably housed in a former Japanese hotel, with great food and soft beds. Arriving at the tennis courts, they were given tennis clothes, racquets, and balls, and told to begin practice. Since neither had ever previously held a tennis racquet in his hand, they were scarcely able to hit the ball back and forth to each other, and informed the man in charge that they were going to forfeit their first match. No further orders were given them, and until the tournament ended some days later they enjoyed the pleasures of Osaka. Only after an extended period thereafter during which no travel orders were forthcoming did he finally decide it was time to go back to his unit – but not before taking a train to Kobe to visit a hometown friend on the latter's Navy ship. Upon arrival at his base, he reported to the Company Commander to say that although he had received no orders to return to the base, he thought it prudent to return anyway. The CC informed him that he was on the AWOL list, but after hearing his story reinstated him to active duty!

14 – Flying on a wing and a prayer

I ended the Fall semester with a string of "Bs" – they simply didn't appreciate my hidden capabilities. It was obvious that I had to work a bit harder the next semester, so when I returned from the Christmas break, I determined to plunge into the academic grind with new fervor. I erred, however, in signing up for an important class at 8:00 a.m., and having not yet resumed the routine of a proper bedtime for the first couple of weeks of the second semester, I managed to regularly oversleep and miss my first class. It soon became apparent that I had blown it completely, and would have to quit the class. Moreover, I was running seriously short of cash. When I learned that classes had not yet started at the University of Buffalo, I headed for home, where I could live with my parents, enrolled at UB, and notified Houghton that I had transferred. I was now in my fourth semester of college in my fourth institution of higher learning. With my "B" average at Houghton, my performance at UB would have to improve considerably if I were going to make it into medical school – whenever and wherever that might be.

Just before leaving Houghton, a most remarkable encounter with a fellow student, who was also seeking admission to medical school, appeared to afford the miracle I was vainly hoping for. He was Andy Berger, of Hungarian birth, whose family had emigrated to Colombia, and in his inimitable Hungarian-Spanish accent he excitedly accosted me one day at school, waving a red medical school catalog, with the incredible news: "Eddie! I've found a medical school that still requires only two years of premed!" Good grief! What kind of diploma mill had he written to? "Okay, Andy. Calm down. What's the name of the school?" He flashed the cover of the catalog before my unbelieving eyes – Harvard Medical School! And sure enough, there at the bottom of one page were the amazing words: "Although a minimum of two years of premedical studies is required, we strongly recommend a Bachelor's degree to those applying for admission."

So inconspicuous was that simple statement that I doubt that not one in a thousand applicants would even remotely consider the possibility of applying to the nation's foremost medical school with anything less than an undergraduate degree – and as I was to learn later, a goodly number did so only after acquiring a Master's degree as well. This was 1946, and four years of war that had kept many would-be medical students from continuing their education had resulted in all medical schools being inundated with applicants. But over there in rural western New York, far from the academic centers of America, a naive country lad with more brass than brains duly wrote for an application to "the Harvard Medical School" as it was wont to be called.

But now an additional hurdle arose. Among the references required were the names of two of one's academic instructors, one of whom must be in the field of biology. My biology professor at Houghton was Dr. George Moreland, who possessed the dismal trait of facing his students with the truth about their performance – and had already suggested to me that I was not putting forth my best efforts in his class. Knowing that I was headed for a "B" at best the way things were going thus far, I regarded him as a poor choice of referee. Nor could I identify other of my professors at Houghton who considered me one of their choicer students.

But what about my friend, John Sheffer, who had recently graduated from the University of Buffalo School of Medicine, and had taught the zoology course I took the past summer at Houghton? I certainly could count on him to come up with a proper letter of reference, having received an "A" in his course. So he wasn't quite of academic status, but perhaps those folks at Harvard wouldn't notice that, as long as he had an M.D. after his name. And for my second referee, what better choice than my good friend Dr. Marvin Pryor, a full professor of physics at an Ivy League school, who had previously been on the faculty at Houghton and had given me an "A" in his course at Amherst? What could I lose?

The semester at the University of Buffalo was essentially uneventful. I did manage to bump into my old flame, Betty, a few times, but nothing came of it. Anyhow, I was too busy trying to get into medical school to let anything so crass as romance interfere.

In March 1947 I received a shocking surprise. Earlier, upon learning that the University of Buffalo had not yet changed its wartime 2-year premed requirement, I made application and was granted an interview. Soon thereafter, however, the requirement was raised to 3 years minimum, and I promptly gave up on that one. But on that fateful day in March, I came home from school to find two astonishing letters in the mail. One was from UB informing me that because I had been interviewed prior to the change in premed requirements, they were waiving the new requirement in my case and would admit me to medical school that fall.

The other was from Harvard, from whom I had had no communication whatever since sending them my application for admission. They, too, had accepted me! Now I was on the horns of a real dilemma. With the GI Bill paying my tuition, and living at home with my parents, I could afford four years at UB, but there was no way I could afford living away from home. I proudly showed the letters to my parents, whose advice was a foregone conclusion, given my father's inability to provide any financial aid: "Stay home!" I was to ponder this matter for weeks.

During this trying period, I amused myself with such blatant egocentricity as, for example, sitting in the lecture hall pretending to read both letters prominently displayed before me so that the guys behind me would have to succumb to curiosity by reading them over my shoulder. Needless to say, this produced a rewarding response: "Here we are, desperately trying to get into medical school, and this guy has two acceptances – and one of them to Harvard!" I had not yet learned the virtue of humility.

Torn between the obvious way out and the opportunity to attend what was generally regarded in medical education circles as the foremost medical school in America, if not in the world, I made a tentative decision. I would go to Boston to see what this Mecca of medicine looked like, and perhaps that might somehow help in arriving at a decision. I talked my brother Dick into driving me to Boston in his newly-acquired 1933 Chevrolet, and we headed merrily on our way, hoping his ancient jalopy was up to the 500 mile trip. Staying overnight with an aunt and uncle in Albany, New York, we reached Boston early the following afternoon – just in time to have fate take us past Fenway Park just as a Boston Red Sox game was about to begin.

As is still the case, Buffalo had only a minor league baseball team, and neither of us had ever been afforded the privilege of seeing a major league game. What to do? Calculating that we would still have time to make it to the medical school after the game, we obviously had no choice. By the time these two country bumpkins reached the Harvard Medical School, there was no one in the Admissions Office but one lone secretary. The following conversation ensued:

"I see I'm a bit late to see anyone," said I, "so I'll just come back tomorrow."

"Sorry, but tomorrow's a holiday, so the office will be closed."

"Oh, a holiday? What holiday would that be?"

"You must be from out of town. It's one of our local holidays, Patriot's Day. But perhaps I can help you."

Explaining that I was one of the students accepted for the fall semester, I casually noted that I had also been accepted at the University of Buffalo, and was now trying to arrive at a decision as to where I should attend.

This produced a startling response. Her friendly demeanor changed to one of absolute shock, as she stammered:

"You...mean...you're...thinking...of...not...attending...Harvard?"

Blushing profusely, I blurted out: "But it's only because I don't think I can afford to come here!"

A profound sense of relief swept over her. "Oh, is that all? My goodness, don't let that worry you. We'll take care of that somehow. What's your name?"

She pulled my folder from her files. "Oh, yes, I see that you're from the Buffalo area. Well, the deadline for scholarship applications is over, but we can certainly give you a loan if need be to get started. Here's a loan application form, and you can apply for a scholarship after you've entered.

"I do have another problem, however," said I. "I note in the catalog that the minimum premedical studies include two semesters of organic chemistry and a reading knowledge of a foreign language. Unfortunately, I've had only one semester of organic chemistry, and a year of German. I could possibly take a semester's credit of organic chemistry this summer, but I don't think I could get enough German to be able to pass any kind of reading test."

"Well, you will certainly need the organic chemistry. As for German, don't tell anyone I told you this, but you won't be tested for your language ability, so don't worry about that. I hope that will settle the matter for you." I was ecstatic.

15 – A mystery revealed

This initial contact with the Harvard Medical School revealed a pattern that was to manifest itself repeatedly during the ensuing years. Once accepted, you were a very special person for whom the faculty and administration would allow virtually nothing to stand in the way of your completing your medical studies. To this day, I marvel at the greatness of that institution. As I was to learn, the failure rate was virtually nil – and this at a time when as many as one-third of first year students at many American medical schools failed to make it into the second year. The schools were so overwhelmed with postwar applicants that they simply could not accommodate so many students in the laboratory and hospital facilities required in the later years of medical school.

In later years, however, there arose – and still exists – a very important question relative to my admission that I assumed would never be answered, not in this life in any event. During my postgraduate studies in public health at Harvard many years later, I was seated at lunch one day, with a good friend, Dr. James Shaw, Professor of Biochemistry at the Harvard Dental School. Jim was also a member of the Admissions Committee for both the medical and the dental school, for in those days at least, medical and dental students attended the same classes jointly for the first two years.

Jim had been discussing certain aspects of the admission process with the person on his right, in the course of which he mentioned that every applicant for either school was required to undergo a personal interview before his or her application could be accepted. When I noted that I was admitted without an interview, he was incredulous:

"Oh, you mean you weren't required to come to Boston for an interview because you lived more than 500 miles away, in which case you would have been interviewed by a local alumnus."

"No, Jim. I just sent in my application and never heard another word until I received my letter of acceptance."

"That's impossible!" End of conversation.

Many years later at one of our quinquennial class reunions, I mentioned this conversation to one of our classmates, Dan Federman – by now a Dean at the school. Some weeks later I received a letter from him saying that he had gone through the old files in the basement, and sure enough, there was no record of an interview. Someone wanted me to enter Harvard Medical School. How about this for a possible scenario?

Admissions Committee Meeting, February 12, 1946 (or whenever):

"Now we turn to one of our more interesting applicants, Edwin W. Brown. Here is a guy who thinks he's qualified for admission after a mere four semesters at four different institutions, with what works out to about slightly above a "B" average. An academic hobo with chutzpah, n'est—ce pas? What do you say to taking him in just to see how the crazy lad does?"

Whatever the case, I eagerly signed up for a summer course in organic chemistry at UB – an intensive 3-week session, with lectures in the morning, Monday through Friday, laboratory all afternoon, and an examination ending each week. The total of three such exams would determine the grade for the course. It turned out to be almost a repeat in miniature of my Amherst College experience, missing the middle third of the program, yet arising from the swamp with a rose in my teeth.

On Thursday afternoon of the second week, I carelessly allowed a flask of acid to tip over while bending down to pick up something, splashing some of the stuff in my face. I raced to the sink, lavishly doused my face in water, and was sent off to the doctor's office. He saw no evidence of serious damage, prescribed some eye ointment, and sent me home. On the bus home, whom should I bump into but the chemistry professor himself, who lived in Williamsville and had already become a good friend. Wondering why I was on my way home before the end of the lab session, he expressed concern for my well being and suggested that I stay home the next day and not take the exam. I thus completed only two of the three prescribed exams, but having received an "A" on the first and last ones, he gave me an "A" for the course.

The remainder of the summer I spent working with my friend, Don Weimer, as night greens-keepers at the beautiful Park Country Club in Williamsville. Our job was simple – water a specified portion of the fairways each night, moving the hoses with the help of a tractor every couple of hours. Having soon determined that there was really no need of two people doing that simple job, given the tractor to assist, I bought an Army hammock at the surplus store, strung it up between two trees, and we took turns napping while the other moved the hoses. All went well until one fateful night when ground fog reduced our visibility, and the rising sun (and rising head greens-keeper) greeted us with the news that we had essentially gone in circles with the hoses during the night – and the 7th fairway was now a lake. It was not a pleasant sight, and we were duly terminated.

The job had afforded me one evening of bliss, however. Learning of a pops concert one evening at Kleinhans Music Hall, I screwed up my courage and asked Betty (whom I had not dated in over a year) if she would go with me. She accepted the invitation, and good buddy Don agreed to cover for me until whatever hour I might return to the golf course. It was a moment made in heaven – a fitting farewell prior to my departure for Boston.

By the time I had made up my mind to accept the Harvard offer, whatever the reason for their having made it, there were no more vacancies in Vanderbilt Hall, the distinctive Italianate student residence at 104 Avenue Louis Pasteur, across Longwood Avenue from the medical school. I was disappointed not to be able to have so distinguished an address, but I managed to find digs with a family some blocks away, where at least the address had a quaint New England ring to it – Wigglesworth Street.

Being one of about 150 students, most of whom were from Ivy League schools, and nearly all of whom had Bachelor degrees, plus a scattering of Master degrees and even a couple of PhDs, was a heady experience. The confidence engendered by being academically "a big fish in a little pond" during elementary school, high school, and my first stint at Houghton College quickly gave way to a decided inferiority complex. Having heard that no more than two or three of the class at most were likely to not make it through, I began seeking to identify at least two or three people whom I judged to be less accomplished than I. I never did achieve that goal.

My first semester was short-lived, as it turned out. Physical exams were required of all new students, and by the beginning of November I found myself a ward patient in the Peter Bent Brigham Hospital, Harvard's most prestigious teaching hospital, adjacent to the school. A routine urine specimen during my physical examination had shown some red and white blood cells and other superfluous debris emanating from my kidneys, necessitating whatever studies might be required to diagnose the problem.

16 – A short-lived beginning

The physician assigned to my case was none other than Dr. George W. Thorn, who held the quaint title of Hersey Professor of the Theory and Practice of Physic – and was one of the foremost physicians in the country. He was also one of the most gentle, caring physicians I have ever been privileged to meet. Although he would arrive at one's bedside on morning rounds with an enormous entourage of interns, residents, fellows, and other assorted staff, and would spend no more than a few minutes at the bedside, one had the feeling that there was no more important patient in the hospital than oneself during those moments.

Many years later, long after he had retired, I saw him in the airport in Prague, Czechoslovakia. Approaching him, I said, "Dr. Thorn? I'm Ed Brown, a long-ago patient of yours – but there's no reason you should remember me."

"Of course I remember you!" – and turning to his wife, "This is Ed Brown, a former student of mine from Buffalo."

This brilliant physician, appointed to an endowed professorship at Harvard at the youthful age of 36, died this past year at the age of 98. It was a great privilege to have known him.

Further physical examinations and laboratory studies during the first week in hospital failed to reveal the cause of the initial findings, so he asked me to stay a bit longer while they did some more detailed studies. From time to time he would apologize for having to be out of town for a day or two, and would I mind waiting until he returned for him to explore some other ideas he had. All in all, this went on for more than six weeks, with my occupying a bed the entire time. The semester had gone by without my presence in class and laboratory, and in repeated anticipation of immediate release, I had not bothered to find out where my classmates were in the program and thus try to keep up with them. Thus, as the end of the semester arrived and final exams were imminent, he asked me if I had been able to keep up with my studies – and was duly shocked when I told him I had not done much studying.

We had only two finals – anatomy and histology – so he proposed arranging with the two department heads for me to take only one of the two exams, doing the other at some later date. Anatomy was not my forte in any case, so I elected to take the histology exam. I was given as much time to prepare as I needed, and a week after the class had taken the exam I finally notified the head of the department that I was ready. He summoned me to his office, handed me the examination questions and writing paper, pointed to the clock, saying that I should quit in about two hours – and left for the day! He later informed me that I had successfully passed.

"Pass" or "fail" were the only grades given at the end of each course. The closest one could come to evaluating one's academic accomplishments relative to others in the class would not come until the beginning of one's final year. Only then could one go to the Dean's office and find out whether he or she had been in the lower, middle, or upper third of the class during the prior three years. While this was Harvard's way of attempting to discourage cutthroat competition, in my case it proved to be a disastrous policy. Assuming that I was undoubtedly near the bottom of the lower third and there was no way I could compete with those better-educated brains above me, I had been content to plod along, just hoping to graduate. It was thus with shock that I learned that in my first two years I had been in the middle of the middle third of the class, falling into the lower third only in my junior year. Hopefully, had I known where I stood in those earlier years, I might have put greater effort into my medical studies, rather than just coasting along.

There was, however, another important factor that obviously had its effect on my lackadaisical attitude toward my studies. When Dr. Thorn was at last prepared to discharge me from the hospital, he strongly urged me to consider leaving school for a semester and going where I could rest and, as he artfully put it, "Learn to live with my disease." This, as it turned out, proved to be a further deterrent to my setting important goals in a medical career and working hard to achieve them.

My disease was what in those days was ruefully termed a "wastebasket diagnosis" – the only thing left in the differential diagnosis when everything else has been ruled out. Told only that it was a chronic kidney disease, I learned after sneaking a look at my chart when the nurse was not at hand that it was chronic glomerulonephritis, an ill-defined, then cause-unknown kidney malady for which there was no known treatment and which, according to the medical textbook I consulted, carried an average life expectancy of 15 years from the time of diagnosis.

For me, 15 years would do – it seemed like a long time at that point in my young life, and should afford ample opportunity for an exciting life, however shortened it might be. Thus far the 15 years have stretched to nearly 60.

Harvard's Peter Bent Brigham Hospital, now the Brigham and Women's Hospital, has a long history of major innovations in medicine and surgery, and not only was I a patient of its eminent chief of medicine, Dr. George Thorn, but I was attended by other prominent members of the staff. The June 2004 issue of the *Harvard Medical Alumni Bulletin* carried several photos of that era fifty years before, bringing back vivid memories of that time in my past. One photo was of J. Hartwell Harrison, chief of urology, John P. Merrill, nephrologist, and Joseph E. Murray, chief of plastic surgery, a team who successfully performed the first organ transplant in humans in 1954, thus ushering in the era of transplant surgery. Joe Murray was later to receive the Nobel Prize in Medicine for his pioneering research in organ transplants. All had played some part in my care.

I had already witnessed some of the greatness of the Harvard Medical School through contact with others whose names were on the textbooks we used or otherwise appeared frequently in the medical literature. Most of our lectures were given by the heads of the department, rather than their lesser lights, and in the laboratories and the hospitals it was not uncommon for them to be involved in our day-to-day routine.

It was also not uncommon to see familiar surnames among the members of our class – the sons of eminent physicians and surgeons – one of whose fathers was a Nobel laureate. I admit to having been rather overwhelmed by such, as well as the fact that many of my classmates had advanced degrees. I was, however, always treated as an equal by them, and found none who ever boasted about their heritage or prior educational accomplishments.

17 -- Taking the cure

The venue selected by Dr. Thorn for this period of rest and introspection was a tuberculosis sanatorium in the Adirondack Mountains of New York State, where his friendship with the director would assure me a comfortable life at no expense – a free ride all the way. The New York State Hospital for the Treatment of Incipient Pulmonary Tuberculosis at Ray Brook, New York, proved to be all that and more. One could not have asked for a better arrangement – beautiful grounds, a comfortable room all to myself, excellent cuisine, an interesting 3-hours-a-day job in the laboratory, and a cute little lab technician to teach me the ropes. There was, in fact, no treatment for pulmonary tuberculosis in those days other than bed rest, and not being among those so confined, I was free to enjoy all the pleasures of a beautiful mountain resort with two major lakes nearby, available whenever I could find someone who had a car and wanted to go fishing, boating, golfing, or whatever.

I did indeed learn to live with my disease. The accepted practice for patients and staff alike (most of the latter having themselves been TB patients) was a leisurely lunch followed by no less than two hours of nap time. This, of course, left little of the remainder of the afternoon for work, and to engage in any form of work after dinner was unthinkable – with 9:00 o'clock, more or less, the prescribed bedtime. "Never stand when you can sit, and never sit when you can lie down" was the watchword – and I had no problem following the routine. On average, I spent no less than 12 of every 24 hours in bed, sleeping most of the time. It was a bit of heaven on earth.

I was also determined to take advantage of this singular opportunity to do something I had theretofore been totally unsuccessful in accomplishing – gain weight. I had been a skinny kid in my childhood, a skinny teenager in the Army, and was still a skinny adult. Here at last was my chance – all the food I could eat, all the milk I could drink, and more time in bed than I would ever have again. I drank a quart of milk at every meal, with another at bedtime, eating everything I could put down at every meal. I began this noble experiment at a base weight of 145 pounds and what proved to be my mature height of 6 feet 3 inches, and one year later I had reached the amazing level of 146 pounds. No one else in my family was that thin – what was wrong with my genes? (There must have been something in my genes, however, that kept me from totally destroying my overworked kidneys with the tons of calcium I poured through them that year.)

My grandmother McClellan's repeated advice concerning my weight was to tell me that her son was just like me until his late 20s, "...and look at him now!" This was a bit hard to grasp, for my uncle Don was a very large man – in breadth as well as height. But her prediction was accurate, and soon after being married at age 26, I began gaining weight, eventually reaching 230 pounds. (I'm pleased to say that I trimmed this back to an even 200 a few years ago and have maintained it at that level.)

My intended stay at Ray Brook, as Dr. Thorn had suggested, was the Spring semester plus the summer holiday. But there were two factors that militated against this plan. First, to return to school in the Fall of 1948 would have put me back where I started in the Fall of 1947, simply repeating the courses I had already (or almost already) taken. Of course, I still had an anatomy final to take, but spending another long stint in the abominable anatomy lab had little appeal. (As it turned out, I put off taking that anatomy final year after year, finally biting the bullet and getting it done only when I was nearing the completion of my senior year and would not be able to graduate without passing it.)

Then there was the other factor. Leaving that idyllic setting was going to be difficult at best, but there was the further complication that I had fallen in love with that cute lab technician, and in the summer of 1948 became engaged to her. It was, we both recognized, a union facing an uncertain future. Edna had been a TB patient for much of her then 26 years, having only been discharged as a patient a couple of years before my arrival. I still had almost a full four years of medical school to complete, and there was no possibility of her coming back to Boston with me. For the time being, therefore, the only sensible course of action for me was to remain at Ray Brook and pick up medical school where I had left off. I thus enjoyed an entire one year holiday between my first and second semesters.

That year, however, had put me in close touch with many people with that infectious disease. I learned just how close the following summer when I returned for a visit to Ray Brook before going on home and taking up a summer job in Buffalo. My old buddy, Frank Trowbridge, the x-ray technician, invited me to come down to his shop for a chest x-ray, assuming I hadn't had one for ages. Sloshing the exposed film in the developing tank, he held it up to the light and solemnly proclaimed (with a certain element of glee) that I had an interesting shadow in my left upper apex. "Ed, my friend, I do believe you've joined the club!" Indeed I had, as his boss, the radiologist shortly confirmed. Now what was I to do?

I immediately consulted the medical director, the assistant medical director, and almost everyone else on the staff, but all were of one voice: "Just stay here for the summer. That might be enough to take care of it." But this was not a satisfactory solution—I needed that summer job. Then my buddy Frank suggested I consult the one staff physician who was not an ex-TB patient – the chief of surgery. His response was, "What do *you* want to do?" I told him I wanted to take up the summer job, which would be a light desk job on active duty in the Army Reserve Office in Buffalo. He therefore put in a call to a friend, Dr. Howard Daymon, chief of the TB service of Buffalo's city hospital, the E. J. Meyer Memorial Hospital, who agreed to see me when I arrived home.

There was, however, another matter of grave concern that needed to be resolved before I departed. My fiancé Edna had developed a recurrence of her TB during the previous year, resulting in major surgery to collapse the affected lung. Although she was now up and about, she felt that we should break off the engagement, given her uncertain medical future and my new diagnosis. With great reluctance I accepted return of the engagement ring, and in a state of despondency headed for home. (Many years later I was to learn that she much later married a local resident, and was the happy mother of five children!) As anticipated, Dr. Daymon felt there was no reason for not letting nature take its course. It was a very early lesion, my sputum was negative, and with a healthful lifestyle he saw no reason why I shouldn't go ahead with the summer job, checking back with him once a month.

The job was a pleasant one and the pay was good. It also afforded the opportunity during a two-week absence of my boss, the regular Army captain in charge, for wheedling a double promotion to a five-stripe sergeant first class from the local Army reserve company commander to whose unit I had been assigned for the summer. What a glorious sight was that splash of rank on my sleeve when Captain Rottstedt returned from leave! And what a look of surprise and an unprintable outburst when he saw not one but two new stripes! But the deed was done, he hadn't the authority to reverse the order, and I resigned from the Army Reserve at the end of the summer.

8 – What fools these mortals be!

Having already lost a complete year of medical school because of one chronic disease, however mild, and uncertain as to how the diagnosis of another might affect my future, I began to wonder if medical school was right for me. This weighed so heavily on my mind throughout the summer that only a few weeks before my scheduled return to Boston I decided to quit medical school and pursue a doctorate in psychology at the University of Buffalo. Accordingly, I sent a letter of resignation to the Dean of Students at Harvard, who graciously replied that they would be sorry to lose me, but that the choice was mine to make.

Looking back, I cannot conceive how I could have reached such an utterly stupid decision, given the fact that I would probably have to do one or two years of undergraduate study to qualify for admission to a doctoral program – and at least two or more additional years to receive a Ph.D. I hadn't told my parents or anyone else what I had done, but God graciously intervened with a Fatherly kick in the pants, and in panic I wrote to the Dean of Students only a week before classes were to begin at Harvard, admitting my folly and begging permission to return. I wish I had preserved his priceless reply, which could only have come from a truly great institution – "Dear Brown, Of course you are welcome to return. Please plan to arrive by September 12th when classes begin. Yours, Reginald Fitz, Jr."

Returning to school, I was put under the care of one of Boston's most distinguished chest physicians, Dr. Theodore Badger. He was the epitome of the Proper Bostonian, accent and all, but he was also a marvelously kind and caring physician. He gave me a most thorough physical and x-ray examination, and like Dr. Daymon, decided there was no reason I should not continue in medical school. At monthly visits he carefully examined me, a routine he was to follow the entire school year, without a hint of expectation of reimbursement. It was a noble gesture of professional courtesy to a mere second-year medical student.

I was now a member of a different class of students, but having had little time to develop close friendships in my former class, I quickly found myself with a number of new friends living near me in Vanderbilt Hall. Although, as fate was to decree, I did not eventually graduate with this class, several of them continued to be lifelong friends. Only one has died in the meanwhile, but I miss him. Bill Curran, who occupied the room next to mine, was a graduate of Harvard College, majoring in English literature of all things, and he was the constant source of innumerable delightful quotations from the classics. About his family I knew nothing, but I was soon to learn.

I had acquired an icebox to hold snacks. No, not a refrigerator but an icebox, and cooled my snacks with weekly deliveries of a block of ice from the local ice man. Late one evening, following a good bit of drunken shouting and singing emanating from a room down the hall, Bill awakened me with a knock on my door and requested the loan of the drain pan, filled with frigid water. He had been trying unsuccessfully to prepare for an exam, and had been equally unsuccessful in quieting the perpetrator down the hall. I gave him the pan, and stood in the doorway, curious to know what he intended to do with it. I watched him exit into the quadrangle (our rooms were on the ground floor), and a moment later heard him shout, "This should cool you off, Brad Murphy!" as he heaved the ice water through Murphy's open window. Loud curses ensued, Bill returned the pan with a satisfied smile on his face, and I went back to sleep.

Bill apparently dozed off himself shortly thereafter, for he was not awakened by the strange muted sounds outside his door that soon aroused me. Not wanting to get involved in some altercation, I listened through my door to what I assumed to be Brad Murphy engaged in some sort of nefarious act of revenge. After a bit there was silence, so I cautiously opened the door, to find Bill's door starting to go up in flames from ignited paper that had been shoved beneath it, presumably to fill the room with smoke. I alerted him by pounding on the door, we obtained a bucket of water from the bathroom just opposite, and doused the flames. It was apparent that this combat had gone far enough, so we both retired for the night.

The resident hall manager having been apprised of the damage the following morning, we soon received word that all three of us were to report to the Dean's office, I being viewed as *accessory after the fact*. Dean George Packer Berry, a man of formidable countenance, summarily chewed out Murphy, telling him he would deal with him later, and then turned attention to the two of us. Mildly reprimanding me for providing the instigating weapon, he then solemnly addressed Bill. "Your daddy is a good friend of mine, Mr. Curran, and I am sure that he would be disappointed in you as the result of last night's proceedings. However, I do not intend to inform him. I trust, however, that we shall have no further repetition of such goings on." With that he dismissed us. I could hardly wait until we were out of there before asking Bill how the heck the Dean knew his father?

With some degree of embarrassment, Bill admitted that his father was none other than the Dean of the Long Island College of Medicine in New York. I was duly impressed – and as we shall see later, Dr. Jean Curran, a distinguished alumnus of Harvard Medical School himself, was to become an important factor in my subsequent career in medicine.

While there was no progression of my tuberculosis during that year under Dr. Badger's care, neither did the shadow on my lung disappear. It was therefore with some misgivings that he assented to my plans for the summer of 1950. I had at last completed the second year of medical school and felt that I deserved a real respite. A worldly-wise fourth year student acquaintance had convinced several of us that a great place to spend the summer would be Acapulco, where, he claimed, the beaches were littered with young American school teachers and room and board could be obtained in hotels for $2.00 a day.

I bought the best used car I could find at the cheapest price – a 1948 Kaiser sedan, already a dog on the market – and three of us blithely headed for paradise. Passing through Buffalo, we picked up my brothers Dick and Dave. Dick had provided the funds for the car, having gone to work after his Army stint. Dave had just finished high school and been accepted at John Brown University in Siloam Springs, Arkansas. We would drop him off on the way back from Mexico.

Dick, however, deserted us in Mexico City prior to our arrival in Acapulco, having developed an acute case of homesickness, pining for a young lady in our church, Jean Loeffler, with whom he had entered into a romantic relationship some months earlier. Much against our advice, he packed up, boarded a rickety bus to the border, and traveled back to Buffalo by whatever cheap means of transport he could muster. By the time I arrived back home a month or so later, they had announced their engagement. He certainly made out better than the rest of us insofar as any romance that summer was concerned – and they're still together 56 years later.

We did not intend to stay more than a couple of weeks, having spent more time in Mexico City than originally planned. However, when we found that the only way to get a $2.00 daily rate was to stay in one small hotel for an entire month, we hunkered down for the long haul. It was a great little hotel, actually, located at the top of the hill overlooking the Playa Caleta. (Fifty six years later I returned to Acapulco, disappointed to find an urban sprawl of two million people.) But the other half of the promise that had brought us there was a total loss – there were, to be sure, a considerable number of girls strewn along the beach, but nary a one who didn't appear to have a Mexican male companion.

Dr. Badger was ready to see me as soon as I returned to school. The lesion had not regressed as anticipated, and he advised me to take off the rest of the semester and get the rest I was supposed to have gotten that summer. Obviously reluctant to further delay completion of medical school, I made a deal with him—the deal-maker at it again. If he allowed me to continue, I would agree to spend all my time in bed that was not required for lectures, clinical sessions at the hospitals, and meals at Vanderbilt Hall. He doubted that I could do it, but agreed to let me give it a try. For the next four months I faithfully followed an increasingly boring routine, studying my notes and textbooks while lying in bed. I managed to complete the semester, but now another monkey wrench fell into the works – my last x-ray showed not regression but slight progression. I gave in, and headed back to Ray Brook for a prescribed 4-5 months of bed rest.

Although difficult to be in such close proximity to my ex-fiancée, it was a pleasure to see many old friends, including another Harvard medical student who had become a patient there during my first stay. David Kliewer had served in the Pacific as a fighter pilot, stationed on Wake Island when the Japanese invaded it. He managed to get into the air before being captured, and to shoot down an enemy plane before finally running out of fuel, forcing his return to the island. He spent the next four years in a prison camp in Japan, an experience about which he said very little. When, after a very long time he was allowed to receive mail from home and send one letter a month to his family, he asked them to complete an application for him to Harvard Medical School – on the basis of which he was admitted when the war ended. But prison had taken its toll, although his disease did not manifest itself until his second year of school. He lost two years of school, graduating in 1951.

19 – Reality check

Before bedding down for the duration, I had to go on to Buffalo to get rid of my old car and let my family know what I was up to. My parents had meanwhile moved to Florida, but my brother and other family members were still in Williamsville. While there, I felt that I owed Dr. Daymon the courtesy of a call. While he agreed that the time had come to take more active measures, he came up with a startling proposal. "As a Harvard medical student, you need to see more of the real world. What I think you should do is become a patient on my TB service at the city hospital and see how patients have to deal with their disease in an urban setting, as compared with an idyllic retreat in the Adirondacks." How was that for throwing down the gauntlet?

I would like to say that I accepted the challenge unhesitatingly – but I suspect it was more a matter of wondering how I was going to be able to stay at Ray Brook and see Edna every day now that our engagement had been dissolved. Whatever the case, I did spend the next five months on the ward of the Meyer's TB division, where the difference from life at Ray Brook quickly became apparent. Several of the more severely ill patients died during my stay, but for those who were able to hang on for another year or two, a potential cure at last became available with the advent of streptomycin, soon followed by other drugs. Although I accepted the challenge of remaining in bed almost 24 hours a day in spite of feeling perfectly fit, at one point cabin fever prevailed and I sneaked off the ward, found my street clothes, and walked out in the dead of winter to a movie theater opposite the hospital. In general, however, the bed was comfortable, the food was palatable, and the staff were pleasant – although I found the habit of one night nurse a bit annoying. About 2:00 in the morning I would frequently be awakened by her shining a flashlight in my face, and when I inquired as the purpose of this seemingly bizarre behavior, her reply left me wondering about the logic of the procedure: "I couldn't tell if you were breathing, and I had to be sure that you hadn't died in your sleep." One would have thought that such information could have waited until breakfast was served. I would like to claim that those five months afforded a splendid opportunity to get caught up on my medical studies, but like the six weeks in bed at the Brigham in Boston, I chalked up a total loss in that area.

I did experience another disappointment, this one not of my own making. The only attraction of serving my sentence in Buffalo was the proximity of other family members, as well as those of my church, visits from whom would help break the monotony. As it turned out, however, an inordinate fear of contagion resulted in not one visit from either the pastor of the church or any member thereof other than my brother and his wife. I learned later that some members of the congregation heard near the end of my stay that I was *in extremis*, becoming the object of special prayer that death might not prevail. It was thus a shock to some when I appeared at a Sunday service after my discharge a few weeks later. I should have attributed my miraculous cure to some secret potion and offered bottles of the stuff for sale.

I returned to medical school in late December 1951, reoccupying my old digs at Vanderbilt Hall. It was good to be back, although by this time I had begun to question whether I was ever going to finish medical school. Starting out in the Class of '51, I had drifted into the Class of '52 upon my return from Ray Brook, and now I had joined the Class of '53 – quite possibly the only person to have been a member of three different classes of the medical school.

An abrupt change in my life began very soon thereafter. On the evening of Sunday February 11, 1952, I had decided to attend the last two hours of an auto show at Mechanics Hall, but when I found a vast throng attempting to board the subway train where I was to get off, I inquired why so many were leaving at that moment. "It's the last night – the show ended early!" At this point, the logical move was to cross the platform to the westbound side and return to my room, thereby getting a round trip for the one-way fare. But that would have been an unnecessary waste of 30 cents with having accomplished nothing, so I made a swift decision to stay on the train and do what I had been wanting to do for a number of years – find a wife.

The hastily-conceived plan was simple -- stay on to the end of the line at Park Street station, and catch the evening service at my church, Park Street Church. This was, after all, an acceptable place to look for one's life partner, and anyhow, it was about time I started going back there, having been considerably delinquent in church attendance since arriving back at school, and contenting myself with listening to Dr. Ockenga's sermon on the radio.

My delinquency had been duly noted by the Rev. Calvin Malefyt, associate minister in charge of the Collegiate Club, so when he caught me sneaking into church, he greeted me warmly and invited me to join some other students at his home after the service. This was not exactly what I had in mind, but weaseling out did not seem to be an option, so I thanked him and headed for the balcony, knowing that the main sanctuary would be filled by that hour. Blocking the entrance and looking down the rows for a likely candidate like some bird of prey, I was shortly addressed by a quiet little female voice saying, "Excuse me, please!", and I stepped aside to allow her passage. She appeared to be a rather attractive young thing, so I followed her into the pew. We shared a hymn book (a neat opening gambit), and I spent the remainder of the service straining for a better view of her out of the corner of my eye, oblivious to the sermon. What I could see was definitely appealing.

The service ended, and now the mighty bird of prey was reduced to a speechless, totally inadequate lump of humanity, frantically attempting to open a conversation. She tried by thanking me for sharing the hymn book, but all that came out of the near-mute on her right was a mumbled, "Uh, you're welcome." Undaunted, she responded with, "It was a good sermon, wasn't it?" Darned if I knew, having heard not a word of it, but I managed a convincing, "Uh, yeah." By now she had given up, so again I heard a sweet, little "Excuse me, please" as she stepped by me, probably to disappear forever from my life.

Disconsolate, I made my way to Calvin's car. He opened the front door for me, and began introducing the occupants in the rear seat – and heaven directed a bolt of lightning straight at me. One of them was she! Her name was Pat Currier.

As I sat opposite her in the Malefyt living room in Cambridge, a new problem presented itself. Seated next to her was another girl whom I had seen in earlier days at the Collegiate Club at church, to whom I had found myself attracted but whom I had never pursued. The longer I studied the two, the more uncertain my choice became. This was something new for me—two girls from whom to choose, in a setting ideal for making a connection. No singles bar this! These were church-going gals. I am embarrassed to reveal the deciding factor, as unlikely as it was. Yes, one was short, the other tall – but I liked short girls, and tall girls, and all sizes in between. The determining factor -- I blush to reveal it -- one shaved her legs and the other did not. Naught but a clean cut American girl for me.

20 – Patience -- a virtue yet to be learned

When I learned that Pat had to take the same subway back to Boston, the next step seemed simple enough. I would accompany her, and by the time we reached her station, I should have been able to work up enough courage to ask her to go the Valentine Day party at church that coming Wednesday. I did, and she accepted. I had just experienced a bit of heaven. I realize that all this sounds a bit absurd – a suave, handsome (well, not a real dork, anyway) Harvard medical student groveling before a demure little Boston University freshman, barely turned 18? But this had been the story of my life insofar as my ability in relating easily to any female for whom I had developed a passion was concerned. As now seems clear to me, it was nothing but the fear of rejection.

That Wednesday evening went swimmingly, and I had little difficulty broaching the possibility of a concert the following week. But then the blow fell! Soon after our second date I received a letter informing me that she could no longer in good conscience continue to see me by reason of a prior commitment – she already had a boyfriend. This was a crushing blow. I poured out my heart to her in a long reply and posted it with much misgiving. I received no immediate reply, and when a friend invited me to double date with him a week later, I reluctantly accepted. The occasion was the visit of his girlfriend's father to town, and this good gentleman was to take his daughter, her best friend, and the two of us to dinner.

The day prior to this impending engagement I received another letter from Pat. She had carefully reconsidered her position, and if I so desired, she would be available the following evening. Gadzooks, what a gift from above – and what a predicament it created. There was simply no way I could back out of the other commitment. The best I could so was to tell her that I would be delighted to see her the next evening – if she didn't mind making a late date, possibly as late as nine. My plan was to get word to my first date, through my friend and his girlfriend, that an emergency had arisen that demanded my attention before the end of the following day, and that I would probably have to excuse myself after dinner. It worked— but how despicable!

Within the next few weeks and several dates later, it became apparent that I had found the girl of my dreams (albeit it for the third time). Announcing that fact to her, however, would demand the utmost patience. Months would have to pass ere I dared reveal my intentions. She was, after all, a mere child – and there were her parents to consider. I simply had to play it cool. Regrettably, that resolve lasted but a few weeks, when a situation arose that demanded immediate action. Pat had applied to the prestigious Harvard-Tufts Forsyth School of Dental Hygiene, left her college studies to await their decision, and had taken a job in a bank. When I called on her one evening in late March she proudly showed me their letter of acceptance. That was all well and good, for I would not yet have to let her know that within scarcely more than a year we would be off to parts unknown following my graduation. (By now my star was shining so brightly that all doubts about finishing school in May 1953 had dissipated.) But there was a fly in the ointment – the letter demanded payment of a $50 nonrefundable acceptance fee.

"Frugality" was not only my middle name, it was the polar star that guided me through all matters fiscal. How could I dare allow her to throw fifty dollars down the drain? I pondered the matter for all of five minutes and then blurted out my intentions. I did not demand an immediate response – I simply wanted her to have time to think it over before parting with a sum of that magnitude. Needless to say, she did not leap with joy. She did, however, tell me that she cared a good deal for me, and whatever decision she was to take, it would not be taken lightly. We then let the matter drop for the time being – meaning that she decided that fifty dollars was not too much to keep her options open.

During the Easter break I took her home to meet my family in Buffalo, without telling them that she was other than a very good friend. She enjoyed the visit, but had to cut it short in order to fly back to her job. As I bid her farewell at the airport, she broke the news – she would marry me and forego her future otherwise. It was an emotional moment. Not long after she left, I had another emotional moment. "You have just made a major commitment, mister – big time!" Had I done the right thing?

Returning to Boston a week later, I received a phone call from her mother, asking if I might join her for lunch at her apartment several days hence. Now the moment of truth had arrived – but what did this portend? Surely she was not taking lightly this frothy relationship between her only child, an innocent babe of 18 short years, and a smooth-talking, fast-moving 26-year-old man of the world. I dreaded the encounter. But like every cloud, it gave promise of a silver lining. If I was going to have to fight for my lady, then I also had the option of giving up and backing out.

Etta Ann Currier was a lady of the highest order – not a Boston Brahmin but a solid New Englander who had grown up under very difficult circumstances (as I learned many years later) and had raised her daughter in the finest tradition of family. She was a most gracious hostess, who immediately put me at my ease – at least at the outset. I still dreaded the ensuing conversation. I still don't recall exactly what was said, but it soon became apparent, contrary to my expectations, that she was thrilled with the whole thing. I was now irrevocably committed.

The engagement was duly announced in all of the Boston papers, complete with a picture of the bride-to-be and the announcement that the marriage would take place on August 9th in Hampton Falls, New Hampshire, the family hometown. My child bride and I were married by the Rev. Everett Scruton in the Baptist church Pat had attended through childhood, and after a brief honeymoon at The Inn in Buck Hills Falls, Pennsylvania, we moved into an apartment at Kenmore Square, overlooking Fenway Park.

The final year at Harvard comprised two months of internal medicine, two months of surgery, a month of pediatrics, and a minimum of three months of electives, with only one month of mandatory holiday at whatever time the student might choose, other than the final month of the academic year. The year began in June, so I carefully chose elective courses that would give me every third month off – August for our wedding and honeymoon and a search for an apartment, November to catch up on domestic details, and February to begin to look at internship possibilities. As it turned out, there was a change in the schedule in April, with the course I had chosen for May no longer offered and none other of interest to me, so that I was permitted to be free in May as well.

Our first son was born during my last year of school – imaginatively named Edwin W. Brown III, but given the name Teddy by his grandmother Brown who said we couldn't hang the name Edwin on that precious little thing. He remains Ted to this day. (At least it's better than Buster!)

21 – Young Doctor Kildare

Although my kidney disorder had become essentially a non-entity, with actual signs of regression, as had the x-ray evidence of tuberculosis, Dr. Thorn felt that I should not undergo the rigors of a typical internship with its inordinate time demands. He therefore proposed a year of research back in Buffalo, where he had arranged a program for me at the Buffalo General Hospital, with an eminent cardiac research team. I was under no obligation to accept this, but since I now had the month of May free, I would go home, have a look at it and then come to a decision.

There were yet two unknowns to be faced, however. The first was that delayed anatomy exam which had been hanging over my head for over five years. How I got through it I will never know, for my knowledge of anatomy was appalling—perhaps best illustrated by an episode that occurred earlier that year in my surgery elective at the Massachusetts General Hospital. On that day I had the privilege of standing alongside one of the world's foremost thoracic surgeons, Dr. Edward Churchill, as he performed a major procedure. As I held a retractor and peered into the open chest cavity, he pointed to a readily discernible, throbbing structure deep inside the mass of heart, lungs, and adjoining tissues and asked, "Tell me, doctor, what is that?" I don't recall exactly what I mumbled, but it was definitely not the right answer, evoking the response: "That's the descending aorta! But forgive me for asking—I forgot that Harvard medical students don't know much anatomy."

The other factor was the uncertainty of whether I would have to return to Boston in early June for another examination. Although Harvard had no overall final examinations as such, they did have a rather strange tradition of subjecting certain final year students to an examination, without offering a clue as to the criteria determining who took the examination. From what anyone outside the administration knew, it included a cross-section of the class, from lowest to highest ranking. Only when the list was posted in the last week of May would one know who had to take it.

I returned home with my lovely bride at the beginning of May, and soon thereafter met with those with whom I had been invited to work for the coming year. The occasion was a dinner at the home of the chief of cardiovascular research, Dr. David Greene, given solely for my benefit, and after a most convivial evening with some of the most friendly and interesting group of people I have ever met, I told Dave (for that is what he insisted on being called) that I would be delighted to begin my duties on June 1st – assuming, of course, that I had in fact graduated.

Sweating out that unknown exam to be given back in Boston, I phoned the Dean's office on the day appointed for posting of the list. The secretary who took the call asked me to wait a moment while she went out in the hall and surveyed the list. After what seemed like an eternity, she returned and happily announced, "I didn't see your name there, so it looks like you've finished medical school. Congratulations!"

Six long years to complete a four-year course – and now that phase of my life was apparently over. Not until I actually had that diploma in my hand, however, would I be completely at ease. Graduation ceremonies were scheduled for mid-June, but I saw no point in traveling all the way to and from Boston just to be handed a piece of paper. While I was sitting in my parents' living room one Saturday in late June (not being prepared to sign a lease for an apartment until the last brick in my medical school education was in place), a Railway Express driver delivered a small, flat package to the door. Therein was the most beautiful piece of paper I had ever seen. Written entirely in Latin, it declared to the world that *Universitas Harvardiana Cantabrigiae* had bestowed upon *Edvinum Wilson Brown* the degree of *Medicinae Doctoris* on the 11th of June in the one thousand nine hundred and fifty-third year of our Lord and three hundred and seventeenth year of Harvard College. I knelt down and thanked my heavenly father for his graciousness. My odyssey was well under way.

The 1953-54 year with Dave Greene, Ivan Bunnell, George Miller, and other distinguished staff of the Buffalo General Hospital and the University of Buffalo School of Medicine, to which I was appointed a Fellow in Cardiopulmonary Physiology, was sheer bliss. They were a fantastic team who treated me as an equal, and I will be ever indebted to them. We were working at what was then the cutting edge of cardiac research, and Dave was a superb teacher. Near the end of that academic year, the time had arrived to put their results on paper and present them at the annual meeting of the American Physiological Society in Madison, Wisconsin. Dave asked me to work on that paper, and when we had together crafted the final version, he insisted that I deliver it at the meeting. I was flying high.

Dave and George have since died, but not long ago I had the pleasure of spending an evening with Ivan and Alice Bunnell. There were many pleasant episodes upon which to reflect, but Ivan's favorite was recalling our move into new quarters at the Buffalo General Hospital, and my having instructed some workmen, in his absence, how to place the sink in the darkroom of our laboratory. Since the task of developing film from our recording device was mine, I had them mount the sink at armpit height so that I could comfortably rest my arms on the drain boards while sloshing film in the sink. After I left for Virginia, Ivan assumed that task – and being a good bit shorter than I, found that he could barely get his arms over the edge of the sink, thus necessitating the construction of a six-inch-high platform on which he could stand.

It was a memorable year in other respects. We were living in a comfortable apartment just ten minutes from work, our second son, John Currier Brown, was born in February at the General, and we had bought our first new car, a 1953 Ford sedan. I had skipped the traditional internship year, but now the problem of New York State medical licensure reared its ugly head. An internship was required. Once again, Dr. Thorn, with the help of Dave Greene, came to the rescue. Dr. Thorn prevailed upon his friend, the director of the Meyer Memorial Hospital (my old alma mater) to take me on as an unpaid intern in excess of their normal quota, to be on duty only from 8:00 to 5:00, five days a week – no nights, no weekends. Dr. Greene then arranged an appointment as Fellow in Cancer Research at the famed Roswell Park Memorial Hospital in Buffalo at a salary of $250 a month (twice the intern pay at Meyer!), in return for which I was required to spend an hour or so each evening on my way home from the Meyer for nine months and then spend the last 3 months of my internship on the wards at Roswell. The rationale for this largesse was that in July 1955 I would then begin a residency at Roswell with Dave's friend, Dr. James Elam, chief of anesthesiology, where I would continue to be involved in a joint research project with Dave, across the street at Buffalo General.

Jim Elam was a remarkable person, the first to seriously promote the use of mouth-to-mouth resuscitation on the basis of the extensive studies he conducted at Roswell. Although mouth-to-mouth resuscitation is described in the Bible and was used for centuries by midwives to resuscitate newborns, it was not considered an adequate method to oxygenate the lungs because expired air contains only 20 percent oxygen, the other 80 percent being carbon dioxide. As the American Heart Association declares in its website, *Highlights of the History of Cardiopulmonary Resuscitation (CPR)*, "In 1954 James Elam was the first to prove that expired air was sufficient to maintain adequate oxygenation."

Like most medical pioneers, he at first met resistance from the American Red Cross and others for whom the time-honored method of resuscitation of victims of drowning and electrical shock was the use of the prone position while pressing on the back of the chest. I had the dubious honor of being the "victim" in his first public demonstration of mouth-to-mouth resuscitation, at a luncheon of the county medical society in Buffalo in 1954. After presentation of his research results and demonstration of the technique on me, I remember hearing such comments from the audience as, "Well, I wouldn't dare try it in an emergency. I would probably be sued if the patient didn't survive!" Fortunately, publication of his results in major medical journals soon changed that attitude, and "the kiss of life" was adopted by the American Red Cross, later to be followed by the pioneering work of others in external heart massage – the birth of CPR.

Our local pharmacist, Ted Dungey, had invited me to join the local Rotary Club, where on one occasion I again heard an "expert opinion" that reminded me of that initial reaction to mouth-to-mouth resuscitation. The speaker one evening was a neighbor of mine, Walter Dornberger, the former German general who directed construction of the German V-2 rocket during World War II. His talk was about the future of rocket flight, in which he described a large stubby-winged aircraft that could travel from coast to coast, powered by a single burst of power at the beginning of its flight and gliding for the rest of the 3000 mile journey to a safe landing. As we were leaving, I heard someone ask a member who was an airline pilot if that prediction made any sense. "Of course not! A heavy aircraft like that could never glide any distance and certainly not land without power!"

With the birth of a second son and payments on a new car, I did physical exams for an insurance agent friend, and at one time responded to a newspaper ad of a lawyer seeking a process server, which seemed an intriguing job. On one occasion, I enlisted the aid of my brother Dave in serving the owner of a Buffalo coffee shop, whom I assumed would deny his identity when I asked his name. Noting the number of the public telephone in his shop and synchronizing our watches, I went down the street to a phone booth to call at the agreed-upon moment while Dave sat near the phone. The man behind the counter went over to answer it, and when. I asked to speak to so-and-so, he said he was so-and-so. Dave then tapped him on the shoulder, said, "This is for you.", handed him the subpoena, and beat a hasty retreat, leaving the poor fellow looking rather bewildered. It was more interesting than doing insurance exams.

22 – "The best-laid schemes o' mice and men......."

An event occurred early in 1955 that was to completely change my direction. During my third year of medical school I had become acquainted with a number of students at the Harvard School of Public Health, adjacent to the medical school, who took their meals in our residence hall. They were fascinating people from other countries, all quite senior in their respective fields of public health. I had become rather disillusioned about the clinical practice of medicine as I experienced it at Harvard. So many of our patients were medical enigmas – not unlike myself that first year – who had been referred from other hospitals from all over the country and other parts of the world. I found that I did not share the thrill of my classmates in trying to unravel these medical mysteries. I was inclined to a more pragmatic approach to medical care – get right at it by establishing the diagnosis and prescribing the accepted treatment. I doubted that I would be a very good doctor and could not see myself tied down day after day, year after year, to a typical medical practice.

Public health, on the other hand, offered much more interesting possibilities, not the least of which was the opportunity to work abroad in a great variety of settings. I had thus decided this was to be my specialty of medicine several months before I graduated. Needless to say, I was in a distinct minority of my classmates in having chosen this field – a minority of two, to be precise.

Early in 1955 I was visited by one of my 1952 classmates who had elected to go into public health. He had finished a traditional internship and was now in a public health residency. He wanted to know, of course, why I had changed directions. I explained that my one-month course in anesthesiology at the Massachusetts General Hospital had been my most interesting and enjoyable elective during my senior year. Thus, when this opportunity for a comfortable solution to the internship problem involved my going into anesthesiology, I felt I would be quite content in that field. "Nonsense!," he responded. "Your reasons for deciding to go into public health were far more valid, and I think you're making a great mistake."

I pondered that statement long and hard in the following weeks. It made good sense. But I had committed myself to this present course and saw no way of gracefully getting out of that commitment. Both Dave Greene and Jim Elam were severely disappointed to hear of my misgivings about going on in anesthesiology, but they were understanding enough not to try to deter me from leaving the program. It was not a decision I was proud of, but in retrospect I believe it to have been the right one.

Residency programs in public health were in their infancy in 1955, and few and far between. The only one appearing at all attractive was a one-year program offered by the Commonwealth of Virginia, involving nine months in the Arlington County Health Department, followed by three months in the rural setting of the Tri-County Health Department in the southeast corner of the state in Suffolk. Its compelling features were two: living in the Washington, D.C. area for most of the year, and an annual stipend of $7500 – more than twice that of clinical residencies. One could live comfortably on $7500 a year in those days.

I contacted the director, Dr. Beachley, the Arlington county health officer, to inquire if the lone position they offered was still open for the coming year. It was, and he appeared eager to fill it, for he invited me to come down at the earliest opportunity and look it over. I did, he was impressed with my Harvard background, and I was impressed with his program. Pat didn't accompany me, having just given birth to Jack, our second child, but the Washington area would certainly be an interesting place in which to live, and a living wage at long last had considerable appeal. Leaving the wee ones with my parents, we shortly embarked on a house-hunting trip and quickly located an excellent rental house in Falls Church, Virginia, only 10 minutes from my future workplace.

One-way truck rentals had not yet come into being, but brother Dave, home from college for the summer, generously offered his services with the move, including driving the empty truck back to Buffalo. The plan was to pick up the vehicle late one afternoon, load it in the evening, and head out early in the morning in order to arrive before nightfall. Despite meticulous preliminary measurements of major pieces of furniture and calculations as to where they would best fit in the space available, the process did not go well, and we did not depart until late afternoon. Goods piled on the passenger side of the truck's cab left just enough room for me to take a deep breath, with Dave at the wheel of our 1953 Ford sedan, Pat in the passenger seat with a couple of large lamp shades in her lap, and two infants buried somewhere among the debris in the back seat.

All went well, however, until our little caravan encountered fog in the hills of southeastern Pennsylvania. Pat was driving ahead, with Dave now holding the lamp shades, and I remained behind her so as to be able to provide succor in the event of a mishap to the car. Mile after mile through the tortuous terrain I kept my unfailing gaze on the taillights, the only thing visible on the car. When the fog at last dissipated, I found that for an unknown length of time I had been following a red Buick, not a green Ford. Failing to catch up with her, I eventually had to pull into a gas station when the needle on my gas gauge was firmly on "E".

Not to worry! I would simply tank up and complete the journey alone if need be, knowing that she could do likewise. It was thus disconcerting when I reached for my wallet, only to recall that it was in the trousers from which I had changed into shorts for comfort at the last fuel stop – and the trousers were in in the Ford. My cash reserve consisted of one thin dime, which I used to call the Pennsylvania State Police, requesting them to be on the lookout for my wife's car, and to give her my location if found. I pulled the truck to the front of the gas station where it would be visible from the highway and prayed for mercy.

Communication lines to the Almighty were in good order that night, for in less than two hours I was blessed with the sight of Pat rolling down the highway whence I had come. She had apparently taken a wrong turn about 40 miles back while Dave was asleep. When he awoke and discovered I had gone missing, he consulted the map and decided their best move was to backtrack to the road they should have been taken, hoping to find me. Reaching our new home at 6:00 a.m., we unloaded the truck, and after Dave had managed a 2-hour nap, we reluctantly bid him farewell, since he had to get back to his summer job in Buffalo.

Dealing with the health of a community, as compared to the care of the individual patient, was every bit as interesting as I had thought it would be. The individual was still very much a part of the life of a public health physician, and the work brought one into contact with an entire cross section of the community. Importantly, the emphasis was on health, not on disease. Health is much more than simply the absence of disease.

Exposure to the myriad functions of the health department of a large community provided an education not to be found in medical school. An army of health professionals unknown to the general public is quietly at work day after day protecting the health of our communities – among them the public health nurse, who is very visible visiting the families of children with reportable infectious diseases or administering shots in an immunization clinic, and the sanitary inspector who meticulously checks every aspect of the kitchen of a public food establishment, from a greasy spoon eatery in the inner city to the restaurant atop the Ritz, and is never seen by the patrons. Most of the work of the public health professionals is not very glamorous; all of it can be very satisfying to those providing the services.

The director of a health department of a large city is the commanding general of this army, and like his counterpart in the military he is dependent upon other agencies for support of various kinds – the legislature, the police, the academic community, the media, etc. In rural areas, much of this contact takes place at a higher level, thereby bypassing the local public health physician, but personal involvement with community members is more intense and generally more rewarding. Near the end of the year I was asked to pay a visit to the health department in a quiet little town in the "horse country" of Virginia about 100 miles from Washington. The director was of retirement age, and the state was anxious to see him retire and have me replace him. Dropping by without informing him of the purpose of my visit, I found him comfortably ensconced in a spacious office overlooking the distant hills, poring over the day's edition of the *Wall Street Journal*. "Not a lot to do here, doctor, and it's a lovely community. You ought to think about taking a job in a place like this some day!" Thanks, but no thanks.

During the Christmas holidays we had packed off to see Pat's folks in Boston. While there I wanted to get an opinion from someone at the Harvard School of Public Health as to at what point in my career it would be desirable to go for a Master of Public Health degree, one of the requirements for specialty board certification. Should I do it early in the game or wait until I had a number of years of experience under my belt?

23 – From southern Virginia to northern Greenland

Dropping by the School of Public Health, I hoped there would be someone, however low in rank, who could offer some advice – like the lone secretary at the medical school next door ten years earlier. As it happened, I did find the place almost completely deserted. I could find only one person in the entire building – the dean himself, John Crayton Snyder, one of the foremost figures of his day in public health. He received me graciously, and after hearing my story, asked, "Have you any interest in teaching preventive medicine to medical students?"

This had, in fact, long been in the back of my mind as the possible culmination of a career in public health – a position to which one might aspire after many years. He then explained: "Well, you might be interested to know that we are starting a new course here next Fall – a two-year program that will be directed by one of our distinguished alumni who has been working in India for the past 10 years, Dr. Carl Taylor. If you would like to consider joining that class, we would be pleased to have you – here's an application. And if you need financial support, the National Foundation for Infantile Paralysis is currently offering fellowships for postgraduate study in public health. Here's their address if you care to write to them."

I applied for the program, received a fellowship from the polio foundation, and by late May, the time had come to look for a house in the Boston area. I offered to look after 13-month-old Jack if Pat could manage with our 3-year-old Ted. By now I was commuting each week to Suffolk, Virginia, renting a room in the home of a very nice widow, and hoped she wouldn't mind my taking in a roommate for a couple of weeks or so. Pat flew to Boston the next day, and I headed south with Jack, bottles, sterilizer and a large supply of diapers. (No Pampers in those ancient days...) Arriving that evening, I left Jack in the car, and with some apprehension explained my predicament to my landlady -- who not only happened to have a crib in the attic but was thrilled with the prospect of caring for the little guy while I was at work. He was no problem whatsoever for either of us, even when I took him with me on an all-day deep sea fishing trip one Saturday.

Although this was to be our first house purchase, Pat was not in the least fazed at going it alone, and did a fantastic job, soon finding a beautiful new tri-level in nearby Framingham that could be financed with a 5% down payment on a Veterans Administration loan. The price was $14,500, and her parents were more than happy to lend us the down payment. The only problem was that I would have to come to Boston to complete the purchase. The next weekend I flew up with Jack, and the deal was done, occupancy to be given July 1st.

This time we had to hire a professional mover. It soon became apparent after settling in that unless I could quickly find a job for the summer, we were going to be in trouble. The necessity of employing a professional mover this time had taken a large bite out of our savings, and my polio foundation fellowship didn't begin until September. The Dean's office at the school went to work on the problem, and soon thereafter I receive a phone call asking me to come to the office of Dr. John E. Gordon, the soon-to-be-retiring professor of epidemiology.

Gordon was a crusty old sort, one of the pioneers in 20th century epidemiology, who had conducted research all over the globe. "How would you like to go to Greenland with me next month? We have a contract with the Army to study intestinal infections in the Arctic, and my field director who did the first two phases in Lapland and northern Alaska has had enough of being away from his family for four months at a time. The final phase is in northern Greenland, and if you can be away from your family for four months next summer, I'll take you with me next month to choose the site for the project."

I had about as much knowledge of where Greenland was as I had about Nova Scotia back in 1946, but that was of no concern. It sounded like a great job. "We probably won't get clearance from the Army and the Danish government for another month, so you can begin right now by going to the library and learning everything you can about Greenland."

Four weeks later we took a commercial flight to the Military Air Transport Command base in Dover, Delaware, and boarded a military passenger plane for the American air base at Sondre Stromsfjord, Greenland. A retired colonel who had served as Eisenhower's chief preventive medicine officer in WWII, Gordon had no difficulty commandeering a small Army float plane for the flight north to Egedesminde, the site recommended by Gordon's Danish colleagues at the Staten Seruminstitut in Copenhagen. Located at the southwestern corner of Disko Bay, some 200 miles north of the Arctic Circle, Egedesminde was named after the Danish missionary, Hans Egede. With its 1100 inhabitants, about 10 percent of whom were Danish government employees, Egedesminde commanded a sweeping view of the mouth of the bay, from the other end of which a mighty glacier spews out a vast array of icebergs that make their way into the Davis Straits. We arrived in style – the first plane that had ever called at that Eskimo village.

There was a small hospital in Egedesminde, staffed by three young Danish doctors who served the villages along the shore of Disko Bay in a small diesel-powered boat in the summer and by dog sled in the winter when the bay was frozen over. Gordon outlined the project to them. The Danish government would provide one of its top microbiologists, a lab technician, and a nurse; I would be the field director of the project; and the doctors would receive extra compensation for their services in helping with the field work. In the meantime, they would have to ready a large room in the hospital to be used as the field laboratory, and find a house suitable for me and the three Danish personnel. If all went according to schedule, the team would arrive at the beginning of June 1957, completing its work at the end of September.

The project comprised an epidemiological survey of the population of Disko Bay, covering several dozen settlements with a total population of several thousand. The purpose of the exercise was to determine the extent of bacteria and parasites in that Arctic environment that could cause intestinal infections – a subject of considerable interest to the U.S. military. To that end, stool specimens would be collected from as many villagers as possible, as well as from the sled dog population – which was about the same size as the human population.

We spent the next three weeks scouting Disko Bay in the doctor's sturdy but very slow boat, visiting the various settlements and assessing them in terms of the design of the project. Only one untoward event momentarily disrupted our routine. The Eskimo – or "inuit" as they're called today -- are a very gentle people, who rarely engaged in physical encounters, even when inebriated – which was a common problem. On that first trip around Disko Bay, we encountered such a problem in Christianhaab. After conducting our business and having lunch with the mayor, we returned to the dock, where a large crowd had gathered – to watch our boat, *Barnov*, merrily circling the bay under the control of a drunken local who had commandeered the boat when no one was on board.

There appeared to be nothing to be done until he tired of his folly, and eventually he brought the boat to a stop by sideswiping the end of the dock – which nearly tore it loose, but fortunately did no obvious damage to the boat. Our captain immediately jumped aboard, but instead of forcing him off the boat or calling for assistance from the crowd, he simply tried reasoning with him – to no avail. "What we need here," observed Gordon, "is an Irish cop." There being none such of any ethnic origin in sight, I decided to take matters in my own hands, climbed aboard, grabbed the miscreant by the collar and the seat of his pants, and gently eased him off the deck.

I suspect he could have turned around and done the same to me, only into the bay instead of on to the dock, but he didn't resist, and we were soon on our way. I learned the following summer that the poor man eventually committed suicide, overcome by remorse for this and other escapades resulting from his drinking.

For the return trip to Sondre Stromfjord, the Air Force plane was not available, so we were forced to hire a boat – a similar "one-lung" diesel with an Eskimo captain and one crew member—for the somewhat formidable 3-day journey back to the air base.

We thus found ourselves cruising along the Davis Strait off the west coast of northern Greenland without a sign of civilization between Egedesminde and Holsteinsborg, 180 miles to the south, and no possibility of imminent rescue in the event of some calamity – such as doing a Titanic with one of the myriad icebergs that dotted the sea lanes. Considering the possibility of such a collision, I decided the first night out that we needed an emergency plan. In the event of a collision, we had only one means of making it to shore, the dinghy towed behind our vessel, which itself would provide only a modicum of security, there being no human habitation other than Holsteinsborg along our entire route. Anticipating a problem in casting it loose in such an emergency, I went to the galley and found the only sharp-bladed knife among the kitchen cutlery, took it to our cramped sleeping quarters, and tucked it under my pillow. Gordon was mildly amused, but agreed that it wasn't too bad an idea.

He proved to be a fascinating companion, regaling me with stories of his world-wide ventures spanning some 40 years. In WWII he had been Eisenhower's chief preventive medicine officer, responsible at the end of the war for feeding the nearly starving populace of Rotterdam, Holland.

Although the Dutch living in the countryside had fared well, those in the cities faced severe food shortages as the war ground to a halt and fleeing German soldiers confiscated all the food they could lay their hands on. Faced with trying to provide thousands of desperately hungry people as quickly as possible, he told of getting huge vats from local breweries and brewing vegetable soup by the ton.

Most of his work after the war had been with the Rockefeller Foundation, with public health research projects throughout the world. Keeping track of these widely scattered interests had required an around-the-world trip every year for more than 30 years – which to this novice traveler sounded like a job created in paradise. Little did I dream that only seven years later I, too, would be taking such annual junkets.

Fortunately, we encountered no problems *en route* and had a spectacular journey along the 165 mile fjord to the air base at its head. On arrival, we learned that we could get home sooner by catching a military cargo C-47 that would take us 900 miles north to the American airbase at Thule, from where we could catch a military transport back to the states. This sounded great, and except for a sizable gap around the cargo door that admitted a steady flow of arctic air, it was an uneventful trip.

The United States Air Force base at Thule occupied the site of the original village of Thule, the northernmost human habitation in the world. Although the settlement dated back some 900 years, it was not known to early Arctic explorers until early in the 20th century. When Thule Air Base was established in 1951, the Eskimo village of 130 persons was moved some 60 miles away to protect its inhabitants from contact with air base personnel and the common communicable diseases that could be devastating to such an isolated population.

Although I spent 3 of our 5 days in Thule in the base hospital for treatment of a severe respiratory infection, it was an exciting place to be, and a fitting conclusion to this first Arctic adventure.

24 – Following the ghost of Robert E. Peary

The first year of the two-year program at the Harvard School of Public Health was the regular Master of Public Health degree program, with the addition of a weekly seminar with Dr. Carl Taylor for those of us in the program for teachers of preventive medicine. As the only American in the latter program, I found myself among an elite group from India, Thailand, Brazil, and Japan, all of them heads of departments of preventive medicine in their respective countries.

Carl, the son of missionaries to India and himself a missionary to India, had established the first department of preventive medicine in an Indian medical school, at the Christian Medical College in Ludhiana. He had also been involved in his early days in India treating casualties of the bloody battles that took place between Hindus and Muslims in the Punjab region after the partition of India and Pakistan in 1947. Muslims fleeing from the Indian side of the border near Amritsar would be attacked by Hindus, and Hindus similarly fleeing from Lahore on the Pakistani side would be slaughtered by Muslims. Carl told of trains arriving in Amritsar from Lahore in which every passenger had been killed, with only the engineer surviving. How tragic that more than 50 years later we still find India and Pakistan fighting at their border in Kashmir!

The most interesting subject in the MPH curriculum was epidemiology – disease detectives at work—although its required "basic science", biostatistics, was anathema to me. In medical school we were given a brief exposure to biostatistics, which was now a complete blank in my memory bank. Although I somehow managed to pass this course, I have no recollection whatever of having grasped its most rudimentary aspects. (This was to prove somewhat distressing just one year later when my first assignment in my first job as a teacher of preventive medicine was to develop a course in biostatistics for my medical students.)

Early in the school year Dr. Gordon introduced me to Dr. Frank Babbott, who had conducted the first two phases of the arctic research project in Lapland and northern Alaska. Frank would be compiling and ordering the list of supplies and equipment required for the Greenland phase, and would accompany me to Egedesminde at the beginning of the summer to help set up things. Frank was a likable, laid-back chap, and we hit it off from the beginning. With two daughters about the same ages as our two sons, he had had his fill of two long absences from his family, and was more than pleased to have a replacement.

With Greenland beckoning, the academic year passed quickly. In preparation, I had availed myself of the opportunity to visit two distinguished old Arctic explorers to discuss the forthcoming expedition – nothing like those they had conducted decades before.

Sir Hubert Wilkins, an Australian, had explored the region of the North Pole in 1931 in a submersible vessel, the *Nautilus*, and in 1957 was a consultant geographer to the U. S. Army, working in their research facility in Natick, Massachusetts, very near our home in Framingham. He received me graciously, and kindly shared some of his memorable experiences. On a more practical basis, since our project was being funded by the military, he also arranged for the supply sergeant at their facility to outfit me with some fine Arctic gear. I was sorry to learn later that he had died the following year.

Vilhjalmur Steffansson, a Canadian of Icelandic origin, was a truly legendary Arctic explorer. Born in 1879, he was an authority on the Canadian and Greenland Arctic regions. He retired from active exploration in 1919, and focused on studying, writing and lecturing about the Arctic, authoring some 20 books and over 400 articles. During World War II, he acted as a military advisor to the United States government, studied the defense of Alaska, and wrote reports and manuals for the armed forces.

I had the rare privilege of visiting him at Dartmouth College, in Hanover, New Hampshire. The Steffansson Collection of printed materials, manuscripts and photographs relating to both the Arctic and Antarctic regions had been purchased by the college some five years earlier, and he was Arctic consultant to their Northern Studies Program. He expressed great interest in our little project, and generously gave me a number of his books, inscribing a special note to me in each one. One of these reads: "For Dr. Edwin W. Brown, with envy of his recent and forthcoming trips to Greenland, from one of his predecessors." He died six years later at the age of 83.

The summer plan was again to fly to Sondre Stromfjord from Dover on an Air Force plane, but in April Frank came up with an intriguing proposal: "I've been talking to the office of the shipping company that will be taking our supplies and equipment to Greenland, and they say that we can ride along with it if we wish. How does a two-week Arctic cruise sound?"

It sounded like a terrific idea, although it would require our leaving sooner than anticipated. I would thus have to again miss a Harvard graduation, leaving immediately upon completion of my final exams, but how could even the impressive fanfare of the graduation ceremonies across the river in Cambridge compare with the delights of an ocean voyage?

In late May, Frank and I flew to Norfolk, Virginia, to board the U.S. Merchant Marine vessel, *Lt. Robert Craig*, which was loaded with supplies for the American airbase at Sondre Stromfjord. We were given the ship's sick bay as our quarters, hoping that none of the crew would need the facility during our voyage. The captain gave us the run of the ship, including the bridge – which privilege I suspect he at times regretted, frequently having to tear me away from the radarscope so he could have a peek himself while we were traversing a dense fog. At that time of year Davis Strait is filled with icebergs from Disko Bay, and I was determined that we would not meet the fate of the *Titanic*.

At the airbase our supplies were transferred to the *Redbud*, a Danish icebreaker used to clear the fjord in the winter and to haul supplies to the western Greenland settlements. Our fellow passengers were two American scientists who were to spend the summer on Disko Island, north of Egedesminde, studying the effects of sunspots on weather during the then International Geophysical Year. There was no tourism in Greenland in those days except for Danish citizens, and the 7000 American airmen at the two bases were not allowed to visit any Greenland settlement – a necessary public health measure. Thus, after Frank had departed, we three would be the only Americans allowed to travel in Greenland that summer. As I was soon to learn, their presence not far from Egedesminde would be a major factor in getting our project under way on schedule.

Our ship arrived in Egedesminde with great fanfare, and there was no end of able-bodied Greenlanders more than willing to help us unload our goods. However, I personally saw to the unloading of one particularly valuable piece of cargo – a box in which I had lovingly packed two cases of Skippy peanut butter and a Smithfield ham. Having observed the previous summer that the local diet leaned heavily toward seal meat and codfish, I had felt the necessity of providing a small supply of emergency rations.

25 – Nanook of the North

We were shown to my new home, a modern 2-bedroom frame house prefabricated in Denmark, which I would share with a distinguished Danish virologist, Dr. Eyvind Freundt; a Danish laboratory technologist, Ana Pedersen; and a Danish nurse, Ida Warthoe, all of whom had arrived a short time before. The hospital in which our laboratory was to be housed was another example of Danish prefabrication – small but modern in every detail.

The day after our arrival Danish electricians were busily at work re-wiring the room to be used as our laboratory so as to accommodate our sterilizer, incubation ovens, and other electrical equipment essential to a microbiological lab. Because the project was funded by the U.S. Army, government regulations required the purchase of American equipment – a typical bureaucratic bit of stupidity when all such equipment was wired for 110 volt current. Not to worry, of course! Frank had included transformers on his equipment list, and hastened to unpack them when the electrician informed me that he was ready to hook up the equipment. The electrician was incredulous as Frank handed him several little 50 watt transformers of the kind used in those days to power an electric shaver when traveling abroad. Neither Frank nor I were very savvy when it came to such things.

"I'm sorry, sir, but these are not quite large enough. We need at least two transformers of 5000 watts each." Transformers of the required capacity, it seems, would weigh about 100 pounds each – and none were to be had in Greenland. But then I thought about those two Americans over on Disko Island? Might they not have something that would work for us?

We contacted them by radio, and they confirmed that they did have one transformer they could lend until we could obtain what we needed from Boston. Contacting John Gordon at Harvard was somewhat more complicated. Telegrams originating in Egedesminde were radioed to Copenhagen from the radio station on top of the hill outside the village. From Copenhagen they were then transmitted to the United States via the Atlantic cable – predecessor to today's satellite transmission. Specifications were thus relayed to Boston, and we soon had a reply that they would be purchased ASAP and delivered by the Air Force. Because of their weight, however, a parachute drop into Egedesminde was unfeasible, so they would have to be picked up at Sondre Stromfjord in about two weeks.

This was about the right time for Frank to return home, so with the laboratory up and running and specimens starting to come in from nearby villages, we headed for the airbase two weeks later. Now, however, we were to travel in style, for a Danish passenger ship had just put into Egedesminde, bound for Holsteinsborg and Sondre Stromfjord, and a cabin for two was available. It was a decided improvement over the previous summer's mode of transport.

After seeing Frank off on a military transport, I spent the next week enjoying Army hospitality while awaiting transport back to Egedesminde. The transformers had arrived in timely fashion, but last year's float plane was no longer available, and local transport was virtually non-existent. Spending much of the summer at the airbase wouldn't have been a terrible imposition, given the comfortable quarters, good American food, and short-wave radio-telephone communication home, but I did have a job to do.

My best bet was to bum a ride on a Danish military seaplane that had been chartered by a group of Danish businessman hoping to develop a hotel in Christianshaab at the east end of Disko Bay. This was an ideal site for Danish tourism, adjacent to the glacier that produced the thousands of icebergs that fill the bay all summer. But the plane was fogged in at the airport in Keflavik, Iceland, and until it arrived, the Danish liaison officer at Sondre Stromfjord would be unable to tell me if I would be permitted to board the flight.

A visitor to the base that summer was the famous undersea explorer, Jacques Cousteau, who was testing a new French turbojet helicopter, Alouette II. Both were staying in the same quarters as I, so I asked his pilot if I might have a ride in their magnificent machine. It was a spectacular flight, heading east from the airbase to the very edge of the Greenland ice-cap, where I could take beautiful photographs as we hovered off the face of a magnificent cliff of solid ice hundreds of feet high.

The Danish plane eventually arrived, and I was awakened at 2:00 a.m. with the news that I and my transformers could go with them to Christianshaab if I immediately went to the airstrip. With 24 hours of daylight, the plane was ready to take off as soon as I boarded. That was the good news; the bad news was that I arrived to find all seven passenger seats on the airplane occupied by seven stout Danes, and the three crew seats by the pilot, co-pilot, and radio operator. The pilot gestured me to sit on the floor, and we took off. After all, it was only an hour ride or so!

I asked if they could drop me at Egedesminde, but the pilot said they had only enough fuel for one landing. Arriving over Christianhaab, however, he was unable to land because of too many icebergs, so he headed for Egedesminde, where his well-to-do passengers would be able to charter a boat to take them back to Christianshaab.

Our landing at Egedesminde at 4:00 a.m. seemed to bring out the entire village, and I was warmly greeted by some of the inhabitants who recognized me. My transformers were left on the dock, to be collected later, and I headed up the road to our house, only to realize a few minutes later that I had left my sleeping bag on the plane (taken in case I had to bum a ride back from the airbase on a Greenland cargo boat) – and the plane had already taken off. A moment later, however, it returned, making a low bombing run over the center of the village and discharging my rolled up sleeping bag. Knowing that it would be quite safe where it lay and being too far up the hill to warrant going back for it, I reached the house in time to see Eyvind staring wildly at me through the open bedroom window.

"How did you get here?", he asked in a startled voice. "On that plane," I replied – and suddenly understood the reason for his strange behavior. He had obviously not awakened when the plane landed, only to be aroused by the roar of its engines as it made its return run over the village, and then saw an object tumbling out of the plane in the distance. A few minutes later I appeared. I hadn't the heart to refrain from telling him about the sleeping bag.

Later that morning I collected the sleeping bag, which some thoughtful person had picked up and placed on a bench in front of the post office. I was rather attached to that sleeping bag, and was deeply grateful to the crew member who had found it aboard immediately after takeoff. It was an old Boy Scout sleeping bag acquired long years ago, and had served me well – first, on camping trips in my boyhood; then, rolled up as a soft seat on which to sit on deck of our troop ship to Italy during the war, and while in Italy for a more comfortable sleep in bunk and truck than provided by the standard Army issue of blankets only; and finally, for its intended use on sea voyages in Greenland.

The pleasure of recovering this old friend soon thereafter gave way to a severe disappointment, however, with the arrival of the Danish freighter, *Ove Amsinck*, in Egedesminde a few days later. I was at first delighted to see it, for it was the very ship which would later bring Pat and the boys to stay for the remainder of the summer.

Again, "the best laid schemes o' mice and men gang aft agley..." Earlier that year I had requested their transport by Air Force plane, only to have the request denied by some stuffy bureaucrat in Washington. Dismayed but undaunted, I then wrote to the president of a shipping line in Copenhagen, one of whose vessels regularly carried coal from Philadelphia to the small towns on the west coast of Greenland. I received a gracious reply from him, authorizing my family to come on the trip that was scheduled to leave Philadelphia on or about July 12th.

Letter in hand, I showed the letter to the captain. He had not been informed that he would have passengers on his next voyage north, but he had no problem with it, noting that his wife would be with him next time and would enjoy having another lady on board. He wondered, however, what two little boys would do to occupy their time. My thought that they would doubtless find plenty of ways to amuse themselves on deck abruptly dissipated, however. The tiny cabin that would be their home at sea opened directly onto the only deck available – the huge cargo hatch. This would have provided a fine flat area of considerable size on which they could happily pedal their tricycles to their hearts' content. The only problem was that it extended to the edge of the ship on both sides – with no guard rail! We agreed that confining two hyperactive toddlers to that tiny cabin for two weeks might not be my wife's cup of tea. I thanked him for his courtesy, and cabled Pat the bad news. She would probably have been seasick the entire journey anyhow.

26 – Land of the midnight sun

With temperature in the 50s, 24 hours of sunlight a day, and a steady procession of gleaming icebergs of all sizes and shapes passing offshore, summer in Disko Bay was an idyllic time of year. We spent much time on *Bjarnov*, the doctor's little diesel-powered craft, visiting the settlements around the rim of the bay, and occasionally taking a potshot at a seal that got too close and ended up on our dinner table. At each stop a census was taken, and the inhabitants were requested to provide stool specimens in capped vials left with them. Every few days a small boat would pull into our harbor, bringing to the lab a sack full of filled containers from one or another village, and keeping our technician busy most of the time. My own time ashore was spent in tabulating and analyzing the results.

Entertainment was limited, but adequate. The local church also served as the local cinema, and from time to time a movie would be shown, depending upon what visiting Danish ships might have brought. The only one I recall was *From Here to Eternity*, which brought startled gasps from Eskimos who were apparently unaccustomed to seeing violent war scenes.

Although the variety of meat available was distinctly limited, food staples were plentiful enough, including tax-free Danish beer at the equivalent of 10 cents the bottle. This was of no interest to me, thanks to my Baptist heritage, but my Danish colleagues drank it at lunch and dinner. I settled at first for distilled water from our lab, eschewing the tap water which came from melted glacier ice and occasionally included a tiny fish that had made its way through the pipes. This soon gave way, because of its bland taste, to having a go at soft drinks. These, however, were almost equally bland, barely sweetened, and I soon realized that in that ultra-dry climate I was not getting enough liquid.

It was interesting to note that the soft drinks were produced by Tuborg and Carlsberg, from whence came the beers of the same brand. So tasteless were these soft drinks that I concluded they were designed to woo teetotalers to their beers. In desperation, I decided to try the noxious brew one lunch-time, pouring myself about a finger of the stuff. It was awful! Undaunted, however, I tried it again at supper, and found it not quite so vile. Within a few days, I actually began to like the stuff, although it produced the desire for a siesta after lunch, making me consistently late to work back at the lab. Although I did not carry my beer-drinking habit home with me, I was to learn not many years later that beer would become a boon to my well-being when traveling in the tropics. Not only would it be the only safe source of fluid in many places, but it would whet the appetite when stifled by oppressive heat or illness.

One terrible day, however, my colleagues informed me that we were out of beer and none was to be forthcoming until the next ship arrived. A few days later, however, I was pleasantly surprised to see some cases of beer stacked outside the local general store, and joyously lugged one up the hill to our house before the others had arrived. When I proudly pointed out my find, sitting on the back porch which served as our refrigerator, Eyvind looked at it with disgust. To be sure, the label was somewhat different from that to which we were accustomed – *lys ol* – but *ol* meant "beer" and it was Tuborg, so what was the problem? "That's *light* beer – with almost no alcohol, and it tastes terrible! We let our little kids drink the stuff on special occasions. We call it "wee-wee beer"!" I think the cook ended up feeding it to the dogs.

Eyvind was also disdainful of the Skippy peanut butter, of which I needed a fix at most meals. (I still have a fix of a peanut butter sandwich at least once a day when at home. Peanut butter is one of America's truly great contributions to the world.) "How can you eat that stuff?", he would chide. "How can you eat *that* stuff?" would be my rejoinder, pointing to the lard that Danes like to spread on bread in place of butter. Eventually, of course, he had to give it a try – and I was grateful for having had the foresight to bring more than an adequate supply. Over the ensuing decades, I have noted the slow but steady advent of peanut butter in the supermarkets of Europe, beginning in England and eventually making its way throughout the Continent.

As the main settlement in Greenland that far north of the Arctic Circle, Egedesminde's native population was increased by more than 100 Danes who provided services of various kinds – administrative, medical, police, etc. About two weeks after I arrived that summer, I was met along the road by the Danish policeman on his bicycle, asking me for my passport. I fetched it from the house, brought it to his office, and he dutifully stamped a visa in it.

Several Danish families were our immediate neighbors, and one or more couples might drop by in the evening for a chat from time to time. In deference to me, they would always begin the conversation in English, but sooner or later one would have difficulty finding the English equivalent for what he or she wanted to say. Someone else would then reply in Danish, and invariably they were off and running, forsaking English for the rest of the evening, seemingly oblivious to my presence. Danes always keep a decorative box of cigarettes on tables in the sitting room, so out of sheer boredom I would light up – and chain-smoke the rest of the evening. Needless to say, the morning-after cotton-mouth was not pleasant, and the habit ended with my return home. (My only prior venture into the world of tobacco occurred more than 30 years earlier, when I found a still-smoldering butt on the sidewalk on my way to school in the 3rd grade in Williamsville. I shared the pleasure with Dick and his roommate, Ralph Keen, the son of our Baptist minister with whom we were living, and we soon got in the habit of scouting for butts to and from school. The habit was abruptly broken not many days later when Mrs. Keen caught us at it one afternoon. The leather belt of the 1930s proved every bit as effective in breaking the habit as the Nicoderm of the 1990s.)

In preparation for that summer, I tried to learn some Danish back in Boston. The only Danish language course available on records in those days was a couple of old 78 rpm recordings made from a wartime Army course. Danish pronunciation is difficult, often spoken as if one had a mouthful of mush, and I failed to get beyond the most simple tourist phrases. "Can you tell me where to find a hotel?" "Yes, there's a good hotel straight ahead and to the right." "When does the movie begin?" "It begins at 7:00 p.m."....and so on – hardly to be of use in an Eskimo village. Yet one memorable Sunday afternoon I missed my one great opportunity to display my vast knowledge of the language. I was sitting on the porch of our house when I was approached by several Danes who come ashore from a ship in the harbor. "Can you please tell us where is the hotel?", they asked in Danish. We did, in fact, have a small guest-house down the road which served meals, and it was straight ahead and to the right. What a grand opportunity to use that phrase I had practiced over and over months before, just to perfect my pronunciation! But I blew it. Before I realized what I was saying, I had replied apologetically in my native tongue: "I'm sorry, but I speak only English." Obviously surprised at finding an American living there but not flustered, they politely thanked me in English, and I lamely pointed in the direction of the guest-house. "It's that red building just down the road on the right." How sad to have missed what could have been a great moment!

I prized my mailing address -- simply, "Brown, Egedesminde, Greenland". Mail from home went by air to Copenhagen, thence by ship to Greenland – a transit time of about three weeks. In midsummer I conceived a novel plan for mailing our Christmas cards that year. Pat sent our Christmas card mailing list, and I addressed cards bought from a Greenlander artist in Egedesminde. I asked the postmistress when the last ship from Denmark might be expected before the winter freeze, and since the timing seemed right, I gave her the bag of cards with the request to hold them for the last ship, which she kindly agreed to do. It worked perfectly. Just a few days before Christmas all our friends received a card from Greenland bearing that impressive return address.

I noted earlier that Egedesminde was named for Hans Egede, but only recently did I learn from the daily devotional, *One Year Book of Christian History*, what a profound effect this Godly servant had had on the population of Greenland. Born in Norway in 1686, he became a Lutheran minister who eventually went to Greenland as a missionary and later returned to Denmark, where he found a school for training missionaries. As the result of his efforts, all of Greenland's native population eventually embraced Christianity.

Although I attended church each Sunday with the ladies in our house, the service was in Danish and the hymns were not familiar tunes. I was therefore grateful that I had taken some George Beverly Shea records with me to make up for that deficit – and at the worldwide Congress on Evangelism in Lausanne, Switzerland, many years later where I first met him, I was able to thank him personally for having thus contributed to the pleasure of my stay in Greenland.

27 – "Westward, ho!"

The return home was uneventful – a passenger ship to the airbase, a military flight to Dover, Delaware, and a commercial flight to Boston, where Pat and the boys met me at Logan Airport. It was a great homecoming, but I soon found I had missed an important phase in the development of our younger son. Jack had barely begun talking, using only two- or three-word phrases at most, when I left. Four months later, sitting between us in the front seat as I drove home, he chattered like a magpie all the way home. Pat later regaled me with stories of some of their antics in my absence, things never done before and not repeated after my return—clearly reactions to having an absentee father even for a few months.

The second year of the program for teachers of preventive medicine was of a more practical nature. Each of us were assigned from September through April to a different department of preventive medicine in one of eight American medical schools, each department having been selected by Carl Taylor for some special aspect of its program. Once a month we would assemble as a group at one of the eight medical schools for a 2-day seminar, and in May we would all return to Boston to complete the program with a final series of seminars. The summer would be devoted to an optional tour of some preventive medicine programs in the U.K. and on the Continent.

There was no question, of course, of not opting for the European tour, small children or no. Pat was perhaps not as keen on the idea, not the least of her hesitation due to our not having the foggiest idea of what it would cost or how we would pay for it. Such mundane considerations would not deter me, however, and she did not resist my making preliminary plans – such as going to the Cunard Line office in Boston and reserving a cabin to England in June of the following year.

Since I was the only member of the group without a job to which to return and the disposal of a house to consider, the only prudent move was to sell the house. While I might have inherited the dubious distinction of being a born traveler, Pat had seemingly inherited the ability to choose a house by those three essential features so loudly proclaimed by realtors – location, location, and location. With no more than a FOR SALE sign in front of the house, we were able to sell it to the first couple who came along. (Which reminds me of the story of the tourist in New York City who stopped a man on the street carrying a violin case under his arm. "Please, sir, can you tell me how one gets to Carnegie Hall?" "Certainly, sir – practice, practice, practice.")

Finding an attorney to assist with the closing on the sale of the house, packing those possessions required for six months in Cleveland, and putting the rest of our goods in storage would require some little time, however. I therefore flew to Cleveland as soon as we knew the house had been sold, to look for accommodations. We had no desire to move into an apartment, and six-month rental opportunities were virtually unheard of. However, I was fortunate to find a splendid old home in the posh Shaker Heights suburb, belonging to an elderly widow who regularly spent the winter in Florida. It would not be available until November, but with our delayed departure from Massachusetts, we could manage temporary quarters in a hotel if necessary.

Arriving in Cleveland in mid-October, we found an affordable suite in an ancient hotel not far from the medical school – a somewhat dismal establishment, but one that would be our home for only a couple of weeks. I began my stint at the medical school, late for work as it were but warmly welcomed by the department members. The most notable of these was an older gentleman who sat down next to me at lunch the first day, and turned to introduce himself: "Hello! I don't believe we've met. My name's Ben Spock." However today's young parents may view Dr. Benjamin Spock's advice for rearing children, I found him a delightful person with whom to be associated.

Eager to tell my lovely wife of this encounter, I returned to the hotel that evening to be greeted with some disconcerting news: "I think I'm pregnant!" Under the best of circumstances, this would have been unwelcome news, for with the birth of our second son, we had been quite content to call a halt to any further enlargement of the family. With a European trip awaiting us only six months hence, it was a disastrous announcement.

By the time Cleveland was blasted with its first major snowfall of the season, there was no question that a third child was in the works. But life must go on, and I dug into the activities of the department. The office to which I was assigned was also occupied by a visiting Scotsman, Dr. Alexander Robertson, with whom I discussed my plight. Sandy described how the British dealt with pregnancies, using midwives for prenatal care and routine deliveries, and assured me that he could arrange for such care for my wife. This would require spending most of the summer in England and Scotland, but there were plenty of outstanding departments of preventive medicine there that I could visit – and upon our return, he would be pleased to have me join him in the new department of preventive medicine at the University of Saskatchewan, where he was soon to become chairman. What a coup! A solution to our problem, and a job offer to boot!

The time went well, the monthly visits to other departments were great fun, and the future looked rosy indeed. I did let Sandy know early on that I deeply appreciated his job offer, but (although I didn't express it quite this way) the wind-swept plains and sometimes 60 degrees-below-zero temperatures of the Canadian wilds inclined me to keep my options open for the time being. (I was to learn some years later that Sandy turned out to be not so keen either on the Saskatchewan climate, both physical and political, and ended up with the World Health Organization in Egypt.)

Meanwhile, Pat continued to develop impressively, and by the time we returned to Boston, she had given new meaning to the term "heavy with child". We were obviously not going to Europe. We found a suitable rental in the Boston suburb of Belmont until we could look for a house, and I soon found myself faced with a very difficult, albeit welcome, choice.

28 – Opportunity knocks – but which door to open?

One of those peripatetic seminars of our group was at the University of Vermont in Burlington – and some weeks later I received a letter from the department chairman, offering me an assistant professorship. It was a perfect setting, on the shore of Lake Champlain, at a beautiful New England campus, in a town of modest size – and the salary was most satisfactory for 1958: $12,000 a year. Pat was born in Newport, Vermont, and until we met had always lived in New England. It was all that either of us could ask for.

Very soon thereafter, Carl Taylor received a call from the chairman of the recently established department of preventive medicine at Tufts University School of Medicine in Boston. He was recruiting staff, and would appreciate any recommendations. Carl advised me to make an appointment to visit. Dr. Count D. Gibson, Jr., an internist from the Medical College of Virginia, was ideally suited for the clinical responsibilities of the department – the Home Medical Service of the venerable Boston Dispensary – but he needed someone to take over non-clinical teaching responsibilities. I would be given a free hand in developing the lecture program in the second, third, and fourth years of the medical school. The best salary he could offer, however, was $8500 – and the cost of living in the Boston area was distinctly higher than that in Burlington.

I was now in a real quandary. Vermont clearly had the upper edge, but I needed counsel. I had recently had the privilege of meeting Dr. Jean Curran, father of my old medical school friend, Bill, at our first Harvard Medical School reunion. He had retired as Dean of the Long Island College of Medicine, and was now in Boston, working on a history of the erstwhile Harvard Medical School in China – established by Harvard faculty members back in the '20s. I could think of no one better qualified to advise me, so I phoned him for an appointment. He kindly invited Pat and me to dinner at his home, after which we two adjourned to his study. He understood perfectly why I was so attracted to Vermont, but wisely pointed out that this would take me out of the mainstream of activity in my field. Being in Boston, whatever its disadvantages, would put me in the forefront of such development. It was a meeting arranged in heaven, and my choice was clear.

We soon found a new home in Norfolk, Massachusetts, some 25 miles from downtown Boston, where the medical school was located. Although it was some distance from both my work and our church, I was either able to carpool or go by train to work, and Pat's parents' apartment on Beacon Hill, only a few blocks from the church, afforded a pleasant Sunday afternoon respite before returning to Norfolk in the evening. We thus got in the habit of having Sunday dinner there each week, and giving the grandparents plenty of time with their grandchildren. Those were happy days for all of us.

By August our third child was due. If we were to have our preference, it would be a boy. We knew about boys, and we had an abundance of leftover boys' clothing. Pat went into labor early one morning, and because of the distance to the Boston Lying-In Hospital, we drove to her parents' apartment to await the moment of truth. Several hours passed without noticeable progression of labor, so we took a drive along the waterfront, whose cobblestone pavement worked wonders. Rushing her to the hospital, I soon received a call in the waiting room from our obstetrician, informing me we had a lovely new daughter. In her room, Pat asked what I thought about. "I thought it sounded rather nice!" "So did I", was her reply.

Having hoped for a boy, we had given no thought to a name for a girl. We asked the boys for suggestions, and they immediately came up with Wendy, the name of a little English girl, who had been a next-door neighbor with whom they had often played. We thought this a splendid choice, with Patricia as her middle name. However, when the staff person responsible for filling out the birth certificate asked for the spelling of her name, I unthinkingly gave it as "Wende" – which it remains to this day. This was a name familiar to me in my youth, living in western New York. Wende was (and I assume still is) a village not far from where we lived. Its sole claim to fame in those days was that it was the site of the county poorhouse. Such a thoughtful father!

The Boston Lying-In Hospital was also the birthplace of our first son, Ted. One of the Harvard Medical School hospitals, on the corner of Longwood Avenue and Avenue Louis Pasteur, it lies directly across the street from Vanderbilt Hall, the medical student residence. Patients in rooms on the Vanderbilt Hall side in my day were not infrequently subjected to late-Saturday-night exuberance of medical students in their cups, loudly singing, "Every day is labor day at the Boston Lying-In". I'm pleased to report that the most notorious of these celebrants all became distinguished medical professors after they grew up.

As fate would have it, Pat was unable to return to our new home when her period of confinement came to an end. Back in the Currier apartment the evening of Wende's birth, 3-year-old Jack, who had been feeling ill all day, spiked a high fever and suddenly went into a mild convulsion. I rushed him to the emergency room at Children's Hospital, just down the street from the Lying-In, where a spinal tap was gratifyingly negative. The diagnosis was ECHO virus infection, at the time epidemic in the Boston area. Fortunately, it was self-limited infection but highly contagious, so we made arrangements with our former next-door neighbors in Framingham, Peggy and Andy Anderson, for Pat and Wende to stay with them. Jack had recovered by the time they arrived there, but now Ted and I had both succumbed. It was not an auspicious week at the Brown household.

What we soon learned, once reunited with mother and daughter, was that we never knew what we were missing until our home was blessed with this dear child. Sons are great, but there's nothing quite like a daughter. (I am told that fathers have a certain bias in this regard.)

I also soon learned that I had a love – and, I think, a gift—for teaching. The first series of preventive medicine lectures came in the second year of the Tufts curriculum. I was immensely pleased to have three hours a week allotted to me, and while preventive medicine is possibly the least favored subject in the curriculum, I was determined to make it interesting. My enthusiasm was somewhat dampened, however, when I discovered that my three hours were back-to-back – on Friday afternoon from 1:00 to 4:00. It positively melted away when I was told that it was customary to begin with biostatistics.

Panic-stricken, I went over to the School of Public Health to consult with one of my former professors. I was too embarrassed to confess that I remembered nothing of the course I had taken the year before, expressing only concern that I had no knowledge of a textbook appropriate for medical students. She graciously recommended a very basic textbook written by a Tulane University School of Medicine professor, and kindly gave me a copy. I went home and began reading it that very evening.

I finished the first chapter with about as much understanding as I had of the fundamentals of rocket propellants. I re-read it. Same result. I again re-read it – and suddenly it was abundantly clear. I was astonished, and hastily went to work preparing my first lecture. It went very well, and each week for the next 3 months I devoted the first hour of the three to biostatistics – and each week I went through exactly the same routine with the next chapter in the textbook. I never did tell the students about that textbook, but made them rely on notes taken in class. Thanks to some innovative props, slides, and impromptu research of my own, (and above all, thanks to a brilliant lady down at Tulane whom I never had the privilege of meeting), the course was definitely a success. Many years later I bumped into one of my former students, who told me how much he enjoyed it.

One particularly gratifying, albeit momentarily disconcerting, episode took place one afternoon when the dean of the medical school entered the room by the rear door and took a seat in the last row. His office was just down the hall from the lecture room, and apparently the raucous laughter emanating therefrom had caught his ear. I managed to keep my cool, however, and went on with the lecture, jokes and all, and he quietly left a short time later. I assume he was satisfied that there was nothing amiss.

Preparing and delivering three lectures in a row, on three different topics, with a 15-minute break in between, was not something I could keep up for long, but I was soon able to find a guest lecturer from among the many experts in the Boston area to take over the middle lecture. All in all, it was one of my most rewarding experiences.

At times I would go to considerable lengths to prepare a lecture – such as the time I spent two days in Nashua, New Hampshire, gathering information about an outbreak of intestinal infections among the segment of the population in one area of the city. I had read about it in the newspaper some weeks earlier, and by the time I arrived the local health department and an epidemiologist from the Center for Disease Control in Atlanta, Georgia, had worked out the cause and corrected the underlying problem – a break in the water line from the local reservoir which had allowed sewage from an itinerant laborers' camp along the way to contaminate the water. All in all, it made for an interesting lecture, including the account of my being stopped by a local policeman for some minor traffic violation, the nature of which I've long forgotten in the light of many such episodes before and since.

29 – Decisions, decisions again

Count Gibson was a prince. One could not ask for a better boss. He involved me in the clinical activities of the department as well, and was ever helpful with cases where my limited knowledge and abilities failed me. He was also concerned about my financial situation, for he recognized that the Tufts salary was inadequate and did whatever he could to help supplement it. First, he arranged an appointment in the Boston City Health Department as a part-time assistant health officer – an undemanding job that provided interesting diversion from my academic duties. He also arranged for an appointment at the Harvard School of Public Health, as Research Associate, responsible for keeping the minutes of a blue-ribbon Committee on Early Childhood Accidents, the member of which were of national and international stature.

One of the committee members was Dr. Robert Haggerty, editor of the prestigious New England Journal of Medicine, and he commissioned me to write a series of editorials on childhood accidents. The remuneration wasn't much -- $25 per piece – but for a young assistant professor of medicine it was a heady experience to see oneself in print in such an outstanding medical journal. One of these pieces was a report on an accident that had made the headlines some weeks before in the Boston papers – that of a 2-year-old child who had drowned in a bathtub in only a few inches of water when his mother went to answer the phone. I decided it would be worth my getting more details about it, so I called upon the mother in a somewhat rundown neighborhood over in Cambridge. She was most hospitable, and I spent some little time with her as she described the tragedy in detail. I left with an uneasy feeling, however – and was not entirely surprised a few weeks later when I picked up the evening paper in the train station *en route* home and saw the glaring headlines: MOTHER CONFESSES DROWNING 2-YEAR OLD CHILD.

By my third year at Tufts it was becoming apparent that we would have to make a move. Despite the extra financial help provided by the part-time appointments, we were experiencing a severe pinch in our finances, so I began looking into the possibility of another job. When I learned that Dr. Kirk Moseley, a fellow member of the Christian Medical Society, had become health commissioner of Oklahoma, I sent him my *curriculum vitae* and received an invitation to visit at his expense. The job he offered would be two-fold: half-time in the department of preventive medicine of the Oklahoma University School of Medicine, and half-time as health officer of nearby Norman, Oklahoma, site of the main campus of the university. It was a tempting offer, but Pat found the climate and flat plains of Oklahoma too far a cry from her native New England.

Early in 1961 I applied and was interviewed for the job of Health Commissioner of Worcester, Massachusetts. The salary was $15,000, and there would be no hurry to move there, our home in Norfolk being not all that far away. Soon thereafter I received a call from the head of the search committee offering me the job -- but only the day before had received another call from Washington, D.C. that was to throw us into quandary once again. The call from Worcester came on a Friday afternoon, so I asked the caller if I might have the weekend to consider the matter and would call back within a few days.

Many months earlier I had heard an interesting talk at a missions conference by a friend and fellow board member of the Christian Medical Society, Dr. C. Everett "Chick" Koop (later to become the U. S. Surgeon General), telling of opportunities overseas with the foreign aid arm of the U. S. Department of State. Thinking that I might one day be interested is such work, I later phoned Chick to ask for more information. He referred me to his contact at the International Cooperation Administration (later to be renamed the U. S. Agency for International Development – USAID). While in Washington some months later attending an international health conference, I called upon this contact. At that time, there was only one academic position in preventive medicine for which they were recruiting – a visiting professorship at Osmania University in Hyderabad, India. I realized, of course, that I was much too junior in my career to be considered for anything they might have, but I would like to go on record as being interested at some future date. Nonetheless, he asked me to fill out an application form, in case something at a more junior level should turn up. I returned home and promptly forgot about the matter.

The phone call that fateful day several months later was from my Washington contact. He explained that they had been trying without success to recruit a senior person for the position in Hyderabad, and the Indian government had finally agreed to take someone of lesser rank. If I wanted the job, it was mine. They were sending me all the details.

The details arrived the following Monday, and Pat had obviously perused the various documents before I arrived home. In the margin of the 4-page description of Hyderabad and its surroundings, were scrawled in pencil:

heat – bugs – flat, dusty plains! I had acquiesced in the Oklahoma offer. How was I going to deal with this one? We talked and prayed about it, and kept the Worcester people waiting for a few days. Professionally, it was a challenging position and would be a feather in my cap – and the pay was excellent. Because it was to be only a 2-year assignment, not an indefinite commitment, Pat was reluctantly willing to give it a go, and with great embarrassment I informed the person in Worcester that this very unusual opportunity had presented itself and I regretfully had to decline their offer. He was not happy with my decision.

Since there was no urgency in my taking up this assignment, we had all the time we needed to prepare for the move. I was able to continue my responsibilities at the medical school without interruption, and even recruited a replacement for myself – a junior faculty member at the School of Public Health who had been one of my guest lecturers from time to time. All in all, it was a very smooth transition that caused no disruption in the department, and I was thus able to leave with the blessings of Count and all of my colleagues in the department. It had been a very good three years. (Count later became head of preventive medicine at Stanford University, and I was recently saddened to learn that he died of a stroke at the age of 81 several years earlier.)

For Pat the transition was far more demanding. There was the house to sell, decisions as to what to take and what to store, and myriad other details – but the unanticipated resources that became available to us were astounding. Through contacts at the School of Public Health, we learned of an Indian woman from Hyderabad living in the Boston area. Not only was she a great help in orienting us to the living conditions, but provided us with the name of the principal of the finest private school in the city. Before we left, our two boys were tentatively enrolled in St. George's Grammar School.

Shipping allowances were very generous, considering we would be provided with fully furnished housing – ocean freight for those things not needed for some weeks after arrival (including an automobile), air freight for early essentials, and generous baggage allowances for our air travel. Your government's employees are well cared for, taxpayers! The steel container era had not yet arrived, so it was necessary to hire a firm specializing in such things to prepare a wooden container – not a problem in a port city such as Boston.

Transport by first class air was the accepted mode for government employees in those days, and new employees were expected to fly immediately to their overseas assignment upon completion of a 4-week orientation course at the Foreign Service Institute in Washington. However, the travel instructions noted that dependents were free to travel by whatever means desired, so I immediately requested an exception for myself. Pointing out that there appeared to be no urgency in my taking this assignment, I asked for permission to travel by sea with my family to Europe, a 3-week holiday there at my own expense, thence onward by air to India. This at first met with a typical bureaucratic response: "This has never been done before, but we will forward your request to the appropriate office." Like several efforts earlier in life to "buck the system", it worked, and I immediately went to the office of the United States Lines in Boston to make reservations. We were given the finest accommodations in their space allotment, as well as a reservation for the new air-conditioned (a considerable luxury in those days) 1961 Ford station wagon we had just purchased to take with us. This was not exactly a typical missionary voyage we were undertaking.

Again Pat's flair for selecting the right kind of and location for a home resulted in our selling the house almost immediately it went on the market. She was thus able to devote all the time necessary for purchasing such things as might be needed for a 2-year stay – including Christmas gifts for the kids and gift wrapping for them! I had only to choose the few text books and files that I might need professionally. (Years later, while visiting a professor at Fuller Theological Seminary who had been a missionary in Hyderabad during our stay, his wife received a phone call from their daughter in Arizona. When told of my visit and asked if she remembered the Browns—she was then six years old — her response was, "Of course, they were the ones who gave me those beautifully wrapped gifts for my birthday.")

We broke in the new car by taking a circuitous route to Washington by way of Boston to visit Pat's folks in Plymouth; Akron, Ohio, to visit my paternal grandparents; and St. Petersburg, Florida, to visit my parents. In St. Pete, a medical school classmate, Art Sherman, and his wife generously gave us the use of their luxurious home and swimming pool while they were on holiday for two weeks. In Washington, Bob and Jane Brubaker, lifelong friends since our Falls Church, Virginia days took in the wandering gypsies for the entire month at the Foreign Service Institute. We were indeed blessed!

30 --"From Greenland's icy mountains to India's coral strands...."

Little did I dream as a young lad, singing that old missionary hymn, that life's journey would literally take me from Greenland to India in my first two professional overseas assignments.

On to New York, we booked in at a hotel and deposited most of our baggage, as well as the car, at the United States Line dock in preparation for an early boarding the next day. The trip was a delight, and 3-year-old Wende even obliged us by giving up diapers *en route*, leaving me with a 2-year supply of polishing cloths for the car. (As noted earlier, Pampers had not yet been invented.)

One could not have asked for a more pleasant way to travel. One of the highlights was the shooting aboard ship of a Disney film starring Fred MacMurray and Jane Wyman, with Disney himself in charge. Of course, all this was in First Class and we were in Cabin Class, but there's always a way to crash a party. Discovering that one of the exits from the ship's theater led to the First Class deck, the boys and I mingled with those exiting after a morning show, and took a seat in the back row of bleacher-like seats. To our surprise and delight, we soon realized that this was part of the movie, and we were to be among the "extras".

As I was to learn some years later after becoming acquainted with two well-known movie actors whose sets at Universal Studios I visited each time while in Los Angeles on business, movie making is a tedious business. After sitting there for an interminable length of time waiting to be "shot", our moment finally arrived. First, however, a production assistant had to consult a photograph of the "audience" taken the day before, to be sure that everyone was seated in the same seat, having filmed part of this scene before the sun faded. Faces trading places on the silver screen in the midst of a scene would look a bit odd. Unfortunately, she checked a bit too closely, suddenly looking up at the back row and shouting, "You there, in the red shirt and the two kids next to you! You weren't there yesterday! Move out!" Thus ended our Hollywood career before it began. Anyhow, that scene would probably have ended on the cutting room floor.

The SS United States was the fastest passenger liner in the world in those days, and we docked in Le Havre, France, only five days later. After clearing Customs, we were escorted to our car, along with the vast amount of baggage required for 3 weeks travel in Europe with three kids. A local French passerby, noting this mountain of stuff, asked if we intended to put all that in our car, and when I replied affirmatively, had the nerve to respond: "All zat weel not feet, monsieur!" Such Gallic gall!

At that point the U.S. Lines attendant who had escorted us asked a more disturbing question: "Have you ze key, monsieur?" The key? What key? The car key? I left it in the ignition switch when I deposited the car at the dock in New York." "But zere eez no key, monsieur." "So how did you get it off the ship?" "We pooshed eet."

My mind raced as we proceeded to load the car. Surely someone can jump start it, and we can head for Paris where there is surely a Ford dealer who will know how to make a key. But then what do we do every time we have to stop along the way? Let the motor run while everyone but me eats in a restaurant while I guard the car? And how will the Paris dealer know the code for the key? I'll have to find a phone and call the dealer in Franklin, Massachusetts, for the code – if he has it. But it's 2:00 a.m. in Franklin. How could I have been so stupid not to bring an extra set of keys? (By then, at least I could give the passerby, who hadn't left his post, a disdainful look as the loading was completed. It took some doing, but it was all inside the car.)

Suddenly a feeble light flickered in my overworked brain. Trembling, I leaned down in front of the car and reached under the bumper. Arising with a triumphant look, I displayed the muddy object clutched in my hot little hand – a magnetic key box which I had forgotten, containing a spare key. Shouts of joy erupted from all present – except the arrogant passerby, who now slunk off. We were on our way.

Now with no need to go to Paris, we headed directly north-northeast for Brussels, thence through Germany, our destination Copenhagen to visit our Danish friends from the Greenland days. Seeing Europe for the first time (other than war-torn Italy) was a heady experience. We arrived in Copenhagen on the third day, and found a marvelous guest-house in the suburbs.

Calling upon a Danish couple whose names had been given us by someone at home, we were told that an American friend of theirs would be delighted to take care of Wende while we took the boys to Tivoli Gardens, Copenhagen's renowned amusement park. With a 5-year-old of her own who spoke only Danish, she welcomed having an English-speaking house guest even if it was only a 3-year-old. When we asked her where she was from in the U. S, she said she had grown up in Buffalo – but when we pinned her down to a more specific location, we were pleasantly surprised to know that she was from Williamsville.

Tivoli was a wonderful place, but at one point we suddenly became aware that 6-year-old Jack was nowhere in view. Having panicked earlier in our trip when he disappeared from Pat's parents' home in Plymouth, where we feared he had fallen down an abandoned well, we should have kept him on a leash. Frantically searching the immediate area without success, I told Pat to take Ted with her and begin circling in one direction while I did likewise in the other, continually expanding the radius of our circles. Only after a considerable period of time and increasing anxiety did we at last see a small boy in a bright red jacket wandering with joyous abandon as he took in the sights – and was perilously close to an exit through which he would have undoubtedly continued on into the heart of the city.

A week exploring the delights of Copenhagen and visiting Danish friends from Greenland days, and we were on our way south to Rome, from where we would fly to New Delhi after I had deposited the car with the American consulate in Naples. The stories one could tell of the joys and the woes of traveling with three offspring, ages 3, 6, and 8, in a huge American station wagon filled to the roof with personal belongings and acquired treasures would fill a book of its own.

From Copenhagen, we traveled south through Germany again, visiting this time some of the smaller towns, through which I was often forced to maneuver our behemoth with two wheels on the sidewalk of some very narrow streets. Crossing the Swiss-Italian border on a high mountain pass, a very young Italian border guard adopted his most official demeanor in examining our passports. The Department of State required each member of a family to have his or her own passport, rather than putting all on one, and with a stony face the young man carefully examined each picture and then stared sternly at the respective occupant. I had taken the pictures myself, in color, and when he came to the picture of the chubby red-cheeked 3-year-old, he blew his cool. Looking up, he broke into a broad grin as his eyes alighted upon this little cherub, and with a flourish he handed back the passports and waved us on our way. I still have a duplicate of that picture on my desk at home, along with that of Wende's second daughter, Kayla – a clone of her mother at the same age.

Our next stop was Milano, and I have already detailed the memorable events that took place with the detour through Saronno in seeking my long-lost wartime Italian girlfriend, then age 13. Heading south through

Firenze, we missed all of the Florentine attractions by wasting more than two hours trying to find the office where discount gasoline coupons could be obtained – only to be told that we didn't qualify for some reason I no longer recall. Rome beckoned, with only two days before our flight to India was to depart. It was not until more than forty years later that we had the opportunity to take in all the wonders that Florence has to offer.

Finding the *pension* in Rome recommended by our guide book proved to be a nightmare. It was located on a small street, one of many reached from an enormous traffic circle around the colosseum, and getting from the point at which we entered the circle, with some five or six lanes of traffic, and exiting into that street could only be described as pure agony. It was the evening rush hour, and over and over we circled, like Ben Hur and the chariots of yore, trying to force our way across the endless lines of darting motor scooters, Fiat 500s (the tiny postwar car favored by 99 percent of Italians in those days), and trucks. After innumerable unsuccessful attempts and on the verge of tears with frustration, I finally gave up, heading for the airport in the hope of finding accommodation there. Unfortunately, there was nothing between the city and the airport, and nothing there, so back to Rome we headed. By now the traffic had eased, and we reached our destination without difficulty – but the hour was now late and we fully expected to be quoted a room rate equivalent to that at the Hotel Majestic Roma on Via Veneto. They did not, however, and we settled in for the night after having dinner and transferring the entire contents of our station wagon to our room, since the car had to be delivered to Naples the next day.

Driving to Napoli and returning by train would take the entire day, so I agreed to take Wende with me so that Pat could manage more comfortably with a bit of sightseeing with the boys. It was a lovely day, and the drive afforded a magnificent view of the Bay of Naples as we descended into the city. The American consul had given good directions to the office of the agent who would ship our car to Bombay, and as I was filling out the papers in his second-floor office, he handed the car keys to an assistant. Wende wandered out onto a balcony overlooking the street, just in time to see our car being driven away. "My car! My car!", she cried out in dismay, as the last vestige of home disappeared from view. The agent kindly drove us to the train station, and we caught the first *rapido* back to Rome. The next morning we and our gear were delivered to the airport in two taxis, and we were soon on our way from civilization as we knew it to our unknown destiny in a distant land.

31 -- India's coral strands?

In those days, all Department of State employees were allowed to fly First Class on overseas flights – a delightful respite with three small urchins. The Pan Am flight from Rome stopped in Ankara, from whence we were the only passengers in First Class. Arriving in New Delhi at 2:00 am was a shock. Leaving the incredible food and other creature comforts of the plane, we were sprayed with insecticide at the doorway by an Indian health official and stepped out into the stifling heat and humidity. As we stumbled sleepily along the tarmac, I asked myself, "What have I gotten us into??!!"

We were greeted warmly (how else in that climate?) by an American couple assigned by the embassy to take us to our hotel. Claridge's Hotel was one of Delhi's finest, but its ancient decor was thoroughly depressing. We collapsed in our room, awaking some hours later in time for a late breakfast. The dining room was depressing. The liveried waiters in their white gloves were depressing. The strange food was depressing. Culture shock had taken over with a bang. (Six months later, when I came up to New Delhi to meet my new USAID boss in the embassy, he invited me to dinner in his hotel. What a stunning place! What a magnificent dining room! What marvelous food! It was the same Claridge's Hotel that hadn't changed in a hundred years – only my perceptions had changed.)

In Hyderabad we were met by Dr. Allen White and his wife, another USAID visiting professor at the medical school, who apologetically took us to the second-best hotel in town, the Ritz Hotel being momentarily full. If the Secunderabad Hotel was the city's second-best, we wondered what the third-best must be like. Our room was actually a dirt-floor cottage (covered with a carpet, however) adjacent to the main building, with a single bare light bulb hanging from the ceiling, making Claridge's Hotel look like the Waldorf Astoria. The next day was Sunday, so he suggested we just have a good rest, and on Monday he would take us house-hunting.

Sunday afternoon, lying about in our dismal room, we had an unexpected visitor. A Indian man entered the room and greeted me excitedly, throwing his arms around me with a uncharacteristically Indian bear hug. "Welcome to Hyderabad!" There was something familiar about him, but I had to ask his name. "I'm Prahlad! Don't you remember how I used to come to your office every Friday afternoon at Tufts two years ago when I was in the course for teachers of preventive medicine at Harvard?" "Of course!

Forgive me! But what are you doing here in Hyderabad?" "I'm the new chairman of the department of social and preventive medicine at Osmania Medical College. I'm your new colleague!"

This was incredible news. The excitement of going to India and taking on this new job had been tempered by a good bit of anxiety about how I was going to be received. As I noted earlier, the Indian government had asked for a senior man for the visiting professorship, since the head of the department was a very senior man. What would he think of this young upstart? How the Lord does provide! Not only a man more my own age to work with, but one who had gone through the same course at Harvard as I. Our dingy room brightened as we talked about the good times we were going to have together.

More good news came the next day, when Allen informed us that he had a room for us at the Ritz Hotel, a former palace. There, too, our room was a separate building – a huge one-room miniature palace that had been the royal playroom. It proved to be a real blessing, for as it turned out, we were to spend six weeks there waiting for construction of the house we had found to be completed. We took our meals in the hotel dining room, where the waiters and the management were extremely gracious, especially to our children.

Many years later, our son Ted was sent to New Delhi by Control Data Corporation in Minneapolis to deal with a software emergency that had befallen one of their customers involved in the very important Asian Games being held there that year. He soon resolved the problem, and when he asked his Indian hosts to arrange a reservation at the Ritz Hotel in Hyderabad, he had to explain why he wanted to stay in what was now very much a second-class hotel. To the Ritz he went, and when the management learned of his prior stay, he was treated like royalty.

His crowning moment, however, was his visit to his alma mater, St. George's Grammar School. Now 150 years old, the buildings were as he remembered them. Standing in a hallway near his old room, he was greeted by an older teacher who asked if she could help him. "No, thank you. I attended school here long ago, and am just enjoying the pleasure of seeing it again." "Are you Doctor Brown's son?," she exclaimed in amazement.

Hyderabad was a fascinating city. Prior to the partition of India in 1947, it was the capital of the wealthiest of the princely states of India, ruled by the wealthiest man in the world, the Nizam of Hyderabad. Hyderabad was a Muslim state, and with partition large numbers of Muslims fled to West Pakistan. When we arrived in 1961 the population of the city was more evenly divided between Hindus and Muslims, living in complete harmony. Old Hyderabad, south of the river, where the medical school was located, was almost solidly Muslim, whereas the rest of the city was both Muslim and Hindu. The old Nizam was still there, living in a sprawling palace complex in the center of the city. Like other former princely rulers, the Hindu maharajahs, he received an annual stipend of considerable size from the Indian government, but no longer had any authority.

Our house was quite modern by Indian standards -- unlike some we had been shown with those abominable squat toilets and no seats still found in much of the world -- and USAID furnished it very well indeed, with air conditioners, refrigerator, carpets, and an abundance of new furniture. It was on the edge of the city, with a separate garage in a large compound surrounded by a high wall. Cobras and other venomous snakes were common in the area, but we were not aware of any having made their way into our yard. Nonetheless, it was prudent when walking outside at night to do so with a heavy foot, thereby scaring off any that might have entered the premises. We soon learned, however, to always make sure that screen doors closed securely when Pat found a large scorpion under Wende's pillow one morning while making the bed.

Having young children, and especially an adorable 3-year-old daughter, was a distinct benefit in relating to our Indian neighbors, and although we were one of only a few American families in a city of over one million, we were always very well received wherever we went. At no time were we ever made to feel like "ugly Americans". Nor did we need to have any concerns about the safety of our children when out of our immediate supervision. One day we noticed that Wende suddenly disappeared. A frantic search in the immediate neighborhood was unsuccessful, but when we finally located her some four or five blocks from home, where she had been strolling on the sidewalk along a main street, an Indian lady was already looking after her. She had put on her best dress, and was carrying a little basket over her arm. When asked where she was going, her reply was, "To the 'zaar!" (She had often heard Pat informing me when she was going to the bazaar for food or whatever.)

32 – Britain's jewel in the crown

We soon made contact with Charles and Margaret Chamberlain, missionaries supported by Park Street Church, who introduced us to a church and to many other missionaries, British and American, in the area. Centenary Methodist Church, pastored by an American missionary, the Rev. Bill Moon, became our church home for the next two years. It was an active congregation, with many young people, and the boys were privileged to have a very fine Sunday School teacher, a student at Osmania University, who later attended seminary in Bangalore and eventually became pastor of that church. Militant Hinduism had not yet reared its ugly head, and there were many Christians among the Hindus and Muslims in Hyderabad, who practiced their faith without fear of harassment.

Prahlad generously offered me as much of the departments lecture schedule as I desired, and hoped that I wouldn't mind doing a course in biostatistics. The only course in that subject which he had ever taken was the same one I had taken at the Harvard School of Public Health – and he felt as helpless in teaching it to his students as I at first did to my Tufts students. I agreed to take it on, but wondered if I could bridge the cultural gap. I spent a good bit of time on that one, adapting my Tufts material to the Indian scene, as seemed appropriate.

At Tufts I had been particularly keen to develop audiovisual and other supplemental material of sufficient interest to overcome the inevitable boredom produced by the graphs and charts of which teachers of biostatistics are so fond. While passing a camera shop in downtown Boston one day, I noted their offer of a set of Kodachrome slides of the current Miss America contestants. Surely there must be a way to use such eye-catching material in one of my lectures!

One of the first concepts taught in biostatistics is that of the normal distribution curve – the bell-shaped curve that results, for example, from plotting on a graph the heights, blood pressure, or whatever of a group of normal individuals in any age group. There are a few short ones at one end of the curve and a few tall ones at the other end, but most fall within the middle 90-plus percent of the curve. By arbitrarily assigning heights to each of the young ladies, I could produce a perfect bell-shaped curve. The lecture was an immense hit. Projecting each one and stating her height, the students entered the value on a graph, and thus saw the traditional curve form before their eyes while enjoying the curves on the screen – and I was thus able to use the entire set of slides. It was a hard act to follow in other lectures, but with taped excerpts from some of my comedy records (those flat, round things on which music, etc., was recorded in the Dark Ages), and other sundry aids, I managed to muddle through.

Clearly, however, none of this was suited to the Indian milieu, and I found myself devoting an inordinate amount of time to the preparation of a biostatistics syllabus that I could use and leave behind for Prahlad. (To illustrate the concept of standard deviation, I turned to a somewhat less colorful visual aid — weighing a bunch of mangoes purchased at the bazaar.) I often wondered if this was really what I supposed to be doing at Osmania Medical College. I had never been given a job description by USAID, and surely there were more important aspects of the teaching of preventive medicine than this one, not very exciting, subject.

Two years later I received an answer to that earlier concern. While employed by the Association of American Medical Colleges under a contract with USAID, I was, as director of the AAMC-USAID Project in Medical Education, responsible for evaluating previous contracts between USAID and some dozen or more Third World medical schools, including Osmania Medical College. This required my spending many hours in Washington at the Department of State, going through their files. I was particularly interested, of course, in those on the Osmania project, and for the first time saw the job description for the visiting professor of social and preventive medicine, with a list of priorities to which he was expected to give his attention. At the top of list: "Development of a course in biostatistics". *Quel formidable!*

Driving a huge 1961 American station wagon with left-hand drive on the "wrong" side of the road was a challenge in a large city teaming with trucks, cars, taxis, motor scooters, scooter rickshaws, bicycles, pushcarts—and the ubiquitous cows. Driving on the open highways outside the cities was even more of a challenge, however. Although traffic was considerably less, nearly all the roads in India in those days, including the major highways, were only one lane wide. Thus, hurtling down the highway at 50 or 60 miles an hour, one frequently encountered a car or truck approaching head-on at similar speed. Since neither driver wanted to go on the shoulder of the road until absolutely necessary, it was a constant game of "chicken". One could only hope that the oncoming vehicle was not being driven by a newly-arrived American or European who might reflexly pull to the right instead of the left! In any case, it was always an uncomfortable situation for Pat on the passenger side, as the two vehicles passed inches apart. She was more than happy to take the wheel anytime I was willing to relinquish it – and was delighted to have the car to herself during the week after USAID gave me a brand-new Jeep station wagon and driver for my official use.

We had the pleasure of making many friends among missionaries in that part of India. Among them were two British doctors, Gilbert and Hedi Way, who operated a small hospital in a village about fifty miles north of Hyderabad, and who introduced us to many of their British colleagues. Theirs was an impressive undertaking, with a water supply limited to a well, from which water had to be carried to a tank on the roof of the hospital in order to provide pressure to the sinks below for them to scrub for surgery – often under kerosene lamps when frequent power failures occurred.

Through them I was extended an invitation to deliver the annual Hospital Day sermon at the Anglican church in Medak, a village about 50 miles northwest of Hyderabad, where their mission had a much larger hospital. We made a grand holiday of it, driving there with Pat and the children. As we approached the village we were amazed to see an English cathedral rising from the plain in the distance. It was in this grand structure that I delivered the sermon from a pulpit high above the congregation – all of whom sat on the pew-less floor. While there I received another invitation when they learned that I owned a shotgun – to come up sometime and dispatch the horde of monkeys that would swoop down through the open windows of the ward and snatch food from the patients. However, I never found time to take on this noble assignment.

Although there were two medical schools in Hyderabad, the quality of medical care left much to be desired. Despite the training many of the professors had had in England, they were prone to revert to local practices – such as using the same needle and syringe to vaccinate a roomful of children. The children remained remarkably healthy during our two-year stay. However, when all three had gone through a rough patch with respiratory infections that seemed to drag on forever, we took them to the Christian Medical College in Vellore, some 500 miles south. Professor John Webb, whom we had the pleasure of visiting many years later in Newcastle-on-Tyne, England, graciously checked them out, assuring us that there was nothing to be concerned about. An American dentist, Dick Topazian, and his wife kindly housed us during our week's stay.

It was a great privilege there to become acquainted with two of the world's foremost experts in leprosy, Dr. William Cochrane, who was at that time a visiting professor, and Dr. Paul Brand, chief of surgery. Paul Brand was one of the truly great men in modern medicine. I had previously met him when he was invited by Osmania Medical College to address all the surgeons in the city at their annual meeting. One could see the love of Christ in him as he told how he first became interested in the surgical treatment of leprosy. The disease itself does not directly cause the loss of fingers, toes, feet or hands. Rather, it attacks the sensory nerves to these sites, so that they no longer feel pain – and the loss is thus due to physical injury to parts that can give no warning of such injury as it occurs bit by bit. The audience was enthralled as he described how many leprosy patients were returned to useful occupations by the development of special tools, special shoes, and other means.

He later moved to the United States to become the chief of surgery at our remaining leprosy hospital in Carville, Louisiana, and extended his work into the treatment of diabetes. I was privileged to serve with him years later on a panel at a conference on medical missions at Wheaton College. He earned several distinguishing honors, including Commander of the Order of the British Empire, awarded by Queen Elizabeth II in 1961, and died in June 2003 at the age of 89.

I am also reminded of a long-standing friendship with another Godly man, a modern pioneer of medicine who contributed much to the health of persons worldwide. Denis Burkitt, born in Ireland in 1911, was a surgeon in Uganda where he discovered a rare and deadly form of cancer in children, now known as Burkitt's lymphoma, which he determined to be caused by a virus,. But his greater contribution came from extensive studies of the differences in the frequency of many major diseases between native Africans and Europeans. Having rarely seen such common diseases as appendicitis, gallstones, and many others among his African patients, his studies after he returned to England led him to the conclusion that the difference was dietary in nature – and specifically related to the amount of fiber in one's diet. The impact of Denis's zeal in promoting this knowledge is seen everywhere today.

Denis was a humble man, a thoroughly committed Christian, and a great friend. He died in 1993, and I miss him very much.

33 – A unique opportunity to exercise diplomatic privilege

I later had opportunity to visit the other Christian medical school in India, the Christian Medical College of Ludhiana, in the Punjab, where Carl Taylor had established the first department of preventive medicine. Two old friends were then on the faculty -- my Harvard classmate, Don Wysham, and Dave Barnhouse, son of the eminent Philadelphia preacher, Donald Gray Barnhouse. (Dave, a urologist, in recent years became an Episcopal priest in Pittsburgh.) While making rounds with the Dr. Nambudripad, professor of neurosurgery and later the dean, he introduced me to a foreign patient, a missionary from Indonesia who had been stricken with a serious brain problem while visiting Ludhiana a short time earlier. Dr. Nambudripad had operated on him, but he faced an uncertain future unless provision could be made for continuous drainage of excess cerebrospinal fluid. The solution was a relatively simple one – a tiny tube called a shunt, inserted under the skin, that would carry fluid from the brain into the peritoneal cavity. The problem was that no such shunt was available in India, and getting a license to import one was a major and time-consuming undertaking.

I asked him where a shunt could be obtained, and how big it was. Although State Department employees had access to APO service, it could only be used for letter mail. When he informed me that it could be ordered from a company in Connecticut and coiled up could easily fit in a sturdy envelope, I told him I would see what I could do. Upon my return to Hyderabad, I wrote to the company explaining the problem and told them they could charge the shunt to my American Express credit card, which they did. It arrived shortly thereafter, and I posted it to Dr. Nambudripad. He later wrote to say that the patient was doing well and had returned to his mission station in Indonesia.

Four years later, while again living in the Washington, D.C. area, Pat and I arrived late one morning for our Sunday School class at Fourth Presbyterian Church. A guest speaker was describing his work in Indonesia, so after class I related the foregoing and asked him if by any chance he knew that missionary, whose name I could not recall. "I certainly do know him!," he replied. "I'm he!" Not only does God afford the opportunity to be of service by putting us in just the right place at the right time under the right circumstances, but he often then rewards us later with an exciting reminder such as this for past service.

Opportunities for travel throughout the country were many, occasionally as a guest lecture at other Indian medical schools, and frequently to various medical meetings, including that of the Christian Medical Association of India. Because Pat remained faithfully at home looking after the young ones, I encouraged her to take a holiday by herself at a time when she was going to New Delhi for dental care. That was the highlight of her stay in India – 2 weeks in Srinagar, Kashmir, living on a luxurious houseboat, with servants at her beck and call. What a pity that for many years now it has been too dangerous for tourists to visit that incredibly beautiful part of India.

As I've noted, our house in Hyderabad was on the outskirts of the city at the end of a dirt road, with nothing beyond us but the boulder-strewn Banjara Hills. To reach the few houses – most of them mansions of the very wealthy – scattered throughout the hills, one had to take a long, circuitous route beginning some distance along the highway near our home. When we returned to Hyderabad a few years ago, we had some difficulty finding our house, now surrounded by high-rise office and apartment buildings that actually touched the house on three sides. Ascending our street, now paved and lined with new buildings, and two large luxury hotels at its crest, we were greeted by an entire city now occupying the Banjara Hills. Great change – and no change – for the busy commercial center of the city was virtually as we had left it 30 years before, cows wandering the streets and all.

Our one long drive as a family occurred during our first year, when the Moons invited us to spend the month of May with them in the south Indian hill resort of Kodaikanal, better known as Kodai. May was the hottest month of the year, during which the Americans, Europeans, and wealthy Indians headed for the hills – the Nilgiris in the south and the Himalayan foothills in the north. We had sent our two servants ahead by train – Isaac, our cook, and Mary, an elderly lady who did most of the heavy cleaning and looked after Wende somewhat.

Our own preparations and subsequent departure were painfully reminiscent of our Buffalo-to-Washington move years before. Instead of the early morning start we had planned, fitting everything into the station wagon took much of the day, resulting in a very late start. Driving in the dark late that evening, we at last reached the newly-built bridge over the Krishna river that separated us from the city of Kurnool, our designated stop for the night. It was a beautiful sight, arching upward across that mighty stream, but we were soon brought to a screeching stop by some barrels carelessly left in the middle of the road by workmen who had apparently been putting some finishing touches on the structure. Hurrying to move them aside, I glanced ahead just in time to see that there were indeed some finishing touches to be made – namely, the other half of the bridge, which now reached only to midstream!

Reversing slowly down our semi-bridge back to the highway, and uncertain as to which direction to go along the river until another bridge of a more finished structure might become available, we headed in the direction that seemed most appropriate, based on the distant lights of Kurnool.

The road – or what I thought was the road—became rougher and rougher, and when I made a wide circle for a better look at the terrain, we discovered we were driving down a dry river bed. Not to worry! One can go nowhere in that overpopulated country without being within shouting distance of other humans – and we were soon surrounded by dozens of curious villagers who appeared out of nowhere. Fortunately, the road was only a few miles away, and with their helpful directions, we soon found ourselves on pavement again.

Unfortunately, we were almost out of gas, and Kurnool – which *might* have a petrol station open that late—was still an unknown distance away. Moreover, we hadn't the foggiest idea of the location of the government guest house in Kurnool, where Prahlad had said we would be allowed, as government employees, to stay for the night, and would try to make a reservation for us.

Our guardian angel was still riding on the roof rack, however. We did find an open station, where we learned that the guest house was but a few blocks away. That was the good news. The bad news was that the night watchman had received no message authorizing our stay. Seeing our plight, he finally agreed to let us in, with my promise to be out by 6:00 a.m. before his boss arrived. It was a short night.

Pat frequently shared the driving with me, allowing me the exciting pleasure of sitting on the right front seat where oncoming lorries on those single-lane highways sailed by at 50 mph a millimeter or two from the right side of our vehicle. Pedestrians were likewise a hazard, but she was not quite prepared for a pig which suddenly darted in front of her as she passed through a village. She braked in an effort to avoid it, throwing the great pile of goods behind us tumbling over our heads, but caught the beast about midway between the front wheels, and since we hadn't yet come to a full stop, it passed under the entire length of our car with a series of loud thumps. Exiting from the rear with raucous squeals, it was seen to be having some difficulty in the use of its rear legs, relying solely on its front legs to frantically propel it home. Sighting some locals rushing toward us, I shouted to Pat to get underway lest we be taken prisoners, with ransom exceeding the value of a herd of pigs being demanded. When safely down the road a few furlongs, we stopped to check for possible damage to the car and to restore our cargo to its rightful place. The kids found it all rather exciting.

Kodai was another world. The climate was heavenly, and we had a refreshing holiday. They even had a golf course – possibly the only one in the world where one could find tiger footprints on the sand "greens" first thing in the morning.

The Moons had invited us to stay in one of the cottages in the compound provided by the Methodist Church in India for its missionaries. We had sent Isaac, our cook, and Mary, the housekeeper, on ahead by train. Isaac was the envy of the other cooks there, being amply provided with staples from the embassy commissary in New Delhi, who had shipped our order directly to Kodai. While the others were preparing everything from scratch for their employers, he lounged about until it was time to remove the top from cans of Chef Boy-ar-dee spaghetti for lunch or whip up a cake from a Duncan Hines mix for dessert for our guests. Several years later, while passing through Hyderabad *en route* home from the Far East, I visited him at the home of the missionary family with whom we had found him employment when we left India. They said he was doing fine, but was sadly disappointed the first time he asked the memsahib where the cake mix was when she ordered a cake for dinner.

34 – A pleasant side-trip and further activities in India

This one-month holiday provided the opportunity to do something I had long wanted to do – visit an old friend in Taiwan. Dr. Wei Sia (or Bill, as we knew him) had become a very special friend in Buffalo during my first two years out of medical school, and was the person who introduced us to International Students, Inc., when we moved to Washington, D.C. We had been privileged to provide some minimal support to him in establishing a tuberculosis hospital in the tribal mountainous region of Taiwan, and I was strongly urged not only to visit him but some other outstanding mission endeavors in that country by Bob Pierce, President of World Vision, Inc., who had been our guest in Hyderabad a few months earlier.

I therefore took some time off from our mountain holiday and flew from Madras to Singapore, thence to Taipei. Bill met me at the airport, and the following day drove me to his home in central Taiwan, where I had a most enjoyable stay with his wife and children. After spending some time at the tuberculosis hospital some hours away, he then gave me a grand tour of southern Taiwan, including a flight out to the Pescadores, which in those days was being periodically shelled by artillery on the Chinese mainland – which was always matched round for round by Taiwanese artillery on the islands. Perhaps one of these days the constant bickering between little Taiwan and its mighty neighbor will find a peaceful solution!

At that time Bill did not have a car of his own and had to rely on taxis to for his regular visits caring for the patients in the TB hospital. Some years later he wrote to tell me that he had become the proud owner of a motorcycle, which was now his means of transportation in making his medical rounds. Not long afterward, we learned from another friend in Taiwan that he had been fatally injured when an erratically-driven oncoming car carelessly forced him off the road. On a happier note, however, our Taiwanese connection many years later was our lovely daughter-in-law, Carrie, whom son Ted met in San Francisco.

On my return I stopped briefly in Hong Kong for the purpose of filling a long shopping list given me by American friends in Hyderabad, whom I had apprised of my impending trip to Hong Kong during the holidays – mostly cameras and film, plus a set of golf clubs and a stock of golf balls for myself. Arriving in Madras airport the following Sunday afternoon, I came under the intense scrutiny of the Customs officer. Somehow my diplomatic passport didn't convince him that I was entitled to bring in that enormous haul of goods not available in India, and he was about to seize the entire lot when I asked him if I might speak to the Chief of Customs.

"It's Sunday – he's not here!"

"Would you please call him at home?"

To my surprise, he acquiesced and proceeded to explain the situation with much emotion, followed by a somewhat prolonged silence.

"Yes, sir, I understand – but, sir, he has thirteen cameras!" Again a moment of silence.

"Yes, sir. I understand, sir. Yes, sir. As you wish! Good day, sir."

Regaining his composure, he reached under the table, produced a long form, and instructed me to write down in detail every bit of contraband and its cost, made me sign the sheet, and reluctantly sent me on my way just in time to catch my flight to the inland city from which I could take a taxi to Kodai – 13 cameras and all. I must confess I felt a bit sorry for him.

(I was to visit Hong Kong a number of times in the ensuing years, by which time I had acquired a number of custom-made suits. My tailor was one John Yu, and when I mentioned on a subsequent visit that the last suit he had made for me had developed some looseness at the one of the seams, he assured me he would take care of that the next time he visited his son at Brebeuf Preparatory School in Indianapolis!)

Kodai also offered me the opportunity to make an unexpected contribution to the future health and well-being of travelers in India. Some weeks earlier I learned of an automobile accident involving two of our USAID nurses traveling in a remote part of India. Badly injured, they were taken to the nearest government hospital, where they received rather inadequate care, and some critical days passed before the American embassy in New Delhi was advised of their plight and sent a plane to evacuate them. Clearly there was a need for the dissemination of information to travelers about a particular group of medical facilities throughout the country where one might obtain quality medical care – the many mission hospitals and clinics staffed by skilled foreign medical personnel and their Indian colleagues, the vast majority of which were in remote areas. As an employee of the U. S. Department of State and a member of the Board of

Directors of the Christian Medical Society of the United States, I realized I was in a unique position to assemble such information and have it disseminated by the American embassy.

Knowing that the Christian Medical Association of India would be having its annual meeting in Kodai while we were there, I contacted the secretary in New Delhi for a complete list of Christian medical facilities in the country, with addresses and (where available) phone numbers. With this in hand I polled the doctors attending the meeting to get their appraisal of their own and other facilities well-known to them, including the name of the head physician. I later forwarded this information to my chief in New Delhi, asking him to turn it over to the appropriate people in the embassy who might find it useful, which he did. I never heard another word about it until more than two years later, when someone in our church in Wilmette, Illinois, who had just returned from a mission trip to India showed me a pocket-size manual, encased in a protective plastic envelope, which he had been given upon arrival in India. The title was *Emergency Medical Facilities in India*, published by the U. S. Agency for International Development, duly crediting me for the information therein.

As I've noted earlier, my position as a visiting American professor under the auspices of the U. S. Agency for International Development provided many opportunities for official travel. A medical conference in Baroda in the state of Gujerat was particularly memorable. Baroda had been one of the princely states of India, ruled by the Majarajah of Baroda, whose son had inherited the title and the palace – and who opened the conference the first evening with a welcoming address.

When I found myself seated with him on the plane to Bombay the next day, he proved to be a pleasant traveling companion. When his Rolls Royce limousine pulled up alongside the plane for him to board, I noticed he had no luggage, so I asked him how he would manage when he reached New Delhi, where he was headed. "Oh, I keep a wardrobe in Delhi and London." (The closest I ever came to such luxury was leaving a pair of size 14 tennis shoes with my friends in Kabul many years later, so I could play tennis with them during my frequent visits.)

Noting that he obviously enjoyed the travel his wealth permitted, I commented with great wisdom on the state of some wealthy persons who never seem to enjoy their status. "For example," said I, "J. Paul Getty (the great oil magnate then living in London) doesn't seem to be a very happy man, from stories I've read about him." "Oh, quite the contrary." retorted he. "I always stay with him when I'm in London, and he's a very enjoyable host." Another exacerbation of foot-in-mouth disease! But he was gracious enough to invite me to bring Pat to Baroda sometime and stay with him. I regret that time didn't permit that before having to leave India.

British rule in India began in 1600 under the East India Company, chartered by the British crown and ultimately responsible to the parliament. By the mid-19th century, India had been rocked by a number of revolts attempting to throw the British out of the country. The Revolt of 1857 so severely jolted the British administration in India that in 1858, governing power was transferred from the East India Company to the British crown. The British Raj, as it became known, lasted until 1947, when India gained its independence.

One of its many evidences in Hyderabad was the Secunderabad Club, the former Officers Club in the military. Now a private club to which our special status entitled us to membership, it was a pleasant place to relax at the pool or have dinner in the ancient dining room. Its golf course, however, left something to be desired, with scarcely a blade of grass on its sun-baked fairways, and hordes of monkeys in the trees around the greens. So hard and rocky was the course that five caddies were required for a foursome – the fifth one to go on ahead and track each player's ball as it bounced hither and yon, and to keep monkeys from running off with it. Tipping a caddy generously when he had previously carried one's bag often paid off when that particular caddy later might be fifth caddy. On such occasions it was pleasantly surprising to find that one's ball had miraculously come to rest on the only tuft of grass within 50 feet, neatly teed up for the next shot.

The only other outdoor sport in which I had opportunity to engage, such as it was, was hunting. As an American with diplomatic privileges, I was able to order both guns and ammunition from the United States – and on the advice of an Indian friend, acquired a sizable arsenal. The friend had a brother who lived about 100 miles north of Hyderabad, where he was employed as the chief tobacco buyer for a cigarette manufacturer, and who invited me up for a weekend of hunting wild boar and panther.

35 – Lo, the mighty hunter

Panther hunting with my new friend, Raza Alikhan, was done at night, with the aid of a spotlight. Cruising about in an open jeep, we would sweep the hillside with the light until it was reflected from the beady eyes of the would-be prey. Our first sighting was two pairs of eyes on the crest of the hill, but when I raised my gun and was ready to blast away, Raza deterred me, wanting to get closer. We dismounted and began a stealthy approach, myself with a .30-06 Remington semiautomatic rifle and he with my 12 gauge shotgun. Alert to the possible danger, I was further protected by my trusty sidearm – a pathetic little .32 Colt revolver, the largest caliber one could legally possess.

Creeping up the hill in the pitch dark, I could imagine the male turning to his mate and saying, "Can you believe those two? Let's give them another five minutes just for laughs, and then we'll take off." Five minutes later they were gone, and we raced back to the jeep with Raza shouting, "We'll go round the bottom of the hill and head them off!" As we careened around the bottom of the hill, we startled another panther up ahead, and again I raised my weapon, only to have Raza shout, "Wait until we get closer!" By the time we did, it had disappeared into the brush. Nor did we sight the first two, so he decided it was time to go home and get some sleep in order to be fresh for the wild boar hunt the next morning.

This proved to be a major undertaking, in which we were joined by a couple of his friends. He placed each of us about 500 feet apart along a high ridge out of sight of one another, looking down into a grassy plain on the opposite side of which were about 25 villagers hired as beaters. Their job was to bang on empty 5-liter cans with a stick while advancing toward us in a wide rank, thus forcing any wild boar in the deep grass to run in our direction.

I was assigned a young boy who would keep lookout with me. For an interminable length of time I stood there in the blazing sun, with nothing but a knotted handkerchief over my head, having foolishly forgotten to wear a cap. The beaters reached the base of our hill with no apparent results, for I didn't hear a shot from any of the others. Suddenly my young companion whispered loudly, "Sahib!" and pointed behind me. There less than 100 feet away was a female, trotting along with five little piglets in tow. I swiftly swung my rifle around, only to see a complete blur in the telescopic sight which was set for 300 yards! By the time I adjusted it, she and her offspring had disappeared. That was the end of the hunt, as the cry to reassemble was passed along the ridge.

The desire to kill was in my blood, however, and as we headed for home a flock of ducks landed on a nearby lake. I asked Raza to stop, and leaped from the vehicle, shotgun in hand. Again I sneaked up on the prey, dodging from tree to tree, only to have them take off in a great sound of flapping wings just as I got within range. This was now my third attempt at wild game and I hadn't fired a shot. I was emotionally and weaponry-prepared for anything, so when I spotted a rabbit hopping along in a nearby field a few miles down the road, I cut loose with my .22 rifle – and downed the vicious beast. Thus ended my big-game hunting in India.

We were privileged to host a number of American travelers in our home during the two years in India. Some were old acquaintances, such as Bob Wenninger, one of my Tufts medical students, who was on a summer world tour, and Dr. Benjamin Castleman, professor of pathology at Harvard Medical School, and his wife, whom I had met at a medical conference in New Delhi. Others I had known previously only by reputation, such as Bob Pierce, founder and president of World Vision, and Dr. Carlyle Jacobsen, dean of the medical school at the University of Syracuse. Both of these were to play a prominent role in my future.

I met Bob Pierce when he arrived in Hyderabad *en route* to a pastors' conference in eastern Andhra Pradesh. His two traveling companions, Dr. Paul Rees and Bob's aide-de-camp, had arrived two days earlier without him when he was detained in Europe by some urgent business. The missionary who was to drive him to the conference was concerned about the dependability of his old car for the 300-mile return trip, for which Bob would be on a tight schedule for his onward flight from Hyderabad. I therefore volunteered to pick him up at the conference center and bring him back three days hence, during which trip and his overnight stay with us he shared many things about his work and how his frequent absence from home had affected his relationship with his daughter. (She was later to write an unflattering account of life with her father.)

Our missionary friends who left for the conference before Bob arrived were concerned that a certain Indian pastor in Secunderabad, having heard that Bob Pierce, benefactor of countless Korean orphans, was coming to town, might attempt to accost him at the airport in an effort to seek funding for his own orphanage. It was known that this man received a large monthly income from an unknown American organization for support of his orphanage – which was non-existent. When visitors from this or other organizations came to view his orphanage, he would round up dozens of neighborhood children and herd them into his large home, duly staffed by members of his extended family.

He did not try to connect with Bob, and I heard nothing more about this man during our remaining days in Hyderabad. Many years later, however, I had a visitor in Indianapolis, an orthopedic surgeon from California and Harvard Medical School classmate, who was championing the cause of Fred Schwarz's Christian Anticommunist Crusade. When he told me he was on his way to India to visit an orphanage supported by the CAC in Secunderabad, he was incredulous when I related my tale, certain that his could not be the same one. It was, of course, for there were no orphanages in Secunderabad, and I regret having never followed up on this conversation in later weeks to learn about his trip to India.

Dr. Jacobsen was one of our last visitors, only a few months before my tour of duty was to end. In response to his question as to my future plans, I told him I had none as yet, but hoped there might be some opportunity to become involved in international medical education back home. He told me about the newly-formed Division of International Medical Education at the Association of American Medical Colleges in Evanston, Illinois, and suggested I write to its director, Dr. Henry van Zile Hyde, who was looking for a number two. He also said he would inform Dr. Hyde of my interest when he arrived home a few days hence.

This I did—and less than two weeks later received his offer of appointment as assistant director of the division. Moreover, because the position was funded under a contract with USAID, he had requested the agency to authorize my return ASAP to take up the position. I was thrilled with the job offer, but having planned to exercise an option offered by USAID to extend my tour an additional six months, we were not keen to return home so soon. However, it was apparent that Dr. Hyde felt an urgent need for my services, so I accepted the offer.

With the semester ending in about two months, we began our preparations for departure. A Chinese packing firm in Madras sent a crew to Hyderabad to build a container for our personal effects, which had increased considerably in two years thanks to the memsahib's expertise in scouring the bazaars for both Indian antiquities and modern productions.

Having realized my ambition as a mighty white hunter, I sold my arsenal to eager Indian buyers. It was also necessary to sell our Ford station wagon, and while I should have been able to sell it for more than I paid for it, there were few who would want to buy such a monster, on which they would have had to pay an additional 100 percent import tax. An interesting possibility came to mind, however. Not only did the old Nizam have duty-free import privileges as a perk of his former rank, but the finance minister of His Exalted Highness, who lived just down the street from us, had earlier commented on the beauty of our behemoth. Surely he could arrange the purchase by his employer, and for the car to become his personal conveyance.

Soon thereafter, when Mr. Taraporewala and I found ourselves seatmates (aided by a bit of maneuvering on my part at the ticket counter) on a flight to New Delhi, I casually brought up the subject, and he took the bait. Before the transaction could be completed, however, it was dealt a fatal blow by the Indian parliament, who, having become increasingly unhappy with all the financial benefits doled out to former heads of local states, passed a law revoking these privileges. Instead, I was forced to sell the car to the State Trading Corporation for use by its bureaucrats – and not only did the STC put a price on it far below what the Nizam would have paid, they rubbed salt in the wound by requiring me to take it 500 miles to Madras to be inspected and left there.

Imported goods were in short supply in India in those days, and the locals were eager to buy anything departing foreigners might wish to sell. We thus rid ourselves of all the 220 volt equipment we had purchased in the U.S. to ship to India, as well as other items not needed at home, much of it to one person, whose brother, M. G. Pittie, and his wife later visited us several times in Indianapolis. In 1995, we returned to Hyderabad on holiday, where we were royally treated by both the Pitties and my old hunting partner, Raza Alikhan. Scarcely a year later we were saddened to learn that Raza had died suddenly of a heart attack.

36 – 'merica and a new career

Our trip home was a leisurely one—two days in New Delhi to complete formalities at the American embassy, then off for a three-day stay in Bombay to await the ship that would take us to Naples. The two-week sea voyage would require a fair amount of hand luggage, so each time we arrived at an airport, hailed a taxi, or otherwise changed modes of transport, the sahib had to do a rapid luggage and head count – 22 pieces of luggage and 5 heads. Wende, now almost 5, knew we were headed for America – and at each stop between Hyderabad and Boston she would ask, "Is this 'merica?"

Our Italian liner offered superb cuisine – although only the boys and I were able to enjoy it for the first few days of the voyage. It was the monsoon season, and until we reached the Suez Canal, most of the passengers, including Wende and Pat, were seasick. To add to these woes, a 2-3 day viral illness, consisting mostly of fever and malaise, swept through the ship. The two boys were the first to succumb, but were fully recovered by the time we reached the canal. By now, however, Pat and Wende were on the sick list, so at Suez they were unable to take the shore excursion to Cairo with us, remaining on the ship until we rejoined it at Port Said 36 hours later. Our daylong visit to Cairo and the Pyramids was the highlight of the voyage.

By the time we reached Naples, all were fully recovered. Turning over to the American consular representative the checked baggage that would go on by sea to America, we boarded the train to Rome – by which time I had now succumbed to the offending virus. An overnight stay in Rome took care of it, however, and we were soon on our way to London for a delightful 3-day stay.

Awaiting the flight to Boston in the Pan American departure lounge at Heathrow, I took one final luggage-and-head count as our flight was called – and came up with 22 pieces of luggage but only 4 heads. Wende had disappeared. A frantic search of the departure area proved fruitless, but as the last of the passengers were boarding the plane we saw a Pan Am employee in the distance, racing toward us with a wheel chair – in which Wende was obviously enjoying the ride. The lady told us she had been picked up as she tried to make her way back through the immigration checkpoint – and fortunately had a tag with her name and flight number pinned to her dress.

Arriving in Boston, we were met by Pat's parents, with whom we were to stay until I had found temporary quarters in the Chicago area, and Pat had arranged the moving of the furniture we had stored in Boston. Dr. and Mrs. Hyde graciously hosted me for the first few days and then offered us their apartment while they went on holiday. Pat and the boys joined me, and we soon found a fine home in Wilmette, only five minutes from the AAMC office. It needed a good bit of fixing up, but I enjoyed the challenge and went to work on it, painting, repapering, and converting the attic to a room for one of the boys.

Working in this national office was a heady experience, the constituency of the AAMC being the deans and vice-presidents for medical affairs of all the medical schools in the United States and, at that time, Canada. Soon after my arrival, I was feted, along with another newcomer, at a grand staff dinner attended as well by medical notables in the Chicago area. The other newcomer to the AAMC was none other than Dr. Bill Moloney, erstwhile dean of the Tufts University School of Medicine, my first employer.

Van Hyde, as he was known to all his friends and colleagues, had recently retired from a distinguished career in the U.S. Public Health Service, during which time he was a key player in the founding of the World Health Organization. Slated to become its Director-General several years earlier, he lost the appointment to a European in an international political coup – a disappointment that never left him. His worldwide contacts brought a steady stream of distinguished medical people to our office, and he was always generous in including me in their luncheons. I particularly recall one memorable luncheon with a somewhat less distinguished visitor, a medical missionary from Congo, who was seeking advice about funding a teaching hospital at his mission station. As he and Van talked, I began putting pieces of memory together. During a lull in their conversation, I asked him if he had been in the Army in World War II. He had. I then asked if his last post was Ft. Sill, Oklahoma, just after the war. It was – and Master Sergeant Bob White, my predecessor as leader of the Lawton, Oklahoma, "Voice of Christian Youth", and I were thus reunited some 20 years later.

One of my notable accomplishments at the AAMC – although I was not to learn of it until years later – was being instrumental in salvaging the career of a fine young medical student. I received a call one day from Ray Knighton of the Christian Medical Society in suburban Chicago asking if I would try to help this person find a place in a foreign medical school, so that he could realize his dream of becoming a medical missionary. His name was Bruce Gale, and he had had the misfortune of failing one major basic science course at the University of Illinois School of Medicine, which was enough to cause his dismissal.

Knowing I could find him a place in one of the new private medical schools in India, where the teaching would be in English, I invited him to my office for an interview. When he told me he was fluent in Spanish and had hoped to eventually serve in Latin America, I realized that God had clearly sent him to me. In an office one floor below me, spending a sabbatical with the AAMC, was the one person who could get him into a Latin American medical school – Dr. Bill Frye, Dean of the Louisiana University School of Medicine, who had been instrumental in establishing Costa Rica's first medical school.

(When Bill first joined us, he related a tale of having one day years before received notice from the U. S. Customs in New Orleans that a shipment addressed to him had arrived from Denmark. Wondering what treasure some kind friend had purchased for him, he eagerly opened the crate, only to discover it contained hundreds of small vials of dog doo, collected in Greenland. He had forgotten his promise to Dr. John Gordon to do the laboratory studies thereon. I proudly told him I had personally packed and labeled that crate in Egedesminde – for which he appeared to be somewhat subdued in expressing his appreciation.)

I told Bruce I had an idea, and would he please excuse me for a moment. I went to Bill's office, told him the story, and asked if he would interview the lad. He did, and was sufficiently impressed with him that he was sure he could make the necessary arrangements – and I soon forgot about the matter.

Some ten years later, while on a visit to Costa Rica, I was touring the Christian hospital, Clinica Biblica, in San Jose when one of the staff doctors introduced himself. The name didn't ring a bell – until he told me I was responsible for his being there. It was none other than Bruce Gale, who had completed medical school there, done well enough to get a pediatric residency in the United States, become certified by the American Board of Pediatrics, and return to San Jose as chief of pediatrics at the hospital – the only American ever to be given a license to practice medicine in that country.

37 -- Afghanistan beckons

During Bill Frye's sabbatical with us, USAID commissioned the AAMC to undertake a study of medical education in the developing countries to provide the agency with guidelines for its further involvement therein. I was appointed Project Director, and Van, Bill, and I divided up the Third World among us, for visits to a sampling of its medical schools. I was to cover South Asia and the Middle East, with visits to India, Afghanistan, and Iraq, Bill took Latin America, and Van headed for Africa. At last – my first round-the-world trip, and in less than seven years from the time Dr. John Gordon at the Harvard School of Public Health put that dream in my head with stories of his own travels that took him around the world every year for decades.

This provided, of course, a splendid opportunity to see my former colleagues in India, and to visit Afghanistan after being frustrated in doing so while in India by reason of Van's having cut short my tour of duty there. More important, it provided the means of evaluating the medical school in Mosul, Iraq, as requested by Dr. Daoud Sani, professor of physiology and newly-appointed dean of what was to become Iraq's third medical school in Basra. He had previously visited us at the AAMC to request help in finding an American medical school to partner with their second medical school in Mosul., and I had meanwhile obtained the interest of the Dean of Boston University School of Medicine in doing so.

I was particularly looking forward to my next stop, having learned of the great work done by Dr. J. Christy Wilson, Jr. in finding places for Christian "tentmakers" in Afghanistan – persons who wanted to serve in secular jobs in that country as a means of bringing the Gospel of Jesus Christ to that country. Until Christy arrived there years before to teach in Kabul's foremost high school, Afghanistan had been completely closed to any onsite Christian witness. My good friend Hal Guffey, president of International Students, Inc., on whose board I served, put me in touch with Christy, who was at that moment on leave in the United States. Christy graciously met me at Idlewild Airport (now JFK International Airport) on the eve of my departure and spent several hours briefing me on the situation in Afghanistan, encouraging me in particular to visit a new school in Jalalabad in hope of my being able to provide assistance there.

He also encouraged me to meet with the American ambassador, whom he was sure would be interested in such a project – and, most importantly, briefed me in detail about the man. Ambassador John Steeves had made a notable impression on the expatriate American Christian community in Kabul in this, his first ambassadorship. Once a Seventh Day Adventist missionary in India many years earlier, Steeves had divorced his wife, left the church, and joined the U. S. Foreign Service. He had now reached the top rank in the Foreign Service.

Upon arriving in Kabul, he was unhappy to learn that some of his top American officials were involved with a newly established Christian school, the Ahlman Academy, to which most American embassy employees were sending their children because of the inferior quality of the American International School of Kabul. The latter, supported heavily by State Department funds, was obviously suffering as the result, and Steeves was determined to rectify the situation.

His first move was to withdraw the educational allowances of embassy personnel who would not enroll their children in the AISK. He then succeeded in firing several key embassy staff for refusing to give up their positions on the Ahlman board of directors, including the head of USAID in Afghanistan and the two embassy doctors, the husband and wife team of Drs. Rex and Jean Blumhagen. The official reason was insubordination, but as I was later to learn from the ambassador himself, the real reason was "proselytizing".

Rex and Jean, whom I have since been privileged to number among my best of friends, had not yet left Kabul, and with additional information gleaned from them, I was able to deal comfortably with the ambassador when I reported to him what I had found in Jalalabad. As Christy had predicted, he eagerly encouraged me to find an American medical school to partner with the Nangrahar University Faculty of Medicine, which I assured him I would do.

What I found in Jalalabad was the most pathetic excuse for a medical school I have ever seen anywhere in the world. Its thirty students had just completed their first year under the tutelage of two professors sent from Kabul University Faculty of Medicine – a school started by Turks in 1932. They were housed in dormitories at the university campus on the edge of town, and their medical school consisted of three rented rooms in the provincial courthouse building in the center of the city. With some embarrassment, the dean, Dr. Khader Baha, formerly professor of anatomy in Kabul, showed me their facilities – the lecture room, with a table, a blackboard of sorts, and thirty chairs; the laboratory room, with a few tables, yet to be equipped with anything else; and the library, with a table, bookshelves, and no books. I assured him I would do everything possible to find help.

It was August 1964, and while Kabul was hot enough for me at 7000 feet altitude, Jalalabad, only 80 miles down the road but at 1000 feet, was a furnace. However, arriving in Baghdad on the third leg of my journey, I thought I was experiencing something of the fires of Hades. I was met at the airport by Dr. Sani, who consoled me with, "It's good you didn't arrive last month, as you originally planned. It was really hot then." These days, every time I see news reports from Iraq, with pictures of our military men and women in the heavy gear they wear and carry, I wonder how they can possibly cope with the heat.

Even 40 years ago Baghdad was in most respects a very modern city with all the amenities one would expect in an oil-rich state. Its medical schools and hospitals were quite impressive, and its well-preserved ancient areas a delight to explore. After showing me around Baghdad over the course of several days. Dr. Sani arranged for me to take an overnight sleeper train to Mosul, where the Dean of the medical school treated me most graciously. I interviewed key faculty members and took many pictures in order to prepare a presentation to the faculty of Boston University School of Medicine. I do regret, however, that the stifling heat deterred me from the sight of ancient Nineveh, across the Tigris River from Mosul (as it had also done with visiting Babylon, on the east bank of the Euphrates 90 km south of Baghdad).

Upon my return home there was an article in the current issue of *TIME* describing an assassination attempt that was to have taken place on the day I left Baghdad. According to the *TIME* report, Abdel Salam Arif, the Iraqi president who had seized power less than a year earlier, was to have been the target of a dissident group of Iraqi air force pilots who had conspired to shoot down the plane taking him to a meeting in Cairo that day. Unfortunately for them, the plot was discovered, and the pilots were arrested and summarily executed.

Such a commonplace event in the turbulent history of the Middle East would not be worth noting were it not for an unusual encounter 45 years later, while on my way by taxi to the airport in Seattle. The accent and appearance of the taxi driver, owner of his small taxi fleet, suggested a Middle East origin, and when I learned he was from Baghdad, I related the foregoing tale. His amazing response: "No, actually we all escaped!" He then told me he had gone to Egypt but did not know where the others ended up. What a very small world we live in these days – and how often I've thought of those days and places during the present war in Iraq!

My presentation on Mosul to the Dean of the Boston University School of Medicine was met with considerable enthusiasm and his assurance that he would do his best to get his faculty members involved. It seems that all went well until Jewish faculty members insisted that any contract to be drawn up between the two schools should specifically make it clear that Jews from Boston University would be welcome. Given the tension between the Arab countries and Israel, I knew that such a written agreement would be impossible – but I also knew that no objection would be made to having visiting Jewish faculty members. This did not satisfy the objecting faculty members, and the project came to naught.

Such handling of a delicate matter again came to light years later when the Blumhagens had returned to Afghanistan under the auspices of the Christian organization, Medical Assistance Programs, Inc., to establish a hospital in the Hazarajat. Some months after their arrival, and having received the approval of the Afghan government to do so, Rex was asked by the government official to whom he reported, "Dr. Blumhagen, when can we expect the first American doctors?" Rex explained that several were "in the pipeline" but that it took considerable time for them to settle their affairs at home before they could leave. He then added with a smile, "But you know what kind of doctors these will be!", meaning that they would be Christians in that Muslim country. "I don't want to know anything about them other than that they are qualified medical doctors!" was the reply, also with a smile.

38 – The incautious ambassador

From Baghdad I stopped in Munich to visit Dr. Hans Borst, a Harvard Medical School classmate, and since it would be the beginning of the Labor Day weekend by the time I was to arrive home, I took Hans' advice and rented a car to drive down to the Bavarian Alps. Gross Glockner, the highest peak in Germany, was the main attraction, but by the time I began my descent night had begun to fall, it began to snow, and I was still high on the mountain road, uncertain where I would find a place for the night. Halfway down was a small inn I had passed on the way up, so I headed for there, hoping for a meal and a room. By now the snow had become heavy, and the lights of the inn were a beautiful sight. A meal was no problem, but when I asked the waitress in my limited German if they had a room for the night, she quickly excused herself and crossed the room to consult with the desk clerk. I saw them look at me, begin to giggle, and then look at the only other diner, across the room. Did I really look that amusing?

She then went and spoke to the other diner, who looked at me and then nodded his head. I had not a clue as to what was going on. From what I could understand when she returned to my table, the other man had just taken the last room – and it had only a double bed, which he had offered to share with me. He spoke no English, but had a German-English pocket dictionary with him, so with the help of that and my meager German – and with the hope that it was not his gender preference but only his kindness to a stranded stranger that prompted his offer, I graciously accepted. Sleep came somewhat uneasily, and several times I almost fell out of the bed in avoiding trespassing on his turf, but all's well that ends well, and we enjoyed a fine breakfast together before going our separate ways, the roads having now been cleared by the efficient German highway department.

Upon my return to work I began contacting several medical school deans who I thought might be interested in working with the school in Jalalabad. Their response was only lukewarm at best – and then had a call from Dr. Gordon Hadley, associate dean of the Seventh Day Adventist medical school at Loma Linda University in California.

Prior to my departure for Afghanistan I had visited Loma Linda to learn something of its international programs. My host, Dr. John Peterson, chief of medicine, told me about Dr. Hadley, who had spent the past two years working in Kabul for the World Health Organization. Gordon would soon be returning, and Jack (a wonderfully warm man who became an instant friend) encouraged me to try to meet Gordon if our paths should cross while I was headed for Afghanistan. I wrote to Gordon, and several weeks later I stopped overnight in Tokyo to spend several hours with him before heading to my next stop in Hyderabad to visit friends there before proceeding to Kabul.

Gordon had been teaching pathology at the Kabul University Faculty of Medicine, and was very familiar with the effort to start a new medical school in Jalalabad. He did not feel that Loma Linda was prepared to go it alone in providing assistance to that effort, but if I were successful in finding one or more other American medical schools that were interested, Loma Linda would surely want to partner with them.

After returning to his job at Loma Linda, however, he became much more positive about the possibility of their becoming part of the effort in Jalalabad and was calling to tell me that they would surely like to become involved in a major capacity if I could find another medical school which would join them in such an undertaking. I was delighted – and by an amazing coincidence received a call the following day from none other than Ambassador Steeves. He was in Washington on official business, and was calling to see if I had had any success in finding an American medical school interested in becoming involved in Jalalabad.

"Your timing is impeccable, Mr. Ambassador. Only yesterday did I succeed in doing that!"

"Marvelous! What school is it?"

"Loma Linda University." And no sooner were the words out of my mouth than I recalled Christy Wilson's tale of the ambassador's defection as a Seventh Day Adventist missionary in India. There was a long pause, then-

"Uh, would it be possible for you to come to Washington to discuss this with me?"

"Certainly! As a matter of fact, I have some business in Washington tomorrow, and can meet you late in the afternoon, if that would be convenient."

"That will be fine. Meet me at the Cosmos Club at 4:00 p.m."

"Good. I'll be there."

The Cosmos Club is one of Washington's posh establishments, and as we sat in those hallowed halls, Steeves proceeded to tell me that Loma Linda University would not be acceptable to the Afghan government because it was a Christian religious institution that would be anathema in that Muslim country. I didn't bother to tell him that Dr. Gordon Hadley, a devout Christian and Adventist, had already established a very warm relationship with his Muslim colleagues, including the Minister of Health himself. These devout Muslims had great respect for his adherence to Adventist dietary restrictions – including his refusal of the offer of tea in a country where tea was offered whenever one sat down with an Afghan. (Years later, while a guest in the home of the Minister of Health, Dr. Ibrahim Majid Seraj, I was asked how Gordon was getting along. He then turned to the other guest, a Muslim friend, and explained that Gordon was a mutual friend of ours who had done much good work in Afghanistan. "He's a real saint!," he added.)

Steeves then went on to tell me of his problem with embassy personnel and others in Kabul who had come to the country with ulterior motives. "Why, I even had to fire my two embassy doctors for proselytizing!" "Really?!", I responded, with a straight face, wondering how he could be so indiscrete in discussing such a matter with me, about whose background he knew almost nothing. If I had then told him that I knew the official reason for dismissing the Blumhagens was "insubordination" (when Rex had refused to resign as a director of Ahlman Academy), he would have had apoplexy!

By now he was waxing eloquent on the subject of "proselytizing". He told me there was an organization in America that recruited such people for jobs in Afghanistan. When I asked what that organization might be, he pulled out a little black book and hastily thumbed it. "The National Association of Evangelicals!"

By now I was becoming thoroughly amused. Although I was aware that Christy Wilson and others were actively involved in finding Christians who would work in Afghanistan, I knew very well that the NAE, although certainly sympathetic to such a cause, was not itself acting as recruiter.

And then he excitedly proclaimed, "Why, do you know that there's an organization here that sends its people to university campuses to obtain the names of Afghan students, so they can proselytize them?"

"Is that right?!!", I responded in feigned amazement. I've often since wondered if I was, as a Christian, remiss in thus leading him on, but I couldn't resist the opportunity. When I asked him if he knew the name of that organization, he declared that he did not, but had someone working on the matter. In his wildest imagination he could not have dreamed that my next appointment was just up Connecticut Avenue a bit, at the headquarters of that very organization, International Students, Inc., for a meeting of the Executive Committee of its Board of Trustees, of which I was chairman!

(ISI, now in Colorado Springs, has for more than 50 years had a highly successful friendship ministry to students from abroad studying in our colleges and universities, and I was privileged to serve on its board for some forty years).

I thanked him for his time and left for my other meeting – wondering if the Loma Linda interest would bear fruit, for I would now have to find another medical school to partner with them. Given my previous difficulty in finding a medical school interested in Jalalabad until Loma Linda entered the picture, I was not overly confident in my ability to find them a partner. But God had a plan for me that I could not have foreseen – one which would lead me in a very different direction before putting me in what was to become the base for my final twenty years of employment prior to official retirement.

As for Ambassador Steeves, his future was severely affected by the vehemence with which he dealt with those U.S. government employees in Kabul who dared to stand up for their Christian faith and remain on the board of Ahlman Academy. Dr. Clyde Taylor, then head of the National Association of Evangelicals – that organization the ambassador mistakenly believed to be recruiting Christians for Afghanistan – became so incensed over the firings of the Blumhagens and others that he brought the matter before his friends in the U.S. Congress. From pressure brought by them on the Department of State, the ambassador was not given another such post when his term in Kabul ended, as is normally the case with career Foreign Service officers. He was instead assigned to a temporary position in Washington, from which he retired soon thereafter.

39 – Life in the fast lane -- with a call from the White House

Life with Van Hyde at the AAMC was anything but dull. He had no end of stories about the fascinating people he had known, with many of whom he was still in touch. He was also an inveterate traveler, and while off to the Middle East one time for reasons I don't recall, I took advantage of his absence by getting in a bit of travel myself – a junket that he would have taken had he been at home, leaving me to mind the store. The AAMC was asked to send a delegate to the annual meeting in Dakar, Senegal, of the newly-formed Association of Medical Schools in Africa, and being, in my humble opinion, the most likely candidate, I convinced USAID (under whose contract with the AAMC I was employed) to issue travel orders for that purpose. Not knowing when I might again have the opportunity to travel to that part of the world, I scheduled several other visits following the meeting.

One of my fellow board members at ISI was Jim Kraakevik, a professor at Wheaton College in Illinois. He was at that time on sabbatical leave, teaching at a Sudan Interior Mission (SIM) school in the bush of northern Nigeria, so I wrote to suggest a visit following my meeting in Dakar. He was delighted with the prospect, and arranged for me to be picked up in Lagos by a SIMAIR plane – one of the myriad small planes still being flown in remote areas by brave pilots belonging to mission organizations such as Missionary Aviation Fellowship (MAF), Jungle Aviation and Radio Service (JARS), and others. On the return flight, I asked the pilot if he could perhaps drop me off in Ibadan, some 80 miles from Lagos, so that I could pay a surprise visit to the dean of its medical school, whom I had met in Dakar. From Ibadan I used my USAID connection to commandeer a ride in an American consulate vehicle to Lagos – a stretch of highway reputed to be the most dangerous in the world, as seemed to be evident from the wreckage of cars and trucks strewn along either side of the highway all the way to Lagos.

From Lagos I took a Nigerian Airways flight to Beirut to visit the president of the American University of Beirut, Dr. Samuel Kirkwood. I had met Sam when he was Commissioner of Health of Massachusetts, and had tentatively offered me a summer job prior to starting my program at the Harvard School of Public Health – which I turned down in preference for the Greenland opportunity. The aircraft was an air-weary Russian model – one of the worst in which I've ever flown – but the flight proved to be uneventful. Beirut was a delight in those days, and all-in-all, it was a splendid trip.

Van Hyde was proud of the perks and acclaim he had earned over the years, and I sensed that he was somewhat dismayed when I acquired a couple of trophies myself during my time with him. The lesser of these by way of distinction, but ever after of considerable value, was a membership in TWA's Ambassador Club, whose private lounges at major airports provided a haven between connections. (Nowadays airline clubs are available to anyone willing to pay dearly for them, but in those days they were offered gratis to their most frequent flyers.)

A more noteworthy distinction but of less tangible benefit was becoming a biographee in *Who's Who in America* (and sometime later, *Who's Who in the World*). Unless one is so gauche as to suggest to an inquirer that "you can find out more about me in any public library", my only substantive benefit of such distinction of which I'm aware occurred during my next job when I sent hundreds of volunteer physicians to Viet Nam on Pan Am. When I asked the Pan Am sales rep how one might become a member of their Clipper Club, he told me they awarded membership to those in any of three categories: members of Congress, persons in *"Who's Who in America"*, and persons who traveled more than 100,000 miles a year on Pan Am. Qualifying in two of the three categories, I was given lifetime membership. (When Reagan was elected president, a newspaper article noted that his aides were searching *Who's Who in America* for likely candidates for top Federal jobs – although needless to say, none contacted me. And it was alleged in the Chicago area that families in the upscale suburb of Winnetka allowed their children to date only those whose parents were listed in *Who's Who in America*!)

After only two years at the AAMC, I was asked by USAID to participate in a meeting in Washington of nongovernmental organizations (NGOs) to discuss a project dreamed up by some staff member in Lyndon Johnson's White House. The war in Viet Nam was heating up by then, and Johnson was taking a lot of flak over napalm bombing and its civilian casualties. The proposal was to recruit American doctors to volunteer for two-month duty in civilian hospitals in Viet Nam, and the purpose of the meeting was to select an NGO which could take it on. This had nothing to do with the AAMC, but because I was working under their contract with USAID, Dr. Phil Lee, my contact there, thought I should attend in the hope they might entice me to head up Project Viet Nam, as it came to be called.

40 – Inside the Beltway and an interesting friendship

The only NGO in those days that utilized short-term physician volunteers for more than one month was Project Hope, whose volunteers signed up for two months on their hospital ship that served Third World countries. Project Hope agreed to take on the project, and while I enjoyed my work at the AAMC, Van thought I should seriously consider it. (As I was to learn later from someone who had worked with him in the US Public Health Service, he had a penchant for taking on deputies, training them for only a couple of years or so, and then sending them on to new pursuits.) Pat wasn't overly thrilled about moving again, but we both liked the Washington area, and the lure of an interesting government-related job there was compelling.

Because the project had fired Lyndon Johnson's enthusiasm, with the usual government desire to then get it underway yesterday, I went on ahead and set up shop at Project Hope's headquarters while Pat remained behind to sell the house and start packing. By now she had successfully purchased and, when the time came, sold each of the three homes to the first couple who looked at it. She was clearly destined for a career in real estate.

The project was a great success. I was invited to the Oval Office to introduce my first volunteer to the president, and the resultant nationwide publicity instigated by the White House brought a flood of applications. All I offered the volunteer physicians was a round-the-world ticket, with an overnight stop in Hong Kong at its most luxurious hotel, The Peninsula, and room, board, and a per diem of $10 while in Viet Nam, but I found myself with four times as many applicants as could be accommodated.

I brought the first group of twenty volunteers to Washington to brief them before sending them on to Hong Kong. Soon thereafter I went to Viet Nam myself to discuss the program with the American Air Force general in charge of it, who suggested I might do the volunteers a favor by briefing them in Los Angeles, instead of bringing them from all over the country and then sending them westward again. Thereafter I went to Los Angeles every three weeks or so to send out a new group of volunteers.

During one of these trips, I was introduced to Raymond Burr, then star of the Perry Mason television series. He had quietly made half a dozen trips to visit servicemen in Viet Nam at the height of that conflict, not to "entertain the troops" as had so many Hollywood figures, but simply to go into the "front lines" by visiting small groups of Green Berets deep in the jungles and chat with them. Thereafter I often visited the Perry Mason set and his office at Universal Studios, and several times was a guest in his Hollywood home.

On one visit to a Green Beret site, the encampment came under attack and his helicopter took off before he was completely on board, leaving him hanging with one arm hooked over the landing gear. He weighed nearly 300 pounds, and sustained severe injury to his right shoulder as the result. The injury was still bothering him when he made the pilot film for the Ironsides series, in which he played a wheel-chair bound San Francisco chief of detectives. Those who have seen the film may recall the scene in which the villain pushed him and his wheel chair down a long flight of stairs. Rather than use a stand-in, he insisted on doing the scene himself, for which he was tied tightly to the wheelchair, which in turn was connected to a long, concealed rope that would bring the chair to a halt at the bottom of the stairs. It did that well, but he was catapulted into the air and landed on the injured shoulder, thus requiring more surgery.

This was only one of his several medical problems, for some of which he was treated at the famed Scripps Clinic in La Jolla, near San Diego. When he happened to mention my name to Dr. Harold Simon, one of his medical team at Scripps, he learned that we were in the same class at Harvard Medical School. He later introduced me to his internist, orthopedist, and general surgeon in Los Angeles, taking the four of us to dinner at one of his favorite restaurants.

Both the internist and the general surgeon later became my personal physicians on one occasion. Some time later I read in a medical publication about a radical new approach to hernia surgery being performed by a Hollywood doctor. Instead of using a general anesthetic, he did the procedure under local anesthesia, and when the underlying sutures in the abdominal muscles were in place, he would have the patient do a sit-up on the operating table (under the influence of a shot of Demerol) to test the suture line. The patient was then taken from the operating room to a long corridor and made to walk back and forth from one end to the other until he had walked a complete mile—a maneuver designed to reduce the possibility of adhesions. Instead of remaining in hospital for the usual 4-5 days following surgery, he was then discharged the following morning.

The name of the surgeon cited in the article sounded familiar, and upon consulting my collection of business cards it proved to be that of Raymond's surgeon, Irving Lichtenstein. I had recently discovered that I had a small inguinal hernia, but the demands of my job at Project Viet Nam didn't allow me the luxury of spending the better part of a week in hospital and carrying nothing heavier than a briefcase for a month thereafter, as was the usual directive in those days. I therefore phoned Irv immediately to confirm that he was indeed the surgeon in the article, and made an appointment to be seen by him on my next trip to Los Angeles. He confirmed the diagnosis, and scheduled the surgery for my next briefing trip thereafter. He did, however, require that I see him four days later, so I remained in L.A., occupying some of the time interviewing volunteer applicants in that area.

The famous Grauman's Chinese Theater (renamed Mann's Chinese Theater in 1973), in front of which are all those sidewalk names and hand impressions of Hollywood stars, was across the street from my hotel. By the second evening after surgery I was feeling chipper enough to take in a movie there. The film, whose name escapes me, starred Kirk Douglas in one of his usual roles – that of a seemingly tall, muscular hero type. The following day, the internist invited me to his beach club in Malibu, and while coming out of the dressing room I noticed a familiar face attached to a muscular but rather short body, attended by a white poodle on a leash. It was, of course, none other than the tall, muscular hero. Film makers could do wonders even in those ancient times, long before today's visual effects.

As I shall relate shortly, we moved to Indianapolis in 1966, and ten years later Raymond came to Indianapolis to do a promotional film at one of our local attractions, Conner Prairie Pioneer Village. Unfortunately, I was due to leave for Saudi Arabia just at that time, so was able to spend only a few hours with him. However, at his suggestion, on my return trip I stopped off in Horta, a small volcanic island in the Azores, and spent several delightful days with him as his guest in a lovely little hotel he owned.

Almost twenty years later, having not seen him since then, I phoned him in Denver, where he was making a series of full length Perry Mason films, to inquire about his health and say that I would like to come out there for a visit. Unfortunately, he was on the verge of leaving for the annual film festival in Cannes, despite a recurrence of his kidney cancer, and suggested I come out a few weeks later. I neglected phoning him again for a number of weeks, until one day while checking out at the supermarket I saw his picture on the cover of one of those lurid "know all-tell all" magazines customarily found at checkout counters. The customer before me having a truckload of goods, I quickly read the article without having to buy the rag, which indicated that he was dying.

As soon as I returned home I phoned his home in Dry Creek Valley, California, where I learned from his partner, Robert Benevides, that was indeed the case. In Cannes he had had a severe reaction to his cancer drugs, was rushed home, and now was so sedated at home that he could no longer tolerate visitors or phone calls. He died a week later. Soon thereafter Robert phoned to ask if we could come to his memorial service the following week at the Pasadena Playhouse, where he had begun his acting career. It was a moving service for a consummate actor who, in addition to two long-running, highly successful television series had acted in 115 full-length Hollywood films, and had given much of his wealth and time to a number of charitable causes. It was a privilege to have been counted among his friends.

My only other association with a Hollywood personality came about as a result of our time in India. Among the small group of Americans working in Hyderabad for the U.S. government was Constantine Savalas, head of the U. S. Information Agency in that city. Gus, as we knew him, often boasted of his brother, Aristotele (Telly, for short), who had established himself as a well-known actor after making a film with Burt Lancaster, *The Bird Man of Alcatraz*. When the movie came to Hyderabad, Gus booked the entire balcony of the cinema for his friends. He was a tall, very handsome Greek-American with a full head of wavy black hair, and we could hardly wait to see his brother, who must surely have outshone him in that regard. We were thus very surprised to see on the screen a somewhat stocky man of only average height, without a visible hair on his head.

As we were leaving Hyderabad at the end of my tour, Gus urged me to get acquainted with Telly if I ever found myself in the Los Angeles area. As it happened, both he and Raymond Burr were at Universal Studios, so I was thus able to visit them both during my frequent visits to L.A. in those days. On one occasion, Telly told me he would be doing some filming on location in the Hollywood hills the following day, where a retake of a scene from "The Dirty Dozen" was scheduled. Early in the morning, I followed the directions he had given me until I came to a fork in the road high above the teeming residential areas below. I was not then familiar with the advice of one of America's great philosophers and baseball players, the inimitable Yogi Berra: "If you come to a fork in the road, take it.", so when I spotted a woman walking a very large dog, I drove over to ask directions. I immediately recognized her as none other than Katharine Hepburn, but playing it cool, I gave no clue to that effect. She was bare-legged and wearing shorts, which, to my surprise, revealed an unsightly skin condition covering both of her legs. (I learned later that this was why she always wore slacks in public.) She kindly directed me, and I drove off, doubtless leaving her wondering how this country bumpkin could have failed to recognize one of the world's best-known actresses.

Telly Savalas, however, was a completely different person from Raymond Burr, who was one of the most respected actors in the business. He had divorced his wife after achieving fame and married a much younger girl, whom I met, along with their two little girls, when I drove him home after he completed his part in the scene just described. I learned much later that he was a womanizer the rest of his life and otherwise lived a profligate life. It was interesting to watch the making of a few of the films in which he starred, and I was pleased to be welcomed by him whenever I appeared at the studio, but he was certainly more of an acquaintance than a friend.

I have never been able to grasp the reason for the excessive adulation shown by most of our society to so-called "celebrities", most of whom are very ordinary people who may (or may not) be skilled in their trade. Some, as was Raymond, are very humble people who strenuously avoid calling attention to themselves, but most seem to have become so enamored of themselves that they revel in the undue attention they receive.

C. S. Lewis addresses this in *Mere Christianity*, where he says,

There is one vice of which no man in the world is free...of which hardly any people, except Christians, even imagine that they are guilty themselves... I do not think I have ever heard anyone who was not a Christian accuse himself of this vice...There is no fault which makes a man more unpopular, and no fault which we are more unconscious of in ourselves. And the more we have it ourselves, the more we dislike it in others. The vice of which I am speaking is Pride.

41 – Alice in Hoosierland

Just a few days after Pat, the children and our furniture arrived in Washington, I received a call from Dr. Kenneth Penrod, who had recently become the Provost of Indiana University, in charge of the Indiana University Medical Center in Indianapolis. He had previously held the same position at the University of West Virginia, at which time we had become friends when he did some overseas consulting for us at the AAMC. Several months earlier, while sitting together at a meeting in New York, he told me he was taking a new job in Indiana and asked if I would be interested in joining him there, to do at Indiana University what I was doing at the AAMC – looking for opportunities to assist Third World medical schools. Indiana University, he said, had long been involved in many Third World university projects, but none of them in the field of medicine. I told him I would certainly consider it, but at the moment I was quite happy where I was.

In this phone call Ken said he had now been at Indiana long enough to be able to create a job for me and wondered if I were interested. He had phoned the AAMC, and was simply told that I could be reached at this number in Washington – assuming I was there on AAMC business.

I was somewhat embarrassed to have to tell him that I had just taken a new job in Washington – and if his call had come a bit earlier I could have had the moving van drop off our things in Indianapolis instead of continuing on to Washington. Project Viet Nam was clearly not a long-term commitment, and I knew I would eventually want to get back into international medical education, so I very much regretted not being able to accept his offer. He was most gracious, however, and since there was no urgency about the matter, I should contact him again when things began to wind down for me in Washington.

Wind down they did – not because of any diminution in the program but only because traveling across the country every three or four weeks, with interim trips to interview applicants, was taking me away from home much more than I had anticipated. Bill Walsh, the president of Project Hope, had become disillusioned with his contract with USAID, so I began looking for another sponsor for the program. The American Medical Association in Chicago had given it a great deal of publicity, so they seemed to be the most likely choice – and when they offered to consider taking it on, I phoned Ken to see if he was still interested in me.

151

He was – and the AMA agreed to take over. Some days later Ken called to make a firm offer, giving me as much time as I needed to think it over. That Sunday at Fourth Presbyterian Church, when I told our pastor, Dick Halverson (later to become Chaplain of the United States Senate) what was in the offing, he asked if my commitment to Indiana University was firm. "Not cast in concrete, but about to be," I replied. He then went on to say that World Vision, of whose board he was chairman, had been in business long enough that its Korean orphanage and other assistance programs throughout the world involved enough medical content that they were in need of a medical director. Would I be willing to go to California to discuss the matter with Bob Pierce? Although not keen to consider a different job and possibly having to disappoint Ken after all he had done, I felt that if God wanted me in a Christian organization I had to consider it.

Later that day he called to say that Bob Pierce (who had already met me in India, as I've noted) would be very pleased to see me, and two days later I flew to Monrovia to meet with Bob and his senior staff. Even in those days World Vision was the most highly financed Christian aid organization in the country, with a budget of over five million dollars (more recently 200 million!), and the job description was very appealing – until he said that I would be expected to spend more than half of my time traveling overseas. "The job is yours if you want it," he said, "so go home and discuss it with your wife."

Recalling my time with Bob in India and his description (also noted earlier) of his family problems, there was little doubt in my mind that the job was not for me, but I promised to talk to Pat about it. We prayed at length about it when I returned home that night, and were in agreement that our future lay in Indiana.

Dick Halverson then asked if I would meet with Clyde Taylor of the National Association of Evangelicals to discuss the possibility of becoming president of World Relief, the NAE' relief arm. Since this would have involved more fund-raising and travel than I felt desirable from my family's perspective, I was likewise led to turn down the offer.

Thus, after only ten months in Washington, the peripatetic Browns were about to move again. So before putting our house on the market, we all packed off for Indianapolis to look for a new home. The one we settled on was indeed a magnificent choice – a beautiful old brick and stone English tudor design with a grand entry way, an enormous backyard leading to an acre or more of open greenery belonging to a large Methodist church just down the street, and more rooms than we had uses for. The owner was the just-divorced wife of a prominent psychiatrist, and with three small children, she was anxious to get out of there. Peeling ceiling paint on the rooms under each of the several bathrooms – the result of bathtubs allowed to overflow – gave evidence of her predicament.

Back in the car we breathlessly asked the kids what they thought about this marvelous property, anticipating shouts of acclamation. Instead there was a sustained silence, until one of the boys spoke up. Reflecting upon those peeling ceilings and the Wilmette house that I never quite finished fixing up, he said, "Oh, dad, you'll never get it fixed up before we have to move again!" At that moment I silently made a firm resolution, not even telling Pat what it was: Under no circumstances would I consider another move for a minimum of at least three years (although I doubted I could spend more than five years before another exciting job opportunity presented itself!).

I truly honored that silent resolution – far more than I could ever have imagined at the time. Two years later, while visiting the Peace Corps in Washington on business, their medical director told me he was retiring and urged me to apply for the job. It would have been a great one, without a doubt, but I told him what I had promised myself for my family's sake. But never did I dream that we would still be in Indianapolis almost 40 years later!

42 – The end of the gypsy life, with a sigh of relief from all

It was a marvelous house, and the next seven years there saw our travel-weary kids though a fine public school system in a city that proved to be a great place to live and grow as a family – and for their kids to grow as well. The first stop on their new educational journey was P.S. 86 – serving a broad cross-section of its school district, comprising a large black population that had begun to move into the north part of the city, a private university community (Butler University), and those who lived in its more affluent fringe. We had learned earlier that the school population was about 30 percent black overall – and almost 50 percent black in the grade in which our number two son, Jack, would be placed.

In Hyderabad, all three children attended schools in which each was the only light-skinned pupil in their respective classes. In Wilmette and suburban Washington there were no black children in any of their classes. We had therefore refrained from telling them what to expect at P.S. 86, wanting to see their reactions. At dinner the evening of their first day in school, our first question was, "Well, what do you think of your new school?" All three responded positively, but with no mention of the racial difference.

"But didn't you notice that all the kids in your classes didn't have the same skin color as you do?" From Wende and Ted, "Uh, gee, I don't think so." From Jack, with white kids in the minority in his class, "Yeah, now that you mention it, I guess there were some that were different!" Then Wende piped up, "Yeah, I did notice something different. When the teacher asked each of us in the back row to walk past the kids in front of us and count them by touching them on the head, I noticed that some of them had hair that felt funny." Our kids had become truly color-blind.

The local high school, Shortridge, had a distinguished history in the annals of Indianapolis secondary education, but by the time we arrived in the city, it had become essentially an inner city school, with the usual problems of a predominately black student population. Our new mayor, Richard Lugar, who was a Shortridge graduate (and has been our U. S. senator for the past several decades), was determined to correct the situation. He did so by declaring it an academic high school, open to students from any school district. The old faculty was still intact, and by the time Ted and Jack had completed the eighth grade, Shortridge had a fine mix of well-motivated white and black students who were receiving a first-class education.

This was not to last, however, due to complaints from parents of children in the Shortridge district who were being bussed to distant parts of the city, and by the time Wende entered the freshman class, she was one of only a handful of white girls. She was, however, very happy there that year. Our house was on North Meridian Street, the main north-south thoroughfare in Indianapolis, and the boys had no trouble hitch-hiking to and from school each day, Shortridge also being on North Meridian Street, twenty blocks south. They would simply stand on our front curb, put out their thumbs, and almost instantly pick up a ride. I had neglected, however, to discuss with Wende how she was going to get to school, and when I looked out the front window on her first day at Shortridge, I was horrified to see my precious darling out at the curb with her thumb in the air – and instantly picked up. The boys had never experienced any sort of problem with this form of transportation, but that evening I informed her that I (or her mother when I was out of town) would be driving her to school each day.

At the I. U. Medical Center I was given a tenured appointment as associate professor in the medical school, a handsome office, and a very simple mandate from Ken: "Get the medical school into international activities." I was completely free to do that in whatever manner I chose. I named my one-man operation the Division of International Affairs of the Indiana University Medical Center, and started looking for projects. Ken suggested I arrange to meet a prominent local businessman, Beurt SerVaas, who was very much interested in the medical school. He had recently returned from a business trip to Jamaica, where he had met the Dean of the Faculty of Medicine of the University of the West Indies in Kingston and expressed to Ken upon his return that he would like to see our medical school involved there.

I met with Beurt, and with his urging visited the school in Kingston. I was pleasantly surprised to find that they had an outstanding department of preventive medicine under a Jamaican head, Dr. Kenneth Standard (years later to become Sir Kenneth Standard). Our department of preventive medicine was virtually non-existent, so I discussed with Ken Standard the possibility of sending small groups of our students to him for a 3-month elective in preventive medicine and community health. It proved to be a splendid experience for a number of such groups over the next two years or so, and during that time two of our faculty member took short-term teaching assignments in other departments in Kingston.

It was a good start, but I soon learned that a far greater opportunity presented itself. My contact with Gordon Hadley at Loma Linda University had been nil after I left the AAMC, and in the interim I had learned that the Peace Corps had sent several young doctors to Jalalabad to teach there. When I learned that Indiana University in Bloomington had an administrative team at Kabul University under a USAID contract, I began to envisage the possibility of Indiana University being the partner I had sought for Loma Linda two years earlier. This pleasant dream prompted me to call Gordon to see if he was still interested, and indeed he was. My next move was to get myself to Jalalabad to see what was going on there.

At that stage I had no funds for international travel – in fact I had no budget whatever for the Division of International Affairs, only an office and a secretary. Ken had funded my position with half the salary from the dean of the medical school and the other half from Dr. Lynne Merritt, the university vice-president responsible for the many international programs on the main campus in Bloomington. Accordingly, Lynne had created a position for me as an assistant director of the university's International Affairs Center in Bloomington, my only responsibility that of becoming acquainted with the university's overall international interests. I had an office in the Center, and its secretaries were available to me should I ever need them. (This arrangement was to prove useful to my secretary in Indianapolis, who was very protective of me. Anytime I was out of the office and received a phone call from someone who she thought should perhaps not be aware of my whereabouts for whatever reason, she would say that I was not in and then add, "Have you tried his Bloomington office?")

The Bloomington connection resulted in my being invited to become a member of a number of interesting committees on that campus, including the prestigious University Committee on International Affairs, chaired by Herman B Wells, the chancellor of the university who as its president for some 25 years had been responsible for raising it from an undistinguished mid-western state university to one of international prominence. (Dr. Wells was also distinguished by having a middle initial with no period. That was all his mother had given him for a middle name – just B!)

My choicest appointment, however, was to the International Grants Committee, as a member of which I had no difficulty advancing my own request for funds to carry on the Jamaica project. Not wanting to push my luck, however, I was reluctant to ask them for funds to get me to Jalalabad so soon after wheedling a grant for the Jamaica project. But another approach seemed worth exploring. I suggested to the head of the Kabul University program that it might be useful to have a short-term medical consultant to advise on the establishment of a student health service at Kabul University – and in short I was again using USAID funds to accomplish my objective.

Arriving in Kabul less than a year after coming to Indiana, I spent a brief but respectable length of time on the Kabul University campus, and then hastily departed for Jalalabad. To my surprise, I was warmly greeted by an Afghan faculty member, Dr. Siddiqui, who had not only been one of my medical students in Hyderabad, but also whose wedding there I had the privilege of attending.

Before leaving Indianapolis I had learned about three of the half dozen or so Peace Corps volunteers working there. One was Dr. Joseph Mamlin, who had joined the Peace Corps upon completing his residency in internal medicine at I.U. and whose return to I.U. was impatiently awaited by Dr. John Hickam, head of the department of medicine, who had a top position in the department awaiting Joe upon his return. Joe was in his first year in Jalalabad, and had been preceded a year earlier by a young couple, Drs. Charles and Lorraine Kelley. I had learned about the Kelleys from my good friend, Ray Knighton, executive director of the Christian Medical Society, on whose board of directors I had served for many years. Knowing that Joe was planning to return to I.U., I had planned to inquire of the Kelleys if they might be interested in coming there also, with Joe to be a cadre of faculty members with overseas experience – in Afghanistan in particular. As it turned out, they were definitely interested because Joe had already proposed their coming there. Both had only completed an internship, so Joe assured me that Dr. Hickam would accept Charles as a resident in medicine upon Joe's recommendation, and if I could find a pediatric residency for Lorraine, that would put icing on the cake. This I was able to do. Upon his return, Joe was offered the position of chief of medicine at the I.U.'s largest teaching hospital, and Charles became his resident – and eventually his number two in the department – while Lorraine pursued a career in pediatrics in Indianapolis.

43 – A dream now to be realized

Jalalabad was clearly ripe for a combined Indiana University-Loma Linda University team, but how would the Peace Corps react to a proposal that we take over from them? Professional jealousies often interfere with progress in any field, and I had no contacts in the Peace Corps in Washington through whom I might work. Once again, I experienced one of the heaven-designed "coincidences" that have characterized so much of my life.

Just before leaving Kabul, my host, Chris Jung, head of the I.U. team in Kabul, invited me to a cocktail party at his home. I'm not a great one for cocktail parties, with everyone standing around with drinks in hand and making small talk, but I couldn't refuse the invitation. As the evening wore on and I was looking forward to getting to bed, I was approached by a personable gentleman who introduced himself as head of the Peace Corps in Afghanistan.

"Chris tells me you're on the medical school faculty at Indiana University and that you visited the medical school in Jalalabad, where we have a number of volunteers. Is that correct?"

"Yes, indeed."

"Well, I'd like to talk to you about that project. It was forced upon me by my superiors in Washington, and quite frankly I don't think we're capable of handling it – and I've told them so. Is there any possibility that Indiana University might be interested in taking it over?"

I assured him that we would be happy to do so!

I could hardly wait to get back to telephone Gordon. The Indiana University—Loma Linda Medical Team at Nangrahar University in Jalalabad was on the verge of becoming a reality. The first step was for Gordon and me to return to Jalalabad. The Dean, Dr. Khader Baha, knew Gordon well from their time together at Kabul University, and we had only to flesh out some sort of agreement as to what we might accomplish there. And so I began the second of what was to become semiannual trips to Jalalabad for the next eight years.

With Gordon's best Afghan friend as Minister of Health, there would be no problem getting Afghan government approval if we could come up with a contract acceptable to it and to both our universities. Loma Linda would certainly agree to provide the salaries and transportation of any of its faculty members who might take part. As for Indiana University, I knew that no major funding was likely to come from its coffers and that no faculty members would be funded by the university should any be interested in participating. This was, unfortunately, to be a somewhat lopsided venture, in which I would have to raise funds, recruit doctors from elsewhere, and generally oversee the project. With Gordon's job as Associate Dean for Student Affairs at Loma Linda allowing him no significant time to devote to the venture at that juncture, my first task was to draw up the contract.

My boss in Bloomington, vice-president Lynne Merritt, was completely behind me in this venture, as was Ken Penrod in Indianapolis, who had given me *carte blanche* to carry on as I saw fit – as long as I was able to raise funds for whatever I undertook. Although Lynne could not provide funds for international travel from his budget, he kindly offered me unlimited funds for travel in the U.S. to raise funds and recruit faculty members.

My top priority at the moment, however, was writing what would be a contract acceptable to the Afghans. But how to do so without committing either university to more than good will, yet making significant financial demands upon the Afghan government?

I labored long and hard over that document. Using such noncommittal language as "to the extent that we may be able, we will endeavor to the best of our abilities to......", I outlined the various aspects of the program that we might undertake. For the Afghans, however, the responsibilities were more specifically laid out, including provision of housing for all our personnel, duty-free entry of personal and professional goods, provision of two salaries at $10,000 per year (enough to pay ongoing expenses at home for any one willing to volunteer his or her services for a year or more), etc. When Gordon was satisfied that it was polished enough to be accepted by Loma Linda, we were ready to have it translated into Dari, the variety of Persian used in Afghanistan, and present it to the powers that be.

Back in Kabul a few weeks later, I contacted the Afghan lawyer who had drafted Afghanistan's first constitution in 1964 when the king declared the country a constitutional monarchy. An alumnus of Indiana University, he willingly offered to do the translation, amused by the fiscal onesidedness, but warned that the bureaucracy moved slowly and it might be some time before it would pass muster. It did languish in various government departments for many months, but I needed that time to begin to raise funds and look for people.

Meanwhile, Gordon presented me with a strategy he was certain would get him a leave of absence to head up the project. As associate dean for student affairs, perhaps the most demanding job in the medical school, he knew the dean would never let him off for another two years in Afghanistan. What I was to do, therefore, was to make an appointment to see the worldwide head of the Seventh Day Adventist Church in suburban Washington, and present our project to him, being assured that he would show an interest since Loma Linda would be involved. Having thus aroused his interest, I was then to make a plea for Gordon's services to head up the team. If he approved – and Gordon was confident he would, Gordon's father having been the founder of the Adventist hospital in Washington – the sequence of events would be thus: The president of Loma Linda University would receive a "request" from the Seventh Day Adventist president for Dr. Gordon Hadley's services for two years, and Dean Hinshaw would then receive a directive from the university president to release Dr. Hadley at the end of the academic year. Gordon's assumption was correct, and we had a team leader. Now we needed a team.

My first recruit came to us in a most unexpected way. While in Washington at the National Prayer Breakfast in February 1968, I was invited to dinner at the home of Bob Strain, associate minister of Fourth Presbyterian Church. Knowing I had taught in India, he asked me if I might be able to find a place on the faculty of an Indian medical school for a young man in his church who wanted to be a "tentmaker" missionary in that country. (Just as the apostle Paul supported himself as a tentmaker while establishing the early church in Asia and Europe, many Christians today—as exemplified by those in Afghanistan – were finding jobs to support themselves as a means of sharing their Christian faith in another country.)

With the many private medical schools then springing up all over India, I was reasonably certain I could help the young man, so I asked Bob to tell me more about him.

"He has finished his residency in internal medicine and is currently engaged in virology research at the National Institutes of Health. His name is Elliott Larson and....."

"Elliott Larson?," I interrupted in amazement. "Do you know if he's from the Buffalo, New York, area?"

Indeed he was. Elliott grew up in our Baptist Church in Williamsville and later went to medical school at the University of Buffalo, where he excelled in his studies. While at the AAMC I was responsible for approving his application for a 3-month fellowship grant during his final year, to work in a mission hospital in Ecuador. I had since lost track of him.

I immediately contacted him and told him I would be pleased to help him find him a place in India, but wondered if he might possibly be interested in teaching in a medical school in Afghanistan instead. When he enthusiastically responded in the affirmative, I had to explain that the project was still on the drawing board, and it would probably be a year before we had the go-ahead and the funds to support him.

"That's perfect! That will give me time to complete my project at the NIH, and I'll raise my own support!" What a God-send! Within a few months he had commitments from his church for the modest $350 a month he would need for living expenses. Meanwhile, Gordon had arranged with Adventist headquarters the transfer to Jalalabad of several of their missionaries in India – an Indian obstetrician-gynecologist and an American lab technician and her administrator husband. Things were looking up.

The Peace Corps director in Kabul had promised to provide English teachers, but someone in Washington dropped the ball, and with considerable embarrassment he cabled me to say that none would be forthcoming. However, he had recently had a visit from a representative of the Medical Mission Sisters, a Catholic order based in Philadelphia, providing doctors, nurses and other health workers to the underprivileged throughout the world since 1925. She was interested in placing some of their nurses in Afghanistan, and he wondered if I would be interested in pursuing this. Needless to say, I did pursue it, and thus we came to be blessed with three outstanding American nurses and an Indian doctor who served for the duration of the project.

44 – Wheeling and dealing

I have never ceased to be amazed at the manner in which divine intervention made itself felt time and time again. Similar projects of assistance to a dozen or more Third World medical schools had been funded in the previous two decades by USAID and several large private foundations, each at a cost of millions of dollars. By now, however, such funding sources had completely dried up—and here we were, offering major assistance to Nangrahar University Faculty of Medicine with nothing much more than goodwill to back it up. And asking other people for money was definitely not my forte – nor did I have a very clear idea as to where to begin, beyond the bounds of the university. Loma Linda University and the Seventh Day Adventist mission board would, of course, take care of all the expenses of their people, but I was on my own to provide for my recruits.

An old friend I had known through the Christian Medical Society was now the medical director of the Methodist Board of Foreign Missions in New York, so he became my first target. He received me warmly, and when I told him of my impecunious state, he thought he might be able to come up with $10,000. Pan American Airways, which was now providing pilots, mechanics, and technical assistance to Ariana, the Afghan airline, was offering a round-trip fare of only $430, utilizing a Pan Am flight from New York to London or Frankfurt, and Ariana from there to Kabul. I should be able to raise that kind of money for travel of our people, and ten thousand dollars would go a long way in funding my own travel back and forth to Afghanistan, as well as that of our team when the time for their departure arrived.

During my first trip to Afghanistan five years earlier, I had met an American surgeon, Dr. Robert Shaw, working for a private relief organization, CARE-MEDICO, on whose board I was now serving. By now he was back in Houston, Texas, as chief of the division of thoracic surgery at the Parkland Hospital – the hospital to which President Kennedy was taken when he was shot. When I called upon him to ask if he might be interested in joining our team, he not only offered to volunteer his services for a year without cost to us, but urged me to contact a surgeon in New York, Dr. James Duke, who might be interested.

Jim "Red" Duke had been Bob Shaw's chief resident at Parkland and was on duty in the emergency department when the Kennedy entourage came screaming in. Seeing that Kennedy was hopelessly wounded, he turned his attention to severely wounded Governor John Connolly, who was in the Kennedy car – and saved his life.

When I presented the project to Jim, noting with some embarrassment that all we could pay him was one of the Afghan salaries of $10,000 for a year of his services, he accepted with enthusiasm. And if I could provide transportation and housing for his secretary, he would ask her to join his family, to home school his and the children of other team members, if need be. (By the time all hands were on board in Jalalabad a year or so later, she had eight pupils, each in a different grade!)

Ray Knighton at the Christian Medical Society had referred me to a young internist, Dr. Andrew Stenhouse, who was on the faculty of the University of Hawaii School of Medicine. I sent him a plane ticket to meet Dr. Hadley and me in Loma Linda, and we offered him the other of the two salaries to be provided by the Afghans. Our team was assuming respectable size.

By 1970, our contract had been approved and the team members began making their preparations for arriving on site as their respective schedules permitted. I had meanwhile acquired additional funding -- a grant of $6000 from the Iran Foundation on whose board of directors I had been invited to serve. Although they had previously only funded projects in Iran, at their annual board meeting in New York that year I screwed up my courage just as we were about to adjourn to ask if they might consider a grant for Afghanistan.

Jalalabad, near the eastern border of Afghanistan, was a sprawling, dusty market town offering few amenities to foreign residents. One of my goals, therefore, was to provide several vehicles for the team to give them opportunity for shopping or other needs in Kabul, 80 miles to the west and Peshawar, Pakistan, 65 miles to the east. I had arranged to purchase an old Volkswagen sedan from Chris Jung, leader of the I.U. team in Kabul, but the other vehicles needed to be of more dependable vintage.

I ordered a Variant, the small VW station wagon, for factory delivery in Germany and a Land Rover for factory delivery in England, each to be picked up by me on my first trip back to Afghanistan after the team was in place. I would then arrange to have them shipped by sea through Russia. This meant a 4-month sea and land journey, so when a young doctor in California who had just finished his residency offered to volunteer his services for four months in Jalalabad, I asked him if he would be interested in driving one of the vehicles to Afghanistan. He thought that was a great idea, and when he mentioned this to his VW mechanic and said there was also a VW to be delivered, the mechanic and his wife decided to join him just for the adventure. Not only could both vehicles be delivered in only a couple of weeks, but the journey would be far less hazardous, with two vehicles and a mechanic.

He flew to London and picked up the Land Rover. I met the mechanic and his wife in New York and flew with then to Heathrow Airport in London, where the Land Rover awaited us. I immediately flew on to Germany, picked up the VW, and drove it back to Brussels, where a friend in the American embassy would turn it over to the others when they arrived from England.

Before reaching Brussels, however, I made two detours. Driving out of the factory in Wolfsburg with the new VW, I noticed on my map that the East German border was but a few miles east. Turning east instead of west, I drove to Berlin to see what that divided city looked like. One was not permitted to leave the autobahn between the border and Berlin, so it was a straight shot – no detours allowed. West Berlin was like any other major West German city – vibrant and prosperous. Then there was The Wall. Leaving my car on a side street near Checkpoint Charlie, I walked into East Berlin border post to get a visa.

While standing in line, I struck up a conversation in English with a blind German student in front of me. He was just a one-day sightseer like me, so I suggested that we do the town together, since my German was *nicht so gut*. He would be my voice and I would be his eyes, describing the incredibly rundown state of the city. It was a splendid arrangement, and when we returned to West Berlin and parted company I headed west.

My next stop was Hannover, to visit my Harvard classmate, Hans Borst, whom I had last seen in Munich. Now the distinguished professor of surgery at the university hospital in Hannover, he entertained me royally that evening and the next morning, after a tour of the hospital, left me in his office to change into driving clothes while he went on rounds. I bade his secretary farewell and took off for Brussels.

After two hundred kilometers or so an accident far down the autobahn slowed traffic so severely and for so long that I was in imminent danger of running out of gas when a rest stop miraculously appeared. It was then I discovered that my wallet, which I had placed on top of a filing cabinet in Hans' office while changing my clothes, was apparently still resting comfortably there. Fortunately, I had sufficient cash in my pocket to buy gas enough to get me to Brussels, where my friend, Dick Martin could help me out, but the wallet contained my driver's license, credit cards, and other items vital to my onward journey – and I had to get rid of the car and fly to Frankfort to catch my flight to Kabul, which allowed no time to go back for it.

Dick was the political officer at the American embassy, and with his help I contacted the American consul in Frankfurt, explaining my predicament and asking if I could arrange for delivery of the wallet to the consulate the following day, to be picked up by me during my change of planes in Frankfurt. He agreed, and since time would be of the essence, he said he would leave it with the Marine guard at the gate. I then phoned Hans' secretary, who confirmed that she could send it by overnight courier service.

I stored the VW in a public parking garage, gave the ticket and all the car documents to Dick, and flew to Frankfurt late in the afternoon. The two hours between flights would necessitate a mad dash to and from the consulate, but my guardian angel was with me all the way, and another mad dash in the terminal got me to the gate in the nick of time. Such would not be possible today, with airport security what it is! Three weeks after my arrival in Afghanistan, the intrepid travelers pulled into Jalalabad, they and the vehicles in fine shape. All in all, I thought it a rather singular accomplishment!

It had taken almost three years to put the project together, traveling to Afghanistan every few months, and for four years it went remarkably well. I visited the team about every six months, always stopping in Europe along the way to acquire needed supplies and equipment. On two of these journeys I interviewed prospective volunteers for the project, Christians whom I knew or to whom I was referred – a pathologist in Munich, a pharmacist in Hamburg, and even a surgeon in Helsinki who was a Harvard Medical School student I had known in Boston many years earlier.

With my limited funds and no financial support from my own medical school, the only consultant from Indiana University for whom I was able to arrange a short-term stay was Joe Mamlin, who was delighted to return, however briefly, with one of his residents, Bob Einterz, to the project in which he had played a key role in its infancy. Thus Loma Linda University School of Medicine became the major contributor of visiting lecturers, as well as providing a number of long-term members to the team -- and long afterward again provided major assistance to the government of Afghanistan during the infamous Taliban era.

Thanks to some unexpected personal income from writing a feature article for *The Saturday Evening Post* (owned by friends of ours in Indianapolis), Pat was able to accompany me on several of my many trips to Afghanistan during those years. (As you may recall, it was while reading that publication when banished to the library one day in high school that the seed of my university education was planted!)

Pat has always been a great traveler, and her initiative in dealing with situations that would deter women less inclined to face potentially hazardous consequences is well-illustrated by a trip she made alone from Kabul to Jalalabad during one of our trips together to Afghanistan. I had left her in Kabul to shop and otherwise enjoy herself while I visited the team in Jalalabad. Two days later, while sitting in the home of our head nurse and reviewing the supply needs, Jane noticed someone going by the living room window.

"Isn't that Pat who just walked by?"

Indeed it was, as there came a knock on the front door and Jane let her in. It seems that she had become bored with shopping and thought it would be more enjoyable to visit Jalalabad. Knowing that the small buses congregated in the market place often went to Jalalabad, she took a taxi to this "bus depot" and found an English-speaking person who could guide her to an appropriate bus, about to depart. It was completely filled with Afghan men, together with a large assortment of chickens and other birds, but she unhesitatingly made her way through this mass of humanity and poultry and took the only available seat, a jump seat in the center of the bus, nodding politely as she pushed her way through. When the driver came to collect the fares, the man nearest her selected from the bunch of currency in her hand the appropriate bills, handed them to the driver, and returned the change to her.

The road from Kabul to Jalalabad is one of the most spectacular in the world, winding down the mountains from an altitude of 7000 feet to 1000 feet in its 80 miles – and also a dangerous one due to the heavy truck traffic, with drivers careening around the bends at breakneck speed. There were many stops along the way, including one at prayer time, when all the passengers disembarked, laid their prayer rugs on the ground, and dutifully paid respects to Allah. It was, all in all, a most interesting trip.

During my many visits to Afghanistan I traveled that amazing road, often with a local friend who wanted to visit Jalalabad or one of our team who happened to be in Kabul at the time. Later, when an Afghan friend loaned me his car for the trip, I drove myself – but was soon advised against this by the head of our I.U. team in Kabul. Under Afghan law, if a passenger or a pedestrian is injured in an auto accident, the driver is not allowed to leave the country until the injured person recovers or dies – and if the latter, must pay damages to the deceased's family. An American doctor working for the Peace Corps learned this the hard way when he took delivery of a new Mercedes in Kabul a few days before he was to drive to Europe at the end of his tour of duty. His first day on the road he had the misfortune to hit a drunken Afghan pedestrian – and spent the next few weeks visiting the patient in the hospital every day until the patient was discharged, to be sure he was getting the best of medical care!

When she later told our friends in Kabul of her adventure, they were amazed that she would dare entrust herself to one of those rickety buses – and as an unaccompanied woman. It had not been many years before that Afghan women were first allowed to appear in public without the cumbersome burkah – if their husbands would permit it – and even in recent years prior to Taliban rule many Afghan women continued to wear the burkah. Foreign women were never put to such lengths, but as she later did when we lived Saudi Arabia, Pat was ever mindful of such customs and always dressed very conservatively – in Saudi Arabia, for example, in dresses that covered her from her neck to her feet, with sleeves down to her wrists, not the most comfortable street wear in 120 degree temperature.

45 – "And my God will meet all your needs...."

One of my major undertakings was seeking sources of equipment and supplies at the lowest possible cost. With little cash available at the outset, I had to rely on donations from Christian organizations in America, England and Germany, at which pharmaceuticals and good used equipment were available for a nominal handling charge. As chairman of the board of directors of the American organization, MAP (Medical Assistance Programs, Inc. – now MAP International), I had access to a broad selection of pharmaceuticals donated by the manufacturers. In England, at ECHO (Equipping Christian Hospitals Overseas) I was able to find good used equipment of a somewhat limited variety, however. A smaller Catholic organization in Germany provided us with a fair number of surgical instruments, a suitcase full of which could sometimes be added to my luggage as I continued on to Kabul.

Two years into the project, however, we struck gold in the form of a grant of $75,000 arranged by our Medical Mission Sisters, who had requested a visit from Father Gordijn, representative of Misereor, a large Catholic organization in Aachen, Germany. I was unaware of this until Sister Jane, head of our nursing team, mentioned the possibility of this during one of my visits, so I arranged a stopover in Aachen on the way home. By the time I arrived, the grant had been approved, to be used solely for supplies and equipment. Moreover, they were agreeable to sending the funds directly to a checking account I had set up for the purpose rather than through the Indiana University Foundation, the recipient of all grants to the university, who exacted a toll of some 22 percent for overhead.

I was now free to wheel and deal with other suppliers, the largest of which was UNICEF in Copenhagen, who maintained a huge warehouse of medical supplies and small laboratory equipment for sale to the governments of developing countries. Again my guardian angel intervened when I approached them to see if they would be willing to classify our project as that of the Afghan government rather than a private undertaking, given our contract with the latter. That, they admitted, was stretching it a bit, but since we had duty-free access of goods, they were willing to ship directly to Jalalabad – and I was thus able to obtain a huge number of surgical instruments, manufactured in Pakistan, at incredibly low prices.

Prior to becoming the object of Misereor's largesse, I had acquired a considerable amount of donated used medical equipment from various sources in the United States, which the manager of the university's warehouse facility on the Indianapolis campus had kindly stored for me until I could figure out how to ship it. Getting goods to Afghanistan in those days was no easy undertaking – and a very expensive one. I finally found a forwarding agency in Baltimore who could arrange the shipping, but the cost of crating and trucking it all from Indianapolis was more than I could afford at the time. However, when my younger brother Dave visited me from California, where he was somewhat footloose and fancy free at the moment, he generously offered to not only help me crate all the stuff, but to take it in a rented truck to Baltimore – another affirmation from the One who was guiding this exciting adventure.

It was exciting to see how God was working in Afghanistan in those days. The Blumhagens, for example, despite a further effort of Ambassador Steeves to keep them out of the country by asking the Foreign Ministry not to give them visas, came back to establish a small hospital in the Hazarajat, about 100 miles west of Kabul under the auspices of MAP. Thus, I became indirectly involved in a highly successful project in that country by reason of my being on the MAP board.

Meanwhile, a number of American and European mission agencies had combined to form a coalition, the International Afghan Mission, that developed a considerable number of aid projects, including a first-class eye hospital in Kabul and other much-needed health facilities. (Although we are accustomed to think of "mission" in the Christian context, it is a widely used term in the secular world, so the name was readily accepted by the Afghan government.)

Satan does not take kindly to such activities, and four years into our project war clouds loomed on the horizon. By this time things were going so well in Jalalabad that I felt comfortable taking my first sabbatical leave from the university. Wende was now in her first year at Shortridge High School, Jack was finishing his final year there, and Ted was halfway through his undergraduate degree program at Indiana University in Bloomington. It seemed like a good time to take all of them with us to Switzerland, where I had arranged a six-month stint at the World Health Organization through its associate director, Dr. Ernani Braga, whom I had known while at the AAMC. Thus, in the spring of 1973 we began preparations for departure.

With one son already away at university and the other to be joining him when we returned from Switzerland, we decided to sell the big house on Meridian Street and put our goods into storage, planning to downsize our housing when we returned. It was probably a wise choice, given the age of the old house and the possibility of major repairs as time went on, but moving from a fourteen-room house with a three-car garage into something much smaller was to tax our ingenuity in finding storage space for contents which had not shrunk in size. Even these many years later, with only two of us now at home, space is at a premium. At times, I almost wish we might have a fire while away from home so that we might start all over again!

Even so relatively minor a matter as buying a car for the sabbatical was the result of divine providence. We had considered a number of popular European models that could be purchased in the United States for overseas delivery, but the larger ones, such as Volvo and Mercedes, were too expensive, while those of more reasonable price were too small to accommodate a family of our size. The choice was finally made through an unanticipated meeting and a new friendship with one of God's great servants, Brother Andrew.

Our pastor, Russ Blowers, had introduced me to his book, *God's Smuggler*, some years earlier, and when I learned that he would be speaking at a church in Indianapolis several months before our departure, I interrupted a meeting in Chicago to fly home for the evening in order to hear him. Introduced to him after the meeting, I was delighted to learn that he was scheduled to fly to Chicago's O'Hare Field the next afternoon, where he would have a four hour layover before his flight home to The Netherlands. My meeting was at a conference room at O'Hare, to which I returned early the next morning, and I again interrupted the meeting in order to spend three hours with him in the international departure lounge. (Gone forever, it seems, are those days when one could not only accompany a friend all the way to the gate, but even on board the plane if necessary – as happened once when Pat accompanied me to the airport, said goodbye at the gate, but after I was seated suddenly rushed on to the plane with two boys, ages 1 and 3, just before the door closed to tell me that I had forgotten to give her the car keys!)

After learning much about his earlier work carrying Bibles behind the Iron Curtain and its subsequent expansion in sending Christian professionals of all kinds as "tentmakers" to work in closed countries, it occurred to me to ask him the kind of car he might recommend for our travel in Europe. Without hesitation he recommended the newest Citroen DS23 station wagon, which I promptly ordered from Citroen USA for delivery in Paris. He also gave me his home address and phone number so that we might keep in touch – and I suspect that I am one of the relatively few who know him simply as Andrew van der Byl.

Our friend, Rod Johnston, director of Young Life in France, had offered Jack the opportunity to work for the summer in their camp in the Praz de Lys, not far from Geneva, so he was the first to leave. The rest of us would follow as soon as we closed on the sale of the house and put our goods in storage. To Pat's dismay, it didn't work out quite that way.

46 – An ill omen

Shortly before our scheduled departure, I received a call from USAID in Washington asking if I could accompany one of their consultants, Dr. Don Rice, to Pakistan to evaluate a project with which I had some involvement several years earlier. This was too good an opportunity to pass up, for the trip would give me the opportunity to visit our Jalalabad project, and the handsome consulting fee would take care of much of the cost of the new Citroen station wagon we had ordered for delivery in Paris. Unfortunately, it would also leave Pat alone to handle the final arrangements for the sale of the house and getting the rest of the family off to Geneva. Reluctantly, she agreed to my deserting her in her hour of need.

When the hour arrived for Pat to drive me to the airport, our goods were in storage, and she, Ted, and Wende would return to a 14-room house, empty save for their belongings yet to be fully packed for an eight-month stay in Europe, a car to put in storage, and both a lake house in Bloomington and a rental house on the other side of Indianapolis to attend to. Theirs was not a pleasant prospect – and I soon received my comeuppance for this act of treachery. Having allowed sufficient time to stop by my office, I picked up the latest mail, got back into our station wagon, and asked Wende to put the mail in my flight bag behind the rear seat.

"What flight bag?"

"You know -- the brightly colored one with all my important stuff in it – tickets, passport, etc.!"

"It's not here. You must have left it at home."

The ensuing panic quickly gave way to rational thought. I had to catch my flight from Indianapolis to New York because I had an immediate connection to Geneva and thence to Karachi, where the other consultant would be awaiting my arrival. It was only a fifteen-minute run from my office to the airport, and I had allowed a generous half-hour for check-in. But my flight bag was twenty minutes in the other direction, and from there it normally took thirty minutes to get to the airport. That would leave minus-five minutes for check-in – not a pretty picture.

"You can't do it, Ed. You'll just have to call and cancel your flight and go later." Women always seem to have a solution for any problem, however impractical.

"I can't do that! I'll make it!" – and off we went, with the two ladies terror-stricken as every rule of the road was broken, pulling into the airport five minutes before the flight was scheduled to leave. The front desk held the plane for me, and I collapsed into my seat, drained of my last drop of adrenaline – only to have the two-hour flight to New York last more than five hours, weather having shut down the airport shortly before our scheduled arrival. After circling for three hours, we were diverted to Philadelphia for refueling, and my flight to Geneva was still on the ground in New York, now scheduled to arrive long after the departure of the flight to Karachi.

Pat never said so, but I suspect she felt I had been given my just deserts. Every cloud has a silver lining, however. Arriving in Geneva I cabled Don in Karachi that I would be a day late, rented a car, and drove over to see Jack at the Young Life camp in France, only two hours away.

Don had been a medical missionary in India for many years, but had never been in Afghanistan, so upon completion of our mission in Pakistan, I suggested that we go up to Kabul from Peshawar instead of returning to Karachi. He could then fly home from there, while I would go on to Paris to pick up the new Citroen station wagon I had ordered before leaving home.

Taking a taxi through the famed Khyber Pass to the border town of Landi Kotal, we picked up an Afghan taxi to Jalalabad. The Pakistani border city was truly in a no-man's land. While waiting outside a shop for him to finish a purchase and be on our way, a swarthy character sidled up to me and showed me a large ball of evil-looking dark stuff in his dirty palm. "You want to buy opium, mister?" I declined.

The program in Jalalabad was going extremely well, despite an undercurrent of suspicion on the part of some local inhabitants that led to accusations that we were American CIA spies – a designation commonly attributed to American aid workers throughout the Third World. By now we had a splendid team of more than 25 long-term personnel and a number of short-term volunteers, most of them committed Christian tentmakers. We had graduated the first class of medical students, a number of whom found excellent postgraduate opportunities in the U.S. and Europe. (Sadly, by the time most had finished their training the Soviet invasion undoubtedly kept many from returning.)

During my first visit to Jalalabad, Joe Mamlin had asked me to obtain approval from Dr. John Hickam, head of I.U.'s department of medicine, to invite the three Afghan doctors whom Joe had been training in Jalalabad to come to Indiana University for an intensive two-year program he would prepare for them. Now a professor of medicine and chief of medicine at Wishard Memorial Hospital, one of I.U.'s major teaching hospitals, Joe now had them under his wing in Indianapolis. The future looked bright indeed.

We spent only a few hours in Jalalabad before heading for Kabul, and once again I had the privilege of traversing the magnificent 80 miles or so of highway that winds its way from 1000 feet elevation to 5900 feet in Kabul – a route in many places even more spectacular than the Khyber Pass. I was scheduled to leave Kabul for Tehran and Paris the following day, very disappointed that my good friend, Ibrahim Majid Seraj, was out of the country with the king, whom he had taken to London for eye surgery. Majid had been shifted from Minister of Health to Minister of Education, but was still personal physician to King Mohammed Zahir Shah. Although his plane was due back that evening, my earlier flight would prevent our meeting. However, the flight was seriously delayed, and by the time the ground agent told us we could go back into town to await our departure, Majid's plane had landed. He gave the agent his home phone number, and I spent the remainder of the evening with him until the airline phoned and he took me to the airport. Neither he nor I could have imagined what a momentous event was to take place in Kabul a few hours later.

Arriving in Paris, I proceeded directly to the Citroen distribution center, picked up the car, and reached Geneva by nightfall. The next day I drove over to see Jack and deliver a case of Skippy peanut butter I had picked up for him at the American embassy commissary in Karachi. The look of joy on his face and those of his roommates made eminently worthwhile the nuisance of lugging the peanut butter all that way.

When one of them asked me from where I had come, he told me he had heard on the radio the day before that the king of Afghanistan had been overthrown. This seemed highly unlikely, but upon my return to Geneva I learned at the American consulate that this was indeed the case – occurring just a few hours after I left Kabul. In a bloodless coup on July 17, 1973, King Mohammed Zahir Shah was deposed by Mohammad Daoud Khan, the king's brother-in-law and head of the army, who proclaimed Afghanistan a republic with himself as its president. The coup in itself would have had no effect on our project, but the cabinet reshuffling that took place resulted in a very unfortunate appointment in the Ministry of Health – and an ominous presage of things to come in Afghanistan.

47 -- The World Health Organization

Having learned on an earlier trip to Geneva that apartment rentals in that city were beyond our budget, I had found a beautiful chalet in the village of Huemoz, the home of Francis Schaeffer's Christian community, L'Abri. Although a two-hour train ride from Geneva, the setting was idyllic and L'Abri would offer splendid opportunities to Pat and the boys for study and exploration of the surrounding countryside. We would enroll Wende as a day student at a British boarding school, Aiglon College in Chesieres-Villars, the next village up the mountain, where the Schaeffers lived.

The chalet was owned by an elderly Swiss couple who lived down on the lake during most of the year but occupied it during the summer. It would thus not be available until mid-September, so we had decided to spend the summer touring Europe. After Pat, Ted, and Wende arrived in Geneva, we drove leisurely through France, Belgium, Luxembourg, and Holland, eventually making our way by ferry to the north of England, where we had arranged to rent a house for a month in East Harrington, a suburb of Sunderland, just north of the beautiful university town of Durham. The owners were Lesley and Michael Kaye-Besley, a young couple who were visiting friends in Indianapolis during that month, and it was a splendid base from which to explore that part of England and as far north as Edinburgh. Jack had hitch-hiked up from France by then, so all of us were able to spend the remainder of the summer visiting friends in Denmark, thence down through Germany, Switzerland and Italy, to the French Riviera, before settling down in Huemoz.

Commuting by train from Aigle, at the foot of the mountain, along the shore of Lac Leman (Lake of Geneva) through Lausanne to Geneva was a delight, passing so close to the Chateau de Chillon on the water's edge – the beautiful 12th century castle made famous by Byron's poem, "The Prisoner of Chillon"—that one could almost touch it. As an unpaid volunteer, I did not always put in a full week at WHO, so from time to time I would drive to work, leaving the office early to take a leisurely drive home on the French side of the lake – or just stay home for the day and go skiing in Villars-sur-Ollon just up the road from Huemoz.

My boss at WHO was a crusty but likeable old Serb named Djukanovic, who had been personal physician during World War II to Josip Broz, better known as Marshall Tito, the undisputed head of the Yugoslav Republic until his death in 1980. He assigned me the task of reviewing reports that had come in from WHO country representatives throughout the Third World in response to an inquiry from his office concerning major government community health projects. The study had been commissioned by UNICEF, for a report to be presented at the International Conference on Primary Health Care, in Alma-Ata, Kazakhstan, the following year.

Notably missing from the report of the WHO representative in India was a very important project with which I had some familiarity, a Christian community health program run by an Indian husband and wife team, Drs, Raj and Mabelle Arole in the village of Jamkhed. Since Dr. Djukanovic and several of his staff were going to visit some of these projects before preparing his final report to UNICEF, I needed more information about Jamkhed before recommending that he go there, so I went over to the nearby Christian Medical Commission office in the headquarters of the World Council of Churches and asked if I could borrow their file on Jamkhed, which they graciously loaned me.

I then wrote to the Aroles to tell them that I was trying to arrange a WHO visit, and could they give me specific directions for reaching Jamkhed from New Delhi – a very tortuous journey, as I thus learned. After I told Djukanovic what I had learned about the project, he wrote to the WHO representative in New Delhi to ask his opinion. I was not surprised at the bureaucratic reply he received – that it was not a government program, was in a very remote location, and would not be worth his taking the trouble to visit. (I suspect the WHO man hadn't the foggiest knowledge of it, and was embarrassed to have been queried about it by his superior in Geneva.)

Before leaving WHO to return home, I spent an hour with Djukanovic, going over the report to UNICEF and strongly urged him to visit Jamkhed when he went to India. Not until many months later, when his office sent me a copy of WHO's *Report of the International Conference on Primary Health Care, Alma-Ata, USSR. 6-12 September 1973* did I learn that not only had he done so, but the Jamkhed project became a major focus at the Alma-Ata conference. This hitherto unknown project under the leadership of two committed Christian Indian doctors thus became known throughout international health circles, receiving countless visitors in the following years who sought to emulate what the Aroles were doing.

One of my new friends in Geneva was the French ambassador to the United Nation Organizations, Jean Fernand-Laurent, to whom I had been introduced by Doug Coe, head of the National Prayer Breakfast fellowship in Washington. While at dinner one evening in his home, I told him how the Christian Medical Commission had assisted me in my work at WHO. He was surprised to learn that there had been essentially no prior contact between these two organizations, and subsequently took it upon himself to arrange for their two heads to meet – a step that was to greatly enhance the image of the CMC in international health affairs. With my name having been mentioned in the WHO report of the Alma-Ata conference as one of the staff responsible for that report, I thank God for putting me in just the right place at the right time to have a part in furthering the work of two worthy Christian endeavors.

One of the WHO staff who had become a very good friend during my short tenure there was an American, Dr. Jerry Stromberg, who one day introduced me to an elderly gentleman in his office when I happened to walk by. His name was Dr. Johannes Holm, who had recently retired as head of the Tuberculosis Division of WHO – and I had the rare privilege, to his great surprise, of telling him that we had already met long ago and that he was, in fact, one of the people responsible for my being at WHO. I then reminded him of the days long ago when he was at the Harvard School of Public Health and was one of the persons, as I've noted in an earlier chapter, who influenced me to go into public health. One does not often have such an opportunity to show appreciation to a mentor from one's distant past.

Life in Huemoz was idyllic. Jack and Ted, both avid photographers, roamed the hills most days, or spent time exploring the neighboring villages. Pat attended Edith Schaeffer's women's group each Monday, and otherwise learned much from listening to Francis Schaeffer's tapes while doing the housework. The kids and I learned to ski, and with my relaxed schedule at WHO we had ample time for family trips through much of Switzerland, some of these with my mother and with friends who came to visit, and on one long weekend we exchanged homes with a family we knew in Geneva for a change of pace.

48 – "Apocalypse Now"

By December 1973 I had found it necessary to interrupt my work at WHO and return to Afghanistan for a week or so, having received some disturbing news from the team. During my first visit to Kabul in 1964 I had met the first real Communist ever encountered in my travels – an anatomy professor by the name of Safi at Kabul University, whose negative and uninformed remarks about the state of health services in America left no doubt as to his political leanings. When Daoud took over the government, he replaced Majid's successor at the Ministry of Health with a physician who had little talent for the job, and some time later Safi became his deputy.

By late 1973 Safi had effectively taken control of the ministry, and the future of our and other health projects had become very uncertain. When I met with him in his office, the extent to which communism had reared its ugly head was immediately apparent. Safi received me politely, but without introducing the grim-looking character who sat silently in the corner during our entire conversation – a typical communist commissar assigned by the party to keep watch on other members of the party. He informed me that the ministry was phasing out foreign aid health projects in the provinces, but any of our people who wished to continue working in Afghanistan were welcome to do so in one of the several health projects in Kabul – meaning, of course, where he could keep a close watch on them. Otherwise, they were to close out their affairs within the next few months and leave the country. The projects most notably affected were those of the Peace Corps, whose volunteers were scattered around the country; the MAP clinic in the Hazarajat; and ours in Jalalabad. He therefore advised me to inform our team members to begin to close up shop, but agreed not to impose a strict deadline, allowing each to make arrangements for his or her future at a reasonable pace.

Only Andrew Stenhouse, our internist, found employment in Kabul, with the Peace Corps. The others sadly began to make their individual arrangements for departure. Soon Elliott and Marty Larson, who had learned Pushtu and established close relationships with many of their neighbors, were the only ones left. They held on as long as they could, until finally the police came to their door one day and told them they had to leave. Slowly they began to pack, wondering what they were going to do, until one evening when the police demanded they leave the following day. Cramming their personal possessions and two little boys, Eric and

Mark into the old VW "beetle" I had bought for them four years earlier, they bid farewell to their Afghan friends and headed for Pakistan.

It was not until many months later that I received a letter from Elliott telling me that they were now in London. No mention was made of how they got there, but I was to be in London soon thereafter and could hear the story then.

Back at the university and with my major effort for the past seven years in ruins, I was forced to face the question of continuing to justify my existence there. As a tenured professor, I had no reason to fear loss of employment, but it was difficult to see how I could justify continuation of the Division of International Affairs as a full-time office of the Indiana University Medical Center. I still had responsibility for the special needs of our many doctors from other countries on temporary visas, but much of this was adequately handled by my secretary. Whether I could find – and fund – further overseas projects was my major concern. The medical school now had a new dean, Dr. Steven Beering, a fine educator and accomplished physician who had been brought in from the outside – and would certainly show more interest in what I was doing than had his predecessor. (So outstanding an educator was Steve that he later became president of Purdue University.)

In any case, I still had to settle accounts with Misereor, who expected a report of how their generous grant had been utilized, now that the project had ended. I've always had a callous disregard for proper recording of expenditures in my private life – much to the dismay of my long-suffering wife – and this, I must confess, likewise characterized my professional life. In Project Viet Nam, the business manager of the parent organization, Project Hope, took care of all of that, leaving me only to run the show. At Indiana University, the job had been created for me by Ken Penrod, who arranged for salaries for myself and a secretary, and whatever budget I might need for my division was my responsibility. Thus, with no formal budget to defend or to which I had to account for to the university, it was now only to a Roman Catholic monseigneur in Germany that I must make my confession.

I labored long and hard, digging through my files and check books to identify the results of all the wheeling and dealing of the past several years. When at last I had juggled enough figures to produce a total expenditure that more or less matched income, I headed for Aachen via London. On arrival, I phoned Elliott, who said to meet him at the Holland Park tube station. "The car's just around the corner," he said as we exited the station – and to my astonishment there sat the beat-up old VW, still with its Afghan license plates. "The customs officer at Hull said I could keep them for a year!"

After working in a mission hospital in Peshawar for some months, Elliott decided to realize his dream of settling in England for a time. They again packed the old VW, this time with a couple of spare tires strapped to the roof and large water bags hanging over the side, for the journey ahead was to be long and arduous. Unable to take the direct route west through Afghanistan because they had been expelled from the country, they headed southwest through Baluchistan and into the Persian desert. Here their faithful machine failed them at last, and they found themselves stranded along the highway, far from the nearest settlement.

A friendly truck driver towed them into the nearest city where the motor could be repaired, but the cost quoted by the mechanic was far more than they could handle. Then from Elliott's memory bank popped up the name of a Christian contact he had been given long ago, who lived in that city. They found this man, who not only took the little family in but arranged for repair of their car at a fraction of the quoted cost. Blessed and refreshed after several days of Christian hospitality, they went on their way, arriving in London without further disaster – a weary family of four who had made their way across more than 4000 miles of Asia and Europe in a car that I would have feared to drive to the next town.

Until they eventually moved to the States some years later, their home was to be my *pied-à-terre* in London. They had long admired the ministry of Francis Schaeffer at L'Abri in Switzerland, which spawned several other L'Abri communities elsewhere, including one in London's Ealing suburb. L'Abri church services were held in a large house at 52 Cleveland Road, the residence of several members of the L'Abri community. Some years later, however, the congregation had the opportunity to buy the chapel of a nearby convent, and the Larsons purchased the house on Cleveland Road. It was here that I watched the Larson boys – now four of them – grow up during my many visits to England. They later moved back to the United States, where they became members of a L'Abri community in Southboro, Massachusetts, where Elliott practiced internal medicine.

Early in 2005 Elliott closed his practice, and he and Marty returned to Afghanistan to work for an indefinite period, joining second son Mark, who was born in Jalalabad, and who had already been working in Kabul for a year. Although they had become proficient in Pushtu, the language spoken in the country's frontier region to the east, they now had to learn Dari, the Persian tongue used in Kabul. Elliott devotes his time to working with the Afghan doctors in a Kabul hospital, while Marty holds classes in English and other subjects. At this writing they are doing well despite the difficult and dangerous conditions, and their youngest son, Carl, recently joined them to begin work on an agricultural project of his design. Somehow all those years devoted to that country seem worthwhile after all.

It was difficult to witness the demise of a project that held so much promise in a country that so desperately needed well-trained medical personnel. As will be seen, some of the key Afghans involved were able to pursue a career in the United States with our help. However, the rise of the Communist party and subsequent Soviet participation in a war that devastated the country forced the emigration of much of the country's best people, including its better-trained doctors.

With the Taliban takeover of the country following the withdrawal of the Soviet troops, there was further deterioration of medical facilities. Yet through it all, many of the expatriates who worked within the International Afghan Mission continued to serve the country under very difficult circumstances – and others who felt led to leave for one reason or another have since returned. Of all the countries in which I have been privileged to know expatriate Christians working there, none has had such an attraction as Afghanistan. The Afghans are a very special people, and I've not met anyone who has worked closely with them who did not want to return to that country.

49 – A temporary detour

Some months after my return to the university, I received a call from Dean Beering. Steve explained that while I was on sabbatical, our new governor, Dr. Otis Bowen, had asked him to supply a medical school faculty member who would volunteer his services half-time as medical director of the Indiana Department of Correction. The health services of the state prison system were a shambles, and our physician governor was determined to improve the situation. This effort was underway, with some progress being made, until the sudden death of the new medical director the previous weekend from a heart attack. Knowing he would soon receive a call from the governor, and knowing that I was hard pressed for something useful to do, Dean Beering asked if I would at least consider the possibility of taking on that responsibility. "You may find the situation not all that different from the health services in Afghanistan!"

I made an appointment with the Commissioner of Correction the following week, and was soon taken on a tour of the Indiana prison system. I had never been in a prison of any kind before, and was appalled at the vast numbers of men and women incarcerated in our prison system. Many of them, as I learned later and as Charles Colson, founder of Prison Fellowship has so often stated, were there for "white collar" crimes that hardly deserved their being locked up for years with hardened criminals. The crying need in the prison medical services was for qualified physicians as opposed to the foreign medical graduates who had failed our licensing examination but were granted temporary licenses allowing them only to serve in prisons. It was clearly a challenging situation, but one in which I felt I could be of some use. I accepted the job.

Colson has more than adequately described prison conditions in the United States in many of his books, so I shall skip their generalities in this accounting. Our largest and oldest is the Indiana State Prison in Michigan City, the home of the department's execution facility, the infamous and absurdly outmoded electric chair. The prison "hospital" was a small wing of one of the main buildings, staffed mostly by inmates with no formal medical training, who sorted out "sick call" and provided general nursing care to inmates occupying its half dozen or so beds. Patients deemed to have problems requiring serious medical attention were transported 130 miles to the IU Medical Center in Indianapolis, an incredibly inefficient, costly, and often wasteful procedure. If needing only outpatient care, they were hauled to Indianapolis early in the morning and returned to the prison late in the day. Those requiring inpatient care were kept in a locked ward in the then largest of the several hospitals on the campus. Here in Indianapolis, at least, prison inmates received adequate medical care.

Local physicians in Michigan City were sometimes brought into the prison to see patients, but it was obvious that my first concern was to find competent physicians who were willing to work full-time in the prison. In addition, there was a crying need for other well-qualified medical personnel. Nurses would have been ideal, both male and female, but the former were in short supply and the warden was adamant in opposing my recommendation that we hire female nurses, whom I had seen successfully employed in other state prisons I had visited after taking this job. There was, however, a new breed of medical personnel ideally suited for this kind of work, the physician assistant – those superbly trained men and women who have now become an essential part of the American medical care system. At that time they were only beginning to be recognized by the physician community as being competent to assume a great many of the tasks until then only the prerogative of an M.D., whereas today we find P.A.s and nurse practitioners working at every level of medical care, from university hospitals to private medical practices.

Not only was I able to find a PA, but within the year I had acquired a full-time former missionary doctor from a nearby town in Michigan, and a full-time psychiatrist for the prison. For a very brief time I also had a second full-time doctor – whose hiring proved to be a nightmare for me and for him.

Shortly before bringing this man on the staff, I received a call from the Indiana Physician Licensing Board asking if I would consider a very special case with which they had been dealing for the past year – that of a defrocked American doctor who had been imprisoned for a rather bizarre sort of intimacy with a female patient who had brought charges against him, and was now applying for reinstatement of his medical license. Even more bizarre, however, was the outcome of his trial, which resulted in his being remanded to the Indiana Hospital for the Criminally Insane – a maximum security institution operated under the Indiana Department of Mental Health. The reasons are too complex to warrant inclusion here, but the man found himself in a completely inappropriate penal facility, with no fixed sentence period – to be held there until it was determined that he was no longer a menace to society. He had been out of the institution for several years, and the licensing board had given him a temporary license, allowing him to work for a year with a physician in northern Indiana who had now advised the board that he was qualified to resume medical practice. The board, however, was reluctant as yet to restore his full medical license, but would be willing to allow him to work in a prison, to which he had agreed.

I agreed to interview him, and he told me his sad story. There was no question that he deserved punishment for his indiscretion – which, as he told me – had involved several of his patients. By no stretch of the imagination, however – mine or any other rational person – did he deserve to be incarcerated at that institution. Neither did the guards feel he belonged there, treating him kindly and protecting him from other prisoners. He was not only permitted visits from his divorced wife and their children, but was even allowed on one Sunday afternoon to treat them to a picnic on the grounds, outside the prison walls. On that fateful day, he simply decided he had had enough and walked away.

In the next few years he found medical jobs in Florida and in Texas, but each time his employer let him go when he learned of the man's past – that he was technically a fugitive from an Indiana prison, although the Department of Mental Health had apparently never tried to find him. The medical licensing board was aware of this, but they too felt that he had been unjustly treated and made no effort to clear things with the Commissioner of Mental Health. Nor did I see any reason to do so. We all felt he had been punished enough. To our pleasure, he began working there a week later.

A short time thereafter I was in Washington, D.C., attending an international health conference. Awaking in my hotel room the day after the conference, I picked up the complimentary copy of the *Washington Post* outside my door. The glaring headline immediately caught my attention: ESCAPED MENTAL PATIENT WORKS AS PRISON DOCTOR. We had become national news!

A frantic phone call to my secretary provided the sordid details supplementing those provided by the national wire service. It seems that the local Michigan City newspaper had carried a small item noting the recent hiring of a new doctor at the prison. A local resident, a psychiatrist formerly with the Indiana Department of Mental Health, recognized the name and phoned his friend, the present Commissioner to tell him the news. The latter in turn immediately phoned the Indiana State Police and told them to pick him up on the old warrant that had been lying dormant for years. By the time I returned home, he was again in the Hospital for the Criminally Insane.

I was furious, and went to the commissioner's office to ask why he had taken such summary action. His lame reply was that there was a warrant and he was obligated to do so. It was an appalling excuse, for I learned later that the man for some unknown reason had a personal grudge against the doctor and seized the opportunity to take revenge.

To my great relief, my name had not been mentioned in the national wire service release I had seen in Washington nor had it appeared in the Indianapolis papers. Neither did Governor Bowen blame me in any way, but when he ordered the medical licensing board to fire their investigator for having failed to learn that there was an old arrest warrant for the doctor, the entire board resigned in protest.

Meanwhile, I visited the poor chap at the hospital, where he was again being treated very well by the guards who likewise felt that he had been treated malevolently. When I asked if there was anything I might be able to do to help him, he told me there was a lawyer in southern Indiana who had taken an interest in his case, and perhaps he might assist. I contacted the lawyer, who was appalled to hear what had happened and not long thereafter obtained his release.

50 – When prisoners take prisoners

The only other negative experience of note during my tenure with the Department of Correction occurred at the same prison. I had just arrived for a routine visit, stopping to greet the warden before proceeding to the medical unit. Our conversation was abruptly interrupted by an emergency phone call, informing him that two inmate patients had just taken my entire staff hostage by holding a home-made knife against the throat of one of them. The warden refused to let me accompany him as he rushed out of his office, where I sat for the next couple of hours waiting for the situation to be resolved. Fortunately, it all ended with all unharmed, their purpose having simply been to get some attention to their complaints about the prison food – doubtless the most frequent complaint in any prison. Needless to say, the menu did not change. Having often eaten the same food during my visits, I must admit that it was not exactly *cordon bleu* cuisine, but it was certainly tolerable – but perhaps not when you had it served to you day after day for years on end. More importantly, none of my new staff members considered leaving, having viewed the episode as being "all in a day's work" prison-wise.

On the positive side, it was overall a gratifying experience. By the time I decided I had done about all I could within the budget limitations of the DOC, I had been able to replace the foreign doctors of questionable ability, arranged for medical and surgical residents from the IU Medical Center to make regular visits to the various institutions, had been able to recruit a considerable number of full-time, well-qualified medical personnel, and had improved the pharmaceutical services.

I also was able to arrange for the parole of two inmates on the basis of their health problems, neither of whom should ever have been incarcerated in a maximum security prison. One was desperately in need of a gastric resection, the only way of dealing with his morbid obesity, and while one of my surgical colleagues at the I. U. Medical Center was willing to do the surgery gratis, he would do so only if the man were released from prison so that he could be closely followed thereafter.

The other was an older man with a heart problem, who should have been sent to the State Farm to serve his sentence for petty theft, but somehow ended up in the Michigan City prison. I arranged for him to work in the prison hospital, but he did not fare well in the prison environment, so I asked the parole board for his release. After he returned to Indianapolis to live with his daughter, I kept in touch with him, and things went well for a time. One day, however, about 4:30 in the afternoon I received a call from him after he had been drinking heavily, thanking me for all I had done for him, but letting me know that he had decided to kill his ex-wife! He told me he had a gun, and before I could get him to admit from where he was calling, he hung up.

Knowing where his wife lived in the nearby suburb of Lawrence, I immediately phoned the Lawrence police to give them the address, jumped in my car, and headed for the tavern on the east side of the city which I knew he frequented. Racing through the beginning of rush hour traffic, and just slowing down for red lights, I screeched up to the tavern, and was informed by the bartender that he had left five minutes earlier. When I pulled into the parking lot of the apartment complex where his wife lived, the only person in sight was a teenage boy. I asked him if anyone had driven in within the past five minutes, to which he replied, "No, but a police car came by a few minutes ago. They're parked there around the corner."

As I walked toward them, my quarry arrived, and when he got out of his car, three policeman tried to wrestle him to the ground. He was a powerful man, so I joined in the fray, sitting on one of his arms, while the officers sat on the other three limbs until they could force him into their car. I followed them to the station, where they placed him in a cell until they could arrange transport to the city hospital. My main concern was the gun he said he had, which fortunately was not on his person. If it were discovered, he would certainly have gone back to Michigan City.

Now he was sitting on the end of the bunk in his cell, banging his head on the wall. I asked the officers to let me in, assuring them he wouldn't hurt me, which they reluctantly did. Putting my arm around his shoulders, I asked in a subdued voice, "Where's the gun, John?" "In my car – but they'll never find it." "Where in the car, John? I need to get it so they won't find it." It was all to no avail, so I decided that my next task was to try to find the gun before the police did.

The car had meanwhile been towed to an impound lot in the city, so I went immediately there and used some harebrained explanation of why, as the prison medical director, I needed to look for something in the car. They let me in, and I spent the next half hour almost tearing it apart. There was no gun.

When he was released from the hospital a week later, I drove him to the impound lot, paid the storage charge, and sent him on his way. He later moved out of town, and with my departure overseas to a new assignment shortly thereafter, I completely lost track of him.

I also had the privilege of becoming acquainted first-hand with Charles Colson's Prison Fellowship ministry in its earliest stages, when I was invited to participate at an unusual luncheon in Washington. Having obtained permission from the Federal Bureau of Prisons for the two-week parole of a dozen carefully selected Christian inmates from various federal prisons, Colson had brought them to Washington for an intensive period of ministry training. They had arrived over the weekend and were being housed in a Washington church. On Monday noon, I joined Chuck and the group at the National Prayer Breakfast's Fellowship House for a kick-off luncheon meeting.

In human terms, they were a "motley crew" – convicted thieves, drug dealers, and the like. In heavenly terms, they were a marvelous group of born-again followers of Jesus Christ committed to working in their respective prisons to bring their fellow inmates into a personal relationship with their Lord. It was a heady experience!

I again had contact with Chuck some months later at the annual meeting of the American Correctional Association in Denver, where he was the speaker at a prayer breakfast arranged by the ACA. Later that day I joined him for lunch with a small group of businessmen at a downtown hotel, where he shared some of his experiences while serving with President Nixon.

The most poignant of these was a sequel to the incident he describes in *Born Again*, when his friend, Tom Phillips, president of the Raytheon Corporation introduced him to genuine Christian faith through C. S. Lewis's *Mere Christianity*. As the result of that encounter, Chuck committed his life to Jesus Christ, leading to his post-prison development of the ministry of Prison Fellowship, which has changed the lives of countless numbers of prison inmates throughout the world. Years after that incident, he commented to Tom one day at the National Prayer Breakfast in Washington that he marveled at the lives Tom must have touched after becoming a Christian himself, before he led Chuck into the Kingdom. There was a long pause before Tom replied.

"Chuck," he said, "during those many months between the time of my conversion and yours, I wanted desperately to share my faith with my colleagues, but somehow I just choked up whenever the opportunity presented itself – until that night you came to my house in Massachusetts. You see, Chuck – you were the first one!" What an incredible harvest the planting of a single seed can sometimes produce!

His initial exposure to the writings of C. S. Lewis has given Chuck a great love for his writings. As he noted in a recent letter in response to my having sent him a copy of *In Pursuit of C. S. Lewis*, "As I've skimmed through your bibliography I've been struck by the extraordinary breadth of Lewis' writings. As a writer myself, I can't imagine how anyone could produce as much material as he did, along with everything else that he spent his time on. Your book will be an extraordinary benefit to researchers and students of Lewis, which of course I consider myself in a modest way to be."

51 -- The search for David Zook

Although most of my international travel was medically related, at times I was able to perform useful service of a completely unrelated sort. One such memorable opportunity involved the search for information about a friend who was missing in action in Viet Nam during the war.

Major David Zook was an Air Force pilot whom we came to know in our Couples Fellowship at Fourth Presbyterian Church in Washington in 1966, just before moving to Indianapolis. Dave came from an Amish background, but felt led to serve his country by joining the U. S. Air Force, later becoming assistant professor of history at the Air Force Academy. As the war in Viet Nam heated up, he volunteered his services there, choosing not to pilot a combat aircraft but, rather, a light single-engine plane used to drop leaflets over Viet Cong territory.

Soon after leaving Washington we learned that he was missing in action. We contacted his wife, Pat, but she had no more information than that, despite many efforts on her own part and those of friends in the Pentagon to determine where and how he disappeared. In February 1968, on one of my early trips to Afghanistan, I decided to go to Saigon to see if I could learn anything about the incident from his commanding officer. It was not the most propitious time to visit that city, now partially occupied by the Viet Cong as the result of the Tet Offensive earlier that month, but it was a convenient time for me.

Fortunately, I still had a good contact there – one of my first volunteers in Project Viet Nam, Dr. Norman Hoover, an orthopedist from the Mayo Clinic who later became the in-country director of our program. When I arrived in Bangkok to connect with a flight to Saigon, I learned that Tan Son Nhut airport had just been closed because of an attack by the VC, so I hunkered down in a Bangkok hotel until the airport reopened. Rather than being an inconvenience, this enabled me to contact three of my classmates in the Teachers of Preventive Program at Harvard, each of whom was head of the Department of Preventive Medicine in his respective medical school in Bangkok. I received the royal treatment from Drs. Suksa, Mukta, and Papasarathorn, and within two days was able to continue my journey.

Tan Son Nhut airport had become what was very likely the busiest airport in the world, with an incredible array of aircraft of every description parked in its vast acreage – a choice target for the VC. Fortunately, they had been temporarily beaten off, with minimal damage to the buildings or the planes. I hailed a taxi, which took me to the hotel in which I thought he most likely was staying, and was informed by the desk clerk that he and his wife were in the dining room. I spotted them before he spotted me, walked up behind him, and said, "Hi!". He wasn't accustomed to having friends casually drop by from the States, so the look on his face was priceless. I joined them for dinner, and then explained my mission, which had become two-fold: one, to visit Dave's commanding officer at Bien Hoa air base, and two, to deliver a gift to a Vietnamese Army captain and his family from their daughter in Indianapolis.

The young lady was Nuong Vu, with whose family my good friends, Ed and Virginia Kornfeld had become best of friends when Captain Vu was one of the many foreign army officers studying at the U. S. Army Finance Center in Indianapolis. When he and his family had to return to Viet Nam, the Kornfelds invited him to leave his daughter with them – and later essentially adopted her, putting her through high school and university, and eventually seeing her happily married to a young Indianapolis man.

The latter errand was performed the next day, since Norm had a number of visits to make to Vietnamese families of doctors he had sent to the States for residency training through the U. S. Agency for International Development, by whom he was employed. He wanted to determine whether these families had suffered any casualties during the Tet offensive a week earlier, before sending messages to their stateside family members. When we located the street on which Nuong's family lived, he said he would park the car at the beginning of their dead-end street, pointing to a huge stadium midway down the block. "There are still some VC holed up in there, which haven't yet been flushed out, and I'd rather not park at the deep end of the street, between there and your friend's house – if you don't mind."

My walk down the street was uneventful, but when Nuong's mother opened the door in response to my knock and I told her why I was there, she ushered me hastily inside and quickly closed the door. "You shouldn't have come – but we're happy that you did." Captain Vu was not at home, having not been allowed to leave his office in downtown Saigon for the past two weeks because of the hostilities, and after a quick cup of tea, she hurried me on my way with tears in her eyes. Norm was waiting patiently, if somewhat nervously, at the end of the street, and was pleased to welcome me back.

The following day we drove to Bien Hoa, about 20 miles from Saigon, using his personal car rather than his official vehicle. "We're less likely to get shot at in a civilian car," he explained. The drive to the airbase was uneventful, but we had some difficulty finding the main gate. Bien Hoa was a huge facility, and had been under sporadic attack during the previous two weeks, but we were surprised to see so many planes parked along the roads on which we were skirting the base – and still no main gate. Finally, we came across a couple of American airmen working in a ditch, who directed us thereto. When we found the main gate, we were shocked to learn that we were *inside* it, not outside. Somehow we had entered and been driving around inside the edge of the base for the past fifteen minutes. We never learned how that could have happened at a military establishment that was supposedly under the tightest security.

The colonel in command of Dave's unit was very cordial when I explained why I had come. "I took command after Major Zook's time so I never met him, but I understand he was a fine pilot and a real gentleman." Walking to a file cabinet, he pulled out a folder and handed it to me. "Here's the whole file. Have a seat and look it over."

The story seemed clear enough. While dropping leaflets in Binh Dong province from his single-engine U10B, Dave's plane was struck by an Air Force cargo plane. The pilot had not seen the plane but felt a bump, and a crew member reported seeing a small plane spiraling into the jungle. A search team was immediately dispatched to the site, but saw only the wreckage of the plane before their helicopter was fired upon and had to leave. An hour later another team was sent. The plane appeared to be empty, but there was no sign of a parachute, so they concluded he had been thrown from the plane and very likely died from the impact. The jungle was too dense to give much hope of finding his body, and in any case was swarming with VC, so they too had to leave the area without absolutely determining his fate.

Upon my return I met with Pat in a restaurant in Dayton, near her home, and sadly delivered my report. Not until I visited the Vietnam Veterans Memorial in Washington many years later did I learn that he had been officially declared dead, his name being inscribed thereon. Much more recently I learned that the Air Force eventually promoted him to colonel, and in 1978 declared him "presumed dead".

52 – In the footsteps of Lawrence of Arabia

I had been involved with the prison system for the better part of two years when I again received a call from Dean Steve Beering. He had been asked by an Indiana alumnus, head of a medical consulting firm in Boston, if there was a faculty member he could recommend for a one-year assignment in Saudi Arabia. I gratefully accepted his offer to grant me a one-year leave of absence if I were interested and headed for Boston to learn the details of the job. I felt no more could be accomplished in my dealing with the Department of Correction bureaucracy and was ready for a change.

A five-man team was being assembled by a group at the Harvard School of Public Health to advise the dean of a new medical school in Dammam, on the east coast of the country. I would be the only academic member of the team, with responsibility for curriculum development. It was not an area in which I felt particularly competent, having no direct experience therewith. However, they had already recruited the other four members of the team, three of whom were already in country, and they were getting desperate. Just as I had previously been selected to fill a position in India years before for which the State Department had long sought a candidate, University Associates, Inc., was willing to overlook my lack of impeccable credentials. After all, as they pointed out, I had spent four years being educated through the curriculum of our foremost medical school, and more recently had at least had some exposure to the curriculum of Indiana University School of Medicine. They even offered to send me to Saudi Arabia to have a look at the situation firsthand. That year proved to be one of the most interesting I've ever experienced.

Thus, in May 1977 I found myself in the coastal city of Al-Khobar, a few miles from Dammam, where University Associates maintained a guest house. The medical school was only a few miles away, and Al-Khobar was next door to Dhahran, the gated community of Aramco, the Arabian-American Oil Company, which offered many amenities to American residents of the nearby communities – including the only church services available in that part of the country. The amenities offered by University Associates were also considerable – an apartment of one's choice anywhere in the city, a new American car of one's choice (or reasonably so), a fine cost-of-living bonus, travel for all of one's children to and from Saudi Arabia twice during the year at the time of one's choice, and enough vacation time to see much of that part of the world. In my case, it also provided the opportunity to return to the States twice during the year to interview prospective faculty. It was certainly appeared to be a comfortable situation, despite the negative climate.

I was eager to take the job, and before returning to Indianapolis to pick up Pat and Wende (who would be with us for the summer), I went house-hunting. The choices here were not as appealing as one might have hoped, and I examined possibilities ranging from a glorified trailer park (with very luxurious mobile homes) to a large suite in the only hotel of any size in town. Rents were atrocious ($3000 monthly and up for an unfurnished 2-bedroom apartment), but the company was paying the bill, so that was no great consideration. I finally settled on a two-story building still under construction that would house two families, one upstairs and one down. The landlord, an officer in the Saudi Arabian navy, assured me he could have it finished within 2-3 weeks.

Pan American was not yet flying into Dhahran airport, so I had to fly to the island nation of Bahrain, only 25 miles away, to catch a flight to Boston for final briefing and contract signing. Since the tour of duty was only for a year, we decided to simply leave our house as it was, except for a few smaller pieces of furniture and other more important items we would hate to lose to fire or theft. The boys could then come home from Bloomington, where both were at Indiana University, anytime they desired. We contracted with a 15-year-old neighbor boy in the next block to cut the lawn and gave him a key so that he could check the interior of the house from time to time. He took this latter responsibility very seriously, as we learned from Ted and Jack, going into the house almost every day and opening and closing various curtains at random to give the appearance of an occupied dwelling to anyone who might be "casing the joint". Upon our return we learned that there had been two burglaries in the neighborhood during that year, and he was very proud, as his father told us, that *his* house was not one of them.

I was expected back in Saudi Arabia within 2-3 weeks, and reluctant to take Pat and Wende back with me to a possibly unfinished flat, I decided to take them only as far as Europe, to a place from which they could get a direct flight to Dhahran. I asked a friend whose company did business in Europe if he could suggest a suitable place to park them for a couple of weeks. He suggested a beautiful little village in Austria, on the German border just west of Salzburg, where British friends of his ran a guest house to accommodate Christian workers going to and from Easter Europe, where they ministered secretly to the needs of the evangelical churches there. I immediately phoned the friend, Brian Bounds, who with his wife Gwynne also frequently made similar visits to the nearby Communist countries, and he said he would be delighted to have them.

Grossgmain was indeed a beautiful village, in as idyllic a hilly setting as any I'd ever seen. Brian met us at the airport in Munich, 60 miles west, and I spent a day or two there before he drove me back to Munich. Ted and Jack still had some classes to attend, but they would try to visit us later in the summer.

It turned out to be a wise move, for soon after my arrival back in Al-Khobar I found my naval officer landlord on his knees polishing the terrazzo floors and cursing out the contractor. A month passed before the flat was ready for occupancy, but I had meanwhile called Pat to come ahead. They could stay in the hotel with me until the place was available, and we could meanwhile be buying furniture, appliances, and a car – all provided by my employer. It was a pleasurable undertaking, despite limited availability of furniture and some household goods, depending upon what had been imported, and by the time we moved in, we had a rather luxurious abode. Connecting American-made appliances to European outlets sometimes posed a challenge, most notably that of hooking up the American threads on the washer to the European threads on the water pipe. However, I managed to jerry-rig a succession of two or three "adapters" obtained by scouring several hardware stores, immensely pleased at my cleverness. That air of confidence lasted only a few weeks, however, when I got up in the middle of the night to investigate what sounded like running water. Swinging out of bed, I found myself standing on very soggy carpeting, soon discovering the source of the moisture to be the laundry room down the hall. I had not had the foresight to turn off the water pressure at the pipe after each washing, and the constant pressure had eventually burst my brilliant piece of plumbing. It was not possible to take up the four rooms of inundated carpeting, since the carpet-layers had simply glued it to the terrazzo floor, so we spent all that day laying down towels, walking on them, drying them in the electric dryer, and thus using them over and over. Fortunately, it's a very dry country, and the air conditioners quickly removed the rest of the moisture.

Later in the year, when I had returned from a one-week recruiting mission and left Pat to enjoy Indianapolis for a couple more weeks before she returned, I came home to a very hot apartment, reeking with the most vile odor ever to assault my nostrils. Although I had been careful to personally pay my monthly electric bill at the electric department just before leaving, some clerk had failed to enter the payment properly and they had summarily shut off our power a week earlier. The temperature had risen to something in excess of 120 degrees, and the full load of meat in the freezer compartment at the top of our refrigerator had been reduced to a vile mass of goo, much of it running down into the refrigerator compartment.

With considerable difficulty I managed to push the machine to the kitchen door leading to a balcony, trundled it over the threshold, and cleaned it out. I then left it there with the door open, went into town to buy a small fridge for temporary use, hoping both it and the entire apartment would be odor-free by the time Pat returned.

53 – Hazards at home and on the road

Other than those two incidents, our domestic tranquility was marred only by a mysterious current leak in our bathroom fixtures, resulting in a mild shock when one would turn the water on or off while sitting in the tub. Given the fact that we were wired with 220 volt current, this was no small concern. An American engineer at the university kindly came over to investigate the problem, but could not identify its source, suggesting only that we refrain from touching the faucets while immersed in the tub. Thankfully no one was electrocuted during our tenure. The entire building, it seems, was a potential death chamber, since the electrical system had not been grounded. He noted that we might consider having it grounded by driving a long copper rod deep into the sand adjacent to the house, but because it would be in sand which would not retain moisture, we would have to water the site several times a day. We decided to take our chances.

Buying a car was an interesting experience. One Saudi businessman, whose Harvard MBA certificate was proudly displayed behind his desk, had a monopoly on car dealerships in Al-Khobar, handling General Motors and Toyota products for the most part. He cordially received me and one of my team-mates into his office, and showed us brochures of his wares. Lest we stretch our employer's budget too far, we each opted for a 1977 Chevrolet Caprice, complete with every conceivable option, that being how he ordered them from America. When we asked to see a model, however, he told us that he didn't keep any on hand, but we were welcome to go to Dammam and make our choice from the huge lot near the docks, where they were stored after being unloaded. This we elected to do, finding a vast array of new vehicles completely coated with sand that clung to the waterproofing with which they had been treated to protect them from ocean saltwater during their voyage. While it was not too difficult to determine the color of the bodies, only by scraping off the windows could one get some idea of the interior. The Cadillacs, Buicks, and Oldsmobiles were very attractive, but we had agreed with our team chief to get Chevrolets, so we wandered throughout the enormous expanse of desert to scout out what was available. We both liked white with blue interior, and so as not to be confused as to which was whose when both were later parked together at the university or elsewhere, he chose one with a single strip of side trim, while I found one without. It's marvelous to see highly-educated, well-disciplined adults come to such decisions on such weighty matters without a hint of rancor.

Despite intensive heat and penetrating dust, the Chevy Caprice performed so well in the nearly 10,000 miles we put on it that it was our choice for a new car when we returned to Indianapolis. Our longest trip was to Riyadh, some 300 miles away, over a narrow two-lane highway that snaked its way through the desert with the main scenic attraction being the wreckage of cars that never made it. Driving in Saudi Arabia was a real hazard. Every Saudi had a car by then, although there was no evidence that any had ever been given any formal instruction in piloting their dangerous weapons. They had little disregard for the rules of the road, and it was not at all uncommon to see a car speed through an intersection at which the light had been red for several seconds. Friends who had come upon a horrific accident just after it happened reported seeing bodies strewn all over the road. Instead of towing away destroyed cars it was the practice of the police to simply push or tow them on to the median strip, if there was one, or the sidewalk at the point where the accident occurred as a reminder to drivers to drive more carefully. It didn't seem to have much effect.

If the desert in that part of Saudi Arabia had consisted of great, shifting sand dunes, the drive to Riyadh would have been a scenic one. Instead, the desert was nothing more than rock-strewn dirt with occasional clumps of weeds and wrecked motor vehicles to break up the monotony. On the return trip after dark, we were proceeding down a long stretch of hill, with a long line of trucks ascending it. Far in the distance, one of them was in our lane, trying to pass. I continued downhill at about 50 mph, assuming he would pull back in line long before we reached the same spot. He did not, and I was forced to swerve off the road on to the rock- and wreckage-strewn shoulder at full speed, praying that we could get back on before careening into an obstruction. Our guardian angel did double duty on that occasion, and we managed to make it back on to the pavement unscathed.

Wende, by then a sophomore at Taylor University in Upland, Indiana, came out to spend the month of January 1978 with us, accepting the offer of a 7th grade teacher at the Aramco school to be her assistant that month. At the Friday morning church service we attended in the gymnasium of the Aramco school she met a young English lad several years her senior, who invited her to a social function of the young adults in the church. They quickly became good friends, and he began taking her out in the evening to such weekly functions. These were unsettling moments for me, for the thought of my precious daughter being exposed to the hazards of the highway at night made me uneasy the entire time she was absent. As the evening wore on and it seemed likely she might soon return, I would go up on the roof and pace around, peering over the edge and down the street every few minutes, hoping to see the lights of their car and praying each time a car came along that it was theirs. Only when one finally pulled into our driveway did I bow my head in thanks.

Women were not allowed to drive a car in Saudi Arabia, and the young Saudis who cruised around town took delight in coming as close as they dared to any foreign woman walking along the edge of the road, there being few sidewalks in the town. On one occasion I had stopped at the edge of the road to let Pat out, so that she could walk across the street to a shop. As she was about to cross the street in front of me, I saw in the rear view mirror a car a block away suddenly speed up, having obviously seen what she was about to do. She jumped back, these maniacs laughing as they flew past.

In Riyad I saw religious police going through the open-air market during the mid-day call to prayer, banging their sticks on the counters of merchants who were a bit slow in shutting down for the prayer time. However, merchants in shops in the rest of the city did not seem to be bothered with this, for I do not recall seeing any close during prayer time. When I returned to Saudi Arabia with a consulting group several years later, however, a marked change was seen. I was in the Pan Am office checking on my onward itinerary one day when the call to prayer could be heard from the loud speakers in mosques throughout the city. The manager quickly herded the customers outside, locked the door, and stood with us in the entry way until 15 minutes or so had passed, after which he unlocked the door and resumed business.

During my many visits to Afghanistan in the '60s and '70s I had occasionally seen workers on construction projects or other outdoor employment stop work at noon, unroll their prayer rugs, and kneel to pray wherever they were. By contrast, I do not recall having seen anyone in Baghdad in 1967 praying outside when the call to prayer could be heard.

If one does a Google search for "adhan", the Islamic call to prayer, all manner of web sites are found which offer assistance in praying to Muslims in non-Muslim countries, including how to know that one is facing Mecca from any point on the earth!

54 – Life under the Saudi version of *shariah*

Criminal justice in the kingdom was something one hoped he would never have to face. For example, the driver of a car striking a pedestrian, even if the pedestrian had heedlessly walked in front of him, might be immediately thrown in jail, without benefit of bail, until his case was decided. Punishment for capital crimes under *shariah* (Islamic law) was swift and harsh. Our friends in Riyadh, Howard and Nora Norrish, lived just down the street from the mosque in front of which public executions were regularly carried out. Although they never desired to see one, some of their visitors did attend and came back with a description of the procedure. A police vehicle with one or more condemned prisoners would pull up to the mosque on Friday some time before prayers ended, and when the men came out of the mosque to be witnesses, a prisoner would be dragged from the vehicle, his head placed on the block, and the executioners sword would quickly dispatch him. If the prisoner was a woman condemned to die for adultery, she would be placed upright in a large sack tied at the top, and the men would stone her to death. Without a doubt, such severe justice was at least somewhat of a deterrent to crime.

One of our more bizarre experiences involved dealing with the dead body of one of our next door neighbors. The adjoining two-story house was occupied by a team of engineers who both lived and did their desk work there. At about 4:00 one morning I was awakened by frantic knocking on our apartment door, to be greeted by the distraught manager of the group, the body of one of his team members having just been found slumped in the doorway of their apartment, presumably dead of a heart attack. The dead man's roommate had been awakened in the wee hours of the morning when his friend complained of feeling ill and had gone downstairs for some fresh air, and when he failed to return after some time, the roommate went looking for him. Fortunately it was still dark, and any passersby had presumably not seen the body.

The body had been placed out of sight in the back of one of their vehicles, and after confirming the death and not having the foggiest idea of how the Saudi authorities would deal with such a situation, I decided the best thing was to move it to the morgue of one of the private hospitals where I knew the director, hoping the vehicle wouldn't be stopped in a routine police check – an unlikely event in any case at that hour of the morning. I led the way in my car, and had them park the other vehicle out of sight on the hospital grounds while I negotiated a transfer with the doctor on duty, which he graciously arranged. In no way did I want to be involved in what might follow, so the director of the hospital kindly kept me out of the picture, as did the head of the engineering team. Being an alien in that strange country, I was loathe to take any chances.

Opportunities for Christian worship in the kingdom were severely limited, but were more readily available in our area because of a number of special privileges afforded those living in Dhahran, the gated Aramco village. In addition to the general Protestant service, there were Anglican, Roman Catholic, and Mormon services. Ours was on Friday morning in the gym, and when it was over, the bulletins were shredded if one chose not to take one home, and every trace of a Christian service (podium, hymn books, piano, etc.) had to be returned to the storage closet, lest any Muslim lad using the gym afterward might be exposed to them. Down in Jeddah, prior to our time Protestant services had been permitted in the compound of the Raytheon Corporation, which managed missile sites for the Saudi military, but had to be transferred to the auditorium of the American Embassy when local religious officials closed down the service at Raytheon.

The only other Christian service allowed was that in Riyadh, but it was eventually closed down and worship had to take place in private homes. The Easter sunrise service we attended in Riyadh was particularly memorable. Held in the parking lot behind an apartment building where a number of foreigners lived, we sang quietly and prayed together as the sun came up. Looking over our shoulders at the rising sun, we saw a cross silhouetted against the sky – a utility pole at the back of the apartment complex. As is still the case in many Muslim countries, the only way in which the good news of the gospel can be passed on by Christian expatriates is on a person-to-person basis with the closest of non-Christian friends or colleagues.

Among the special privileges afforded Aramco employees was a movie theater; a shop where one could buy ham, bacon, and other pork products; and the right to make wine and beer or even distill hard liquor in one's home. This last, however, had produced so many accidents when stills exploded in bathrooms that all the newer houses being constructed had a separate outside room for that purpose, connected to the house by an overhead duct carrying electric wires and air conditioning. Foreign women were allowed to drive within the village itself, so when Wende was with us, we would sometimes go over to Dhahran just so they could cruise around the village behind the wheel. And although Dhahran was the only place in the kingdom where pork products could legally be sold, and only to non-Muslim employees of Aramco, a rather interesting product was available in one of the local supermarkets. If one went up to the meat counter and asked for Polish beef, the attendant would reach under the counter and surreptitiously bring out a foil-wrapped loaf bearing a striking resemblance to good Polish ham, quickly slice off the requested quantity and as quickly wrap it and replace the mother lode under the counter. Similarly, if one wanted an alcohol-based cough syrup, it could be obtained at certain pharmacies, where it was hidden in a locked cupboard.

The Saudis also had imposed a ban on a long list of products of American companies which did major business in Israel, including, for example, all Ford automobiles, anything bearing a Sears Roebuck label, and Coca Cola. Americans headed for Saudi Arabia were therefore advised to remove any Sears labels from their clothing and not to bring any appliances with the Sears name. In Riyadh, I was once taken to the Intercontinental Hotel by my American host to see a large, new car belonging to the Saudi owner of the hotel, which he always parked near the lobby entrance. "Tell me, Ed – what kind of car is that?" "Why, it's obviously a new Lincoln Continental – but I thought Ford products were banned." "They are. But now look at the hood ornament and the wheel covers." I did – and they read "Cadillac"! And when I first drank Kaki Cola which was bottled in Saudi Arabia, its bottle strangely resembled that of Coca Cola, and the Arabic script thereon appeared almost identical to that I'd seen on Coca Cola bottles elsewhere in the Middle East. Any American tasting it would immediately recognize that it was the real thing, contrary to local belief. If you're a Saudi and sufficiently grease the palms of the appropriate government officials, forbidden fruit can miraculously turn into grapes, oranges, or whatever.

55 – A delinquent dean, a welcome change, and a strange interlude

Working with colleagues from many different countries, there as yet being few Saudis sufficiently qualified for major teaching positions, was a pleasure. Working with Dean Torki Al-Torki was not always so. The contract with University Associates had been negotiated with the president of the university, and it appeared that the dean had agreed to it largely for benefits other than the personnel involved. He was cordial enough, but rarely seemed to be around to listen to our counsel. If he wasn't in Riyadh on "business", he spent much of his time over in the girl's classrooms, being the only male allowed on that side of the premises. The girls were taught by female staff and the boys by male staff. The buildings were one-story prefabricated structures, connected to one another by enclosed walkways. When the girls occupied the laboratory facilities in the center of the complex, a sign was posted on the outside of the door leading into the lab from the boys' side: "In use by female students" – in Arabic and English. Thus the boys were never to lay eyes on the girls when the latter were not wearing their burkahs.

My office was adjacent to that of the dean, both of them on the boys' side. Female students occasionally came to the dean's office for various reasons, but they had to be completely shrouded from head to foot while entering or leaving, and any boys who might be nearby were expected to divert their gaze. Girls were also seen in the dean's office during admission interviews, in which the dean would invite me to participate, so he and I were the only males on the staff who ever saw girls with their veils removed. Some of the girls appeared to be somewhat nervous in removing their veils in my presence, but conducting an interview through a piece of cloth would have been as impersonal as that of a priest hearing confession. This strict separation of the sexes was also to be the means of protecting the integrity of examinations, since both sexes didn't always take the exams at the same time. However, one day a girl came in to complain that the brother of one of her classmates, both of whom lived at home, had apparently passed on key questions on an examination he had already taken, and she was thus unfairly able to get a much higher grade.

My impression of the dean's relative indifference to our advice was confirmed when we had a visitor from the medical school in Edinburgh, Scotland. He had met with the dean while I was out, and when he came into my office later, he exclaimed, "I recognized that guy! He had been sent to our hospital for postgraduate training several years ago, but spent most of his time in the library, having made it clear to everyone that he already knew everything they were supposed to teach him."

The dean's inadequacies were also apparent to the president of the university, and not long before I left he was "moved upstairs" to a vice-presidency to make room for a much more qualified person. Dr. Tafiq Tamimi had been chief of surgery at the large Saudi military hospital in Abha, in the southern part of the country, and was a refreshing replacement. When he told me he had spent several years at the University of Maryland hospital in Baltimore under the tutelage of a Dr. John Hankins, we immediately hit it off when I told him that John was an old friend of mine, who had worked in Afghanistan for several years. My only regret was that I hadn't much time left to work with him.

He was a devout Muslim, and would excuse himself if we were together when the call to prayer came three times during the day. One evening, when he had taken me out to dinner, he told me that his friend, the president of the university, had frequently prevailed upon him to come to Dammam. But he was happy where he was, and repeatedly resisted the call. Finally, however, he had no choice, he said, having been ordered to do so. "We Muslims have a special prayer to which we expect an answer, and I prayed for an answer as to what I should do – and got it." I told him I had assumed he meant the order had come from King Fahd, but now I realized that it had come from the King of Kings. He nodded firmly, obviously pleased with the comment. I had not yet learned enough about Islam to know that Allah was not the same God I worshipped.

Having a Dean not interested in taking advice had its advantages. One of the more interesting interludes during our time in Saudi involved my participation in The Sixth International Conference on the Unity of the Sciences in Los Angeles in November 1977. Shortly before leaving home, I had been asked to chair a panel on "Health Care As A Global Problem: Social and Behavioral Aspects", but declined because I would not be in the country at the time. The sponsor assured me that would be no problem. They would pay all the expenses for both me and my wife to come from overseas.

I was somewhat chary about accepting the invitation because of the nature of its sponsorship – the International Cultural Foundation affiliated with the Unification Church of The Rev. Sun Myung Moon. The program featured a large number of distinguished scientists and scholars, some of whom I knew well, including Dr. Claude Villee, chairman of biochemistry at Harvard; John Karefa-Smart, assistant director-general of the World Health Organization; and one of my own panelists, Dr. Elizabeth Kubler-Ross, the Swiss psychiatrist whose book, *On Death and Dying*, was instrumental in the development of the hospice movement in America. Most notable, however, was Charles Habib Malik, the eminent Lebanese statesman and one of the founders of the United Nations, whom I knew to be a committed Christian. If these people had no qualms about the sponsorship, I saw no reason for not accepting the honor.

In all honesty, I had no idea as to why they chose me to chair a panel, but since I wasn't to be a speaker and thereby reveal my ignorance of the subject, I looked forward to the adventure. Pat and I had the great pleasure of becoming personally acquainted with Dr. and Mrs. Malik during the conference, and I was later privileged to hear him as the main speaker at a conference in California at the former headquarters of Campus Crusade for Christ.

An amusing incident took place in the hotel elevator at one point. Pat was headed for our room on the 8th floor, while I had to get off on the 3rd floor to check out the meeting room. We were discussing something or other as we entered the elevator on the ground floor, continuing our conversation until I stepped out. After the door closed, Pat overheard one lady comment to another: "Did you notice that Saudi gentleman who just got off? He spoke perfect English!" Although the name badges of guests such as Pat bore only their name, those of us on the program featured a small flag and the name of the country from which we had come in large letters. She obviously hadn't noticed my name.

As the result of my initial involvement with the International Cultural Foundation, I was invited to participate in their Seventh International Conference in Seoul, Korea. However, while attending the first planning session in the hotel owned by the foundation in New York, I left the meeting at one point to make a phone call, and on my return noticed a marker over the doorway of one of the rooms. It read "Chapel", so I decided to have a look. Around the wall were cushions, and at the front of the room was a table-like furnishing resembling an altar. Behind this was an enormous floor-to-ceiling colored photograph of Sun Myung Moon and his wife in traditional Korean garb. A chill ran up my spine, and I returned to the meeting with no intention of following through on the invitation to the Seoul conference, except to write a letter of regret as soon as I returned home. At the Campus Crusade conference I mentioned to Dr. Malik what I had seen and why it caused me to withdraw from the Seoul conference. He confided in me that he, too, had refused the invitation, having second thoughts about being even tangentially involved with something related to the Moon cult.

56 – Rank hath its privilege

The year in Saudi Arabia also afforded opportunity for travel to Pakistan to recruit faculty members for the medical school. Placing advertisements in major newspapers and visiting friends in the medical schools in Karachi, I later returned with Dean Al-Torki to interview those who had responded.

A more interesting trip, however, was to Iran for a WHO Conference on Medical Education in the Middle East, in Teheran. Pat had never been in Iran, so we decided to make a brief holiday trip of it. We spent two days in Shiraz, where I visited the Dean of Pahlavi University Faculty of Medicine, whom I had met while at the AAMC. A day tour to the ancient site of Persepolis, where Darius the Great built his magnificent palace complex around 500 B.C., completed our stay, and we flew to Teheran, 400 miles to the north, that evening.

We had been unable to book a hotel there, so at 11:00 p.m., with the help of an English-speaking taxi driver, we began our search for accommodations. After many rejections, at one stop he came out of the lobby of a small hotel to inform us that he had found a place. Eagerly we went to have a look – having already learned that one doesn't take a room sight unseen in most of the establishments we had tried. The desk clerk led us through the lobby, outside through the back door, into an apartment complex across an alley, and up several flights of stairs to one of the apartments. Opening the door, he noted that it wasn't exactly a private room, but it was all he could offer. "Semi-private" would not quite have described it either. In the living room, at least half a dozen men were sleeping on the floor. We thanked him, and after explaining that it wasn't quite what my wife could accept, we dragged ourselves on our way.

It was by then 4:00 a.m., and if we didn't find a place within the next hour, we would have been tempted to hire his cab for the next several hours and curl up in the back seat. Several stops later, he came out and apologetically announced that they had a room but a large bribe would be required by the desk clerk. In desperation we agreed to the terms, but by the time we paid off our driver, there was not enough for the bribe. My passionate plea for permission to take the room and return later in the day to pay him his due finally overcame his disappointed resistance to giving us the room, and we staggered up the stairs to our quarters. It was a private room, to be sure, but in fact a conference room into which two single beds had been shoved amidst tables, chairs, and the remains of the day's meeting – empty glasses, empty water and juice bottles, etc. To us, however, it was a bit of heaven. There was, however, no lock on the door, so after shoving a table piled with chairs against the door, we bedded down for what little remained of the night.

With the help of an Iranian friend living in Tehran, whom we had been reluctant to phone in the wee hours of the morning, we found comfortable accommodations the next morning at a hotel across from the American embassy. We could not possibly have imagined what was to take place at the embassy only a year later.

Arriving at the conference center, to my pleasant surprise I immediately bumped into my old AAMC boss, Henry Van Zile Hyde, and we sat together through the entire meeting. Also present were many old friends from Afghanistan and Iraq, among them Kader Baha, dean of the medical school in Jalalabad; Ghazanfar, professor of biochemistry at Kabul University; and Dauod Sani, dean of the new medical school in Basra, Iraq.

At the close of the morning session, it was announced that some of the delegates were invited that evening to the royal palace to meet His Imperial Majesty the Shah of Iran, Mohammed Reza Shah Pahlavi. We had seen his life-size portrait in living color wherever we had gone in Shiraz and Teheran, so I looked forward to meeting the real McCoy. By the next morning, the official photographer for the conference had posted individual photos of each of us so honored, shaking hands with His Excellency. I used to have that photo on display in my office at Indiana University, until I learned that our Iranian students despised the man – a feeling shared by most of the young people in Iran, which led to his downfall in 1979.

We also had the pleasure of meeting the ruler of Saudi Arabia, King Fahd bin Abdul Aziz, when he came to King Faisal University. ("bin" means "son of", the Hebrew equivalent of "bar", as in Bartimaeus, the son of Timaeus, one of the two blind beggars of Jericho of whom we read in Mark 10:46 and Matthew 20:30.) A huge luncheon for the entire faculty was the highlight of that affair, with all of us seated at a line of contiguous tables about 100 feet long set up in the main corridor of one of the buildings. Each group of four, two on each side of the table, were served a variety of delicacies, in the midst of which was placed an enormous silver platter containing a bed of rice on which an entire sheep (devoid of skin and fleece, and well-done) rested comfortably on its back. I and my fellow Westerners eschewed the delicacy of the eyeballs and tore into the carcass with the only instruments provided – our hands. We soon found this required cooperation from one's counterparts across the table, the two on one side each firmly gripping a leg while two opposite pulled chunks of flesh off the bones. (Such meals, we found, were standard fare at Saudi gatherings, referred to irreverently by the outsiders as "goat grabs".)

Throughout the meal we noticed a long line of what we presumed to be servants standing in a row behind us. However, they seemed to have no function to perform, and only when we all arose after having satiated ourselves did we realize that they were the second contingent – persons of lower rank who then eagerly took our places before the piles of leftover debris. A somewhat similar situation occurred when Pat and I were guests of our Saudi friend in Riyadh. On our last day he had invited a number of male friends to a lunch of similar proportions, served on a tablecloth covering the carpet in his dining room. After lunch, the men sat in another room for a chat, and after a couple of hours we had to leave for Al Khobar. As we drove away, I asked Pat if she had lunch as well, having not seen her during the entire proceedings. "Oh, yes." "Did you eat in the kitchen with Mrs. Rasheed and the cook?" "Oh, no. We ate in the dining room." "In the dining room?" "Yes, in the dining room – right after you men vacated it." "Well, what did you ladies have to eat?" "The same thing you did." "Oh, you mean you went to all the trouble of cleaning up our mess and then setting it up again for your lunch?" "Oh, no. We ate what you left." So much for the status of women in that part of the world!

57 – "Vanity of vanities, saith the Preacher; all is vanity."

By the time our year was drawing to a close, the president of the university – probably on advice from Dean Tamimi – decided the contract with University Associates for International Health had contributed about as much as the medical school needed at that stage in its development. He informed Roger that it would not be renewed at the end of the second year. Two of us on the team had no intention of extending our stay, and were pleased to move on to something that might better utilize our expertise. My return home called for a difficult decision, however.

By the time I reached my mid-40s the Brown family DNA had wreaked its toll on what was once a handsome head of hair, and I was now obviously a clone of my father and paternal grandfather. On my first trip to Milan to visit a friend while living in Switzerland, I recalled that the Italians were known for their construction of what were now euphemistically referred to as hairpieces. I asked the hotel clerk for the Italian word for wigs, checked the yellow pages for listings of the purveyors of same, and chose the nearest one. No point in missing the opportunity to thwart the processes of nature and thus restore one's youth! With much fanfare I was ushered into a barber's chair, and multiple measurements made of my skull. I was then told to report back in three weeks for the final fitting.

Three weeks later to the day I reappeared in this house of magic and departed a new man. Such a glorious acquisition! I then picked up the airline tickets at American Express that would get Wende and Pat home from Geneva (for some odd reason they were two-thirds the price demanded in Geneva), that being the excuse I had given her for my trip. It was late at night when I arrived home, and Pat was asleep, so I crawled quietly into bed so as not to disturb her. One can imagine her shock upon awakening to find a hirsute stranger in bed with her. I'm not at all sure that she accepted this new look, but she didn't insist on my consigning it to the trash can. Wende found it amusing.

I wore a hairpiece for the next three years but gave it up temporarily while enduring the heat of Saudi Arabia. On our first trip home, however, I suddenly panicked as we finished the check-in process – I had forgotten the thing! Despite Pat's pleas to stay calm and proceed to the boarding area, I raced out of the airport, grabbed a cab, waved a large bill at the driver to encourage the utmost speed, returned with the prize shoved in my pocket, and ran to the boarding area. It was empty, so I dashed for the plane, where Pat was sitting in the front seat by the door, frantically looking for me. But I made it, thereby avoiding the acute embarrassment of appearing naked among our friends in Indianapolis.

On our final return from Saudi Arabia we arrived home unannounced in the middle of the week. Having become accustomed to the real Ed Brown during the past year, she prevailed upon me to remain that way now that we were home again. "When we get to church tomorrow, no one will really notice the change. They'll just think you must be cutting your hair differently, or some such thing." Nonsense! I avoided the issue until the last minute the next morning. "I've got to put it on!" "No, you don't! Let's get in the car or we'll be late. No one will notice." In a state of utter agony I departed.

The first person to greet us was Russ Blowers, our senior minister. With his usual crushing hand grip he exclaimed, "Hey! It's great to see you back! But where's your hairpiece? You looked great in it!" So much for Pat's harebrained theory! But I was now committed, and haven't worn it since, except to amuse the grandchildren from time to time.

I now decided to look into the possibility of getting back into teaching. The Department of Preventive Medicine had long ceased to exist, its programs having been absorbed by a variety of other departments, leaving no substantial body of curricular material into which my own background easily fit. The Division of Allied Health Sciences was certainly a possibility, but while I was exploring that with the director of the division, another opportunity presented itself.

When I left for Saudi Arabia, responsibility for international students on the Indianapolis campus was transferred to the Office of Student Affairs, and since I was the sole person in the Division of International Affairs, that entity had ceased to exist. During my absence, the university had brought in an outside consultant to evaluate its overall handling of the special needs of its international students, so I called upon the vice-chancellor for our campus to learn what this had produced. He gave me a copy of the report, asking me to study it and then come back with my reactions.

In recent years the Indianapolis campuses of both major state universities, Indiana University and Purdue University, had been combined into a single administrative entity, Indiana University—Purdue University at Indianapolis (IUPUI), with an Indiana University vice-chancellor at the helm. Visa matters for IU international students were handled by Bloomington and those for Purdue students by West Lafayette, Purdue's home campus. With the increasing enrollment of students from overseas at IUPUI, the report recommended that these functions also be combined into an office on the Indianapolis campus. I told our vice-chancellor that I agreed completely with that recommendation, having often experienced problems in dealing with the Bloomington office in particular. He, too, felt this was a necessary change, but as yet no steps had been taken to open such an office. After a moment's pause, he said, "Say, why don't you consider doing that? You're the only one on this campus who's had any experience with these matters, you're already on the payroll, and our new administration building for IUPUI would be an ideal location for the office."

It wasn't exactly what I had in mind for my next assignment, but he was certainly correct, so I told him I would think about it – and the more I did, the more interesting the possibility became. I would do it only for a year or so until I could train someone to take over and get back into more medically-related responsibilities. That was late in 1978, and six years later I was still involved full-time with international students! Although I had a part-time assistant from time to time, the university had never seen fit to assign the full-time person I had envisaged as taking over. Moreover, I had also been given responsibility for evaluating the academic credentials of overseas applicants to determine the level at which they should be placed in our undergraduate and graduate programs – a function formerly performed by the admissions offices on the parent campuses. I thus became not only the Dean for International Students – and the university official responsible for issuing the U.S. government documents by which foreign students obtained their visas to come to the United States – but the admissions officer for these students as well. This visa authority was to prove invaluable in some very special cases.

It was an interesting job, to say the least. The variety of problems affecting students from other countries is, of course, considerably greater than those of domestic students, and my overseas experience proved invaluable in dealing with many of these. Moreover, with the job security afforded a tenured faculty member, compared to that of my untenured counterparts on our main campuses, I felt comfortable dealing with some problems by circumventing ridiculous bureaucratic rules when necessary.

As in the Division of International Affairs, I was responsible primarily to myself, allowing freedom to travel whenever I deemed it appropriate, whether on holiday or what I considered legitimate business. On one occasion, I received a frantic call from the husband of one of our Chinese medical researchers saying that she had gone to Toronto the day before to renew her visa at the American consulate, expecting to fly back to her job and her children the next day. However, the consular underling who interviewed her told her she would have to go back to Hong Kong to get her visa renewed before she could re-enter the United States. I immediately flew to Toronto, successfully plead her case before the American consul himself, and brought her back with me.

On another occasion, after a Libyan graduate student had been treated for a mental breakdown, his physician cleared him to return to Libya but insisted that he be accompanied by a medical person. As the only person this poor chap trusted, I presented the problem to the Libyan embassy, who issued tickets for both of us to London. There we were met by a representative of their embassy who took custody of him, and I had a pleasant weekend with friends in London.

Having accumulated many frequent flyer miles in previous travels, free air travel was always available when needed. On one occasion, on a trip to Israel with Pat I personally delivered the admission and visa documents to a young Arab on the West Bank of Jerusalem, whom I had admitted to the university when his relatives in Indianapolis sought his admission.

At one point I became momentarily involved in politics at the national level, when I received a phone call from an old friend, Dr. Everett "Chick" Coop, who asked what I might know about the position on abortion held by our dean, Dr. Steve Beering. He explained that his Pennsylvania senator was about to propose him for the recently-opened position of Surgeon General of the United States, but was under pressure to nominate another candidate, our dean. If it was known that Steve was not firmly pro-life, then this would augur well for Chick's nomination – but the senator needed an answer within the next twenty-four hours.

I told him I had no knowledge whatever of this, but I would do my best to find out and would call him back. I turned immediately to my friend, Joe Mamlin, professor of medicine, who probably knew as much about the inner workings of the medical school as anyone. Joe had not known Steve to have expressed his views directly on this subject, but in light of other things he knew about Steve, he was reasonably sure that he was pro-life. As it all turned out, Steve had known that he was being considered for a post as undersecretary of the Department of Health and Human Services, of which the Office of the Surgeon General is an agency, and when offered the nomination as surgeon general, he turned it down. Thus Chick was successfully nominated, and became the most publicly visible surgeon general the country has ever had. Although Steve did not become undersecretary of HHS, he distinguished himself in a greater capacity by becoming president of Purdue University.

As noted earlier, it had been my privilege to work for a time for our former governor, Dr. Otis Bowen. He was a fine man and excellent governor, the first governor to serve the maximum eight years since 1851. Like any governor, he received VIP treatment wherever he went, but I recall vividly seeing one day what a difference being out of office makes. It was at the end of our annual Governor's Prayer Breakfast the year after he left office, and instead seeing him hustled off in a limousine, I saw him leave the Convention Center just ahead of me, walking alone to the parking lot. He had just lost his wife, and I hurried to catch up with him, put my arm around his shoulder, and wished him God's best in his bereavement.

At that time he was serving as adjunct professor of family practice at the medical school, but soon thereafter was appointed Secretary of Health and Human Services by President Reagan, the first physician to serve in that position. Chick Koop later told me of his reaction to the appointment, viewing him as somewhat of a "weak sister" when they first met, but soon came to regard him as a very effective boss.

58 – Unorthodox use of official privilege

A much more important use of the authority to issue immigration documents came after the Communist takeover in Afghanistan. Joe Mamlin one day received a letter from his old friend and pupil, Dr. Sami Ahmedzai, whom he had trained both in Jalalabad and Indianapolis. Sami was from a prominent Afghan family, several members of which had been assassinated by the Communists. He had temporarily taken refuge in Kabul, hiding out when the situation in Jalalabad grew untenable, and one day he heard on the radio that he had been appointed dean of the medical school in Jalalabad. This would have been a death sentence for him if he accepted, for the now hostile anticommunist factions among the Pashtuns in Nangrahar province would have killed him for taking the job. Should he refuse the appointment he would have met a similar fate from the Communists for failing to do his duty. He had no choice but to flee the country.

Through his connections in the government, he obtained permission to take his elderly mother to New Delhi for medical treatment. Now he had been there for several months, unable to take a job in India and unable to return to his own country. In his letter he simply told his friend Joe of his predicament, embarrassed to specifically ask for help but just letting a friend know of his situation. Joe brought the letter to me, and together we worked out a solution. The only alternative for him was to declare himself a refugee to the authorities in India, but the Afghan refugee program was only then in its formative stages, so this was not an option. Once on American soil, however, he would be eligible for political asylum, a category which would allow him to work and to stay here indefinitely until his case could be decided – and that could take years.

I would therefore send him visa documents to come to the U.S. under the Exchange Visitor Act, despite there being no exchange program then available to him here. Although such documents were never to be issued without a guarantee of a program and financial support, this was an emergency. The visa officer overseas would not know we had no program, and when he got here I would take him immediately to the U. S. Immigration Service office in Indianapolis, where he could apply for political asylum.

The only problem with this was that exchange visitor visas were normally only issued by the American Embassy in the country in which the person was currently working. If he simply showed up at the embassy in New Delhi and the visa officer became suspicious that he was really a refugee, the visa would be refused. I therefore enclosed with his visa document a letter explaining the situation and instructing him to deliver to it missionary friends in New Delhi, with whom we had become acquainted at L'Abri and who might know an embassy official who would be sympathetic to the problem and see that a visa was issued.

Joe and Marietta Smith were preparing to leave for summer holiday when Sami arrived at their home, but they graciously postponed their plans, prayed about the matter, contacted a friend at the embassy, and took Sami to meet him. He would give him 90 days for his wife and daughter to join him in New Delhi and then issue the visa. If they hadn't been able to get there by then, Sami would have to go on alone.

As we were to learn later, his wife and daughter tried twice to cross the border disguised as tribal nomads, but each time they were turned back. Finally, by selling everything they had, they were able to buy an exit visa and plane ticket, joining Sami just two days before the 90 days were up. Everything worked as planned when they arrived here, Joe was able to give him a job at the hospital, he later passed the medical licensing examination, and today has a successful practice in northern Indiana – hoping someday to get back to his own country.

Some time later Joe received a letter from our other friend, Dr. Nasser Shinwarie, the other professor of medicine in Jalalabad, who had escaped to Peshawar, Pakistan, with his wife and daughter. They were living in a small apartment and he was caring for patients in the Afghan refugee camps there on the Pakistani side of the border, now teeming with inhabitants. He was happy in this role, and all he asked of Joe was if he might be able to raise some financial support for this effort. Again, Joe came to my office with the letter, saying that he felt he must visit him to see how he could best help him. I thought that was a great idea and offered to go along.

It was a wonderful reunion for us, and we made several visits to the refugee camps with him, where on a number of people greeted Joe warmly, remembering when he had treated them in Jalalabad. However, we learned from Shinwaries's wife that he was in imminent danger. Already numerous political factions had developed among the Afghans in Peshawar, and because he was a prominent Afghan physician, each was pressuring him to join them. He wanted no part in this, and his wife was certain that he would eventually be killed by one these militant factions as an example to others who refused to join them.

He didn't agree with her, but we took it seriously enough to go to the American consul in Peshawar and ask for his help in case the need for them to leave the country became imminent. He was completely sympathetic, told me to send Shinwarie a visa document, and gave us his card to give to him. On the back he wrote in Urdu, "Admit this man immediately to my office." He then added, "If he feels he must leave, have him present this card to the guards at the gate, and I will have him and his wife and daughter on a plane to Indianapolis the next day." It was several months before Shinwarie felt that the time had come, and he too is now successfully practicing here in the Indianapolis area. As it turned out, our Jalalabad project was not a total failure.

Although the trip had a happy ending insofar as Shinwarie was concerned, it had its downside. Both Joe and I came down with severe cases of salmonella food poisoning, presumably from exposure in the refugee camps, and while he chose to stay on until he was completely recovered, I felt the need to get home. Traveling by way of Karachi, Beirut, and Athens, I arrived in Geneva, having eaten essentially nothing for two days and still feeling miserable. I phoned my friend Jerry Stromberg to see if he could put me up for the night. He came to the airport for me, and his wife prepared a marvelous but light dinner that rejuvenated me, and I arrived home the following day in good spirits. A friend in need is a friend indeed – especially in far off places.

59 – Dealing with the Communists again

It was gratifying to have been in a position to do things for others of a kind not included in one's job description, just by reason of being in the right place at the right time and having certain privileges afforded by the job. The opportunity to use my authority to issue visa documents in a manner not intended by our Department of State, who granted me that authority, was a case in point. Not always, however, did my efforts of assistance have the desired effect.

Early in my career at Indiana University we had a visiting professor of neurology from Czechoslovakia, Dr. Oldrich Kolar, whose wife Vera was also on our staff as an electron microscopist. They had come during a brief window in time when a benevolent Communist head of state removed the onerous travel restrictions on Czech citizens, but had left their young daughter behind in the care of her grandparents. That summer Vera went home to bring back the child, and shortly thereafter the head of state was replaced with a typical Communist despot who rescinded the privilege of unrestricted travel. Now together as a family, they gratefully accepted the university's invitation to become permanent member of the faculty, and so they defected.

Some time later, another Czech scientist arrived under a Soviet-American exchange program that allowed him six months in one of our research projects. Unfortunately, those in charge of the program who selected him neither determined that he had an adequate command of English or that his expertise was appropriate for the project to which he was assigned. I received a call one day from the head of our instrument maintenance lab saying that there was a Czech gentleman who had been assigned to their lab, and his English was so poor that they didn't know what to do with him. Would I see if there was any way I could help him?

Dr. Juraj Bolf was head of the one of the institutes of the prestigious Slovak Academy of Science in Bratislava and, as I was to learn later, the top scientist in his special branch of mathematics in the entire Soviet Union – and we had relegated him to a basement laboratory that did nothing but repair electronic instruments. The first thing I did was introduce him to the Kolars, who were unaware of his presence, and then began contacting various departments in the medical school where I thought he might be useful. The head of the physiology department was happy to take him on, and for the remaining few months of his stay he was happily occupied.

The Bolfs had been allowed to bring their 11-year-old son with them, leaving behind an older married son. This was unusual, for it was standard practice in the Communist countries to require a younger child to be left behind as a "hostage", to deter the parents from defecting. Assuming that the older son could take care of himself, I approached the Bolfs about the possibility of defecting, since he could be an invaluable asset to our country. They showed some interest, but were concerned about the financial implications. I contacted someone at Purdue University who assured me they could find a position for him, but it would take some time.

I then contacted a friend at the Eli Lilly Company, whose world headquarters is in Indianapolis, to see if they might have something. It didn't appear that his expertise was appropriate to their needs, but they generously offered a "consultancy" at a stipend of $400 a month until something turned up at Purdue, with no expectation of ever demanding his services. That was more than enough to pay his rent and basic living expenses at that time, and he could continue to work in the physiology department. They were ecstatic, and sent a message through some means or other to their son in Bratislava telling him of their plans. However, when he replied with excitement over their good fortune, adding that he and his wife would join them and had already begun formulating an escape plan, his mother went ballistic. "He doesn't know a word of English, so how could he survive in this country?," she told the Kolars. They did their best to reassure her, but when their Czech passports, which were valid for only six months, were about to expire, they decided to return home. Vera was so distraught that she couldn't bear to see them off at the airport.

When he invited me to visit him about six months after their return, as an official guest of the Academy, I was treated royally. He put me up in the best hotel in Bratislava, and when he was not free to take me sightseeing himself he sent his driver to take me in the big black Russian-made ZIS sedan that was a perquisite of his high rank in the Soviet scientific community.

The usual point of entry was from Vienna, only 50 miles from Bratislava, traveling by car or bus. On my first visit I was driving a new VW "beetle", ordered in Indianapolis and picked up in Frankfurt. Just getting a visa at the Czech embassy in Vienna was an experience in itself. The only human being in sight was a low level functionary who handed out forms and instructions, collected the requisite fee, directed one to a table, and after an interminable wait pointed to a shuttered window. Passport and visa application were pushed through an open slot below the window, grabbed by a hand that quickly closed the slot, and that was that until the next day, when, as instructed by a sign, one was to return between the hours of 1:00 and 3:00 to collect the passport – hopeful that it contained the visa, and not a rejection slip.

The border post was an evil sight, with manned machine gun watch towers on each side of the highway, from which a high barbed wire fence stretched to the horizon in each direction – and a long line of trucks and cars waiting to enter. Baggage had to be unloaded and inspected, and the car searched for contraband – with no clue as to what might constitute contraband. Again, one's passport was handed through a slot, presumably examined with great care, and at last returned. One was free to go – into a police state. Bolf had given directions to the hotel where he would meet me after I had checked in. My new yellow VW was the object of considerable attention.

When I left, Juraj, his wife, and their younger son, Peter, who had been with them in Indianapolis, led me to the border in their ancient Skoda. They were allowed to proceed to an exit point about a quarter of a mile from the actual border, also guarded by similar watch towers, with a red-and-white barrier across the road. The barrier was raised, I was waved through, looking back to see my friends waving goodbye behind that ugly red-and-white barrier. It was a sad ending to a delightful visit.

After my third or fourth trip, Bolf commented that I must by now have a thick dossier in the files there at the border. "Oh, I don't think so," said I, to which he just smiled. On my next trip I took the bus that traveled once a day each way between Bratislava and Vienna, carrying workers permitted employment in Vienna and bringing them home in the evening. I had not been able to notify Bolf of my visit, so while documents were collected from the passengers and the baggage inspected, I went to a nearby pay phone. His son Peter answered the phone, said his father was out but would pick me up at the bus station. I told him I would phone from the bus station so they wouldn't have to wait for me.

The line was busy when I tried to phone from the bus station, and continued to be so on repeated attempts for more than an hour. I finally gave up, and since there were no taxis in sight, decided to try to find the house on foot. At that moment, however, a car came careening around the corner, screeched to a halt, and Juraj and Peter jumped from the car, greeting me with warm hugs. When I told him about the busy line, Juraj smiled, and told me they had been at home for the past hour. "I told you they must have a thick dossier on you, and since they monitor all the calls from that border pay phone, they obviously notified the authorities here in the city to cut off my phone service until they got approval to let you through."

60 – The fall of the Wall and a fresh breeze from Moscow

During my first visit to Bratislava, Bolf had introduced me to a young surgeon friend, Jan Slezak. Some years later, when I was on my way to Saudi Arabia as part of a team of consultants to their military medical service, I phoned Jan from London to let him know that I planned to come by on my way back, and asked him to let Bolf know. His son answered the phone, told me his father was at his office, and gave me the number. I gave him time to tell his father to expect the call, and then placed my call. "Hello, Ed!" "Hello, Jan!" – and then a click. The line was dead. I placed the call again a few minutes later, and without explanation Jan continued the conversation, pleased to know that I would be coming by in a few weeks. When I later asked him about that strange interruption, his explanation was simple. "The secret police employee who monitors my phone line must have been dozing, and when he heard the beginning of a conversation in English, he panicked, shutting down the line until he could get his recording device on and running."

Some months after the Bolfs returned home from Indiana, their older son Paul and his wife went through with their escape plan, ending up in Germany. Although he spoke no German either, he managed to learn enough to get into dental school, and is still practicing there. This meant, however, that Juraj would now never be allowed to leave the Soviet bloc. The next time I visited him, he had been stripped of most of his privileges, including the car and driver, and a commissar, like the one I had seen years before in Safi's office in Kabul, had been assigned to keep watch on him when he had visitors in the office. When he sent me postcards during his holiday travels, they were always from some resort in the Communist countries.

His English had not improved much until my third visit, when he informed me that he was trying to learn English from the Bible. We had never been able to communicate to the point that he had ever given me a clue that he was even a "religious person", so when I asked to see his Bible, I was surprised to see it was a King James version that he had been given by a Seventh Day Adventist pastor in Indianapolis. Here I had had a brother in Christ for more than a decade without knowing it—who I thought might even have been a Communist for all I knew! The next time I came I brought him a six version side-by-side Bible, suggesting he try the NIV or Living Bible for his English lessons. I had the pleasure of visiting the Bolfs again in 2002, finding them still in the same apartment, but with a new car, a new TV – gifts from their son in Germany – and enjoying once again the freedom they had known many years ago. Perhaps it wasn't such a shame that they didn't stay in this country after all.

Before his fall from grace because of his son's defection, Bolf had been allowed to travel freely and received many visitors from the West. Now I was the only one from former days who came to see him, so I felt an obligation to do so whenever possible, even if it was only every two or three years. Seeing life under Communism firsthand was an educational experience that will ever remind me how precious is the freedom we in America enjoy.

On another visit, the first on which Pat accompanied me, we had come from Salzburg, where our British missionary friend, Brian Bounds, had described the experience of another missionary at the Bratislava checkpoint. While in the lady's room she threw some innocuous item from her purse into the toilet, and even as it was being flushed down, a female border guard burst into the room, seized her purse, and demanded to know what she had disposed of.

During my later travels to Romania, I learned how thoroughly a Communist government could maintain surveillance on its ordinary citizens. Some years before Ceausescu's demise, that ruthless dictator had ordered the telephone company to design and produce new phones in several styles and a variety of colors. The populace was then informed that everyone would receive a new phone of their choice incorporating the latest technology, as an example of the generosity of their government. They did indeed incorporate the latest technology, but not designed to enable the user to hear better. Rather, each was equipped with a microphone so sensitive that it could pick up a conversation anywhere in the tiny apartment in which most persons lived who had telephones – and every phone was connected to a central listening post in Bucharest. Such was life in the people's republics – with unseen eyes and ears everywhere.

Other than many trips to Czechoslovakia during the Cold War, my experiences with Communist countries during those days was limited to a drive through Hungary from Vienna to Lubliana, Slovenia; an overnight visit to Moscow; and an Aeroflot flight I once took from Lagos, Nigeria, to Beirut. The Russian aircraft was a bare-bones piece of equipment. In the galley was an ordinary, ancient refrigerator (bolted to the floor, I trust), a few small oxygen tanks in one of the overhead racks, and seat belts that looked as if they would separate under the slightest pressure. When we landed with a great bounce in Beirut, the flight attendant muttered something about the captain having his 12-year-old son in the flight deck with him, probably having let him land the plane.

My overnight in Moscow many years ago was on my way from Afghanistan to Denmark. It was in January, and having spent the previous fortnight primarily in Pakistan, I hadn't packed with a stopover in Moscow in mind. Finding a warm restaurant near my hotel was my sole objective for the evening. My plane took off the next morning in a blinding snowstorm for Warsaw, where I had an eight hour stopover, and was to be met by the wife of one of our medical researchers at the I. U. Medical Center for a tour of the city.

Unfortunately, Warsaw airport was temporarily closed because of weather, so the plane landed in Bratislava until it could be cleared onward. While sitting in the waiting room, an Austrian businessman from Vienna, also headed for Copenhagen, decided to cancel his plans and arranged with the Czech immigration officer to allow him to take a taxi to Vienna, only 50 miles away. Fearing that our plane might return to Moscow, I asked him if I might join him, to which he agreed, but before we could do so, the pilot came in, announced that we were leaving for Warsaw and refused to take our bags off the plane.

As we were landing in Warsaw, I saw my SAS flight to Copenhagen taking off. Because I now had no confirmed ongoing flight within twelve hours, I was not allowed to enter Poland for the day, and was detained at the Aeroflot desk, where the ticket agent told me that LOT, the Polish airline, had a flight about to depart for Copenhagen – but I would have to buy a ticket for $300! When I protested that my ticket should cover the charge, I did not have $300, and I was not going back to Moscow, she just glanced over my shoulder, saying nothing. I turned around to see two burly Russians putting Moscow baggage tags on my suitcase. (With no visa for Moscow, I wonder what they would have done with me there!)

I must have looked rather ill at that point, for at that moment a fellow passenger on our Aeroflot flight who was standing nearby stepped up to the counter and asked if he could pay for my ticket with Swiss francs, which she affirmed. As he counted out the money, I could barely hold back the tears as I asked him for his name and address, saying I would repay him as soon as I arrived home. This I did, for which he wrote to thank me – and told me that soon after I left, the Austrian businessman found himself in the same predicament and that the poor guy had been sent back to Moscow because my plane had gone and there was no other flight that day to Copenhagen. I, on the other hand, was given a full refund of the $300 fare by SAS after I complained to them that there had been no SAS representative there to put me on the LOT flight!

Some years later I had a much more pleasant visit to Moscow at the invitation of Komsomol, the Communist Youth Party, one of the leaders of which (whom I had met in my travels) asked me if I could arrange for some bright young Russian doctors to spend a month observing in our hospitals. Seeing the possibility of a Christian witness to such a group, I asked if he would want them to stay with American families during their month's stay, to which he eagerly responded.

During the ensuing months while their departure was being arranged, I was invited to come to Moscow for what proved to be a delightful four days. The Cold War had just ended, Moscow had opened its first MacDonald's, and the hospitality of my host was superb. I had meanwhile arranged home stays with Christian doctor friends, and when the group of four arrived some time later, they were given the royal treatment at the hospitals to which they were assigned. One of them was a very young neurosurgeon – 21 years of age and on the staff of Moscow's foremost hospital. (He had graduated from medical school at the age of 16!) Driving from the airport, as we passed a MacDonald's, he was astonished to see that there were no lines there – the ones in Moscow were several blocks long. That evening I showed him a clipping from our local paper, reporting that the Moscow MacDonald's had raised the pay of its employees from 500 rubles to 800 rubles a month. He told me his salary was 300 rubles a month!

61 – The CIA disconnection

Because of my frequent travels in the Middle East and South Asia, some of my friends were sure that I really worked for the CIA. My response was that they would never hire me – I could never keep a secret. I did, however, have a very tangential association with that agency for a time.

My Indianapolis businessman friend, Beurt SerVaas, was in the Office of Strategic Services in China during World War II, with a friend, Richard Helms. The OSS was the precursor of the CIA, and when I first met Beurt in 1966, he encouraged me to meet Helms the next time I was in Washington. I couldn't imagine why Helms would have any interest in meeting me, but two years later when in Washington I did so. We had taken the kids there on holiday just after Martin Luther King's assassination, and because of the riots that were occurring there at that time, many tourist attractions were closed. Having little to do one afternoon, I phoned the CIA and told Helms's secretary that Mr. Beurt SerVaas had asked me to make an appointment to see Mr. Helms. She called me back a few minutes later to tell me that it was arranged for 10:00 the next morning. He received me most cordially, asked me something of my work, introduced me to a doctor who had joined us, and after 15 minutes of conversation bid me farewell – obviously having no more idea of why Beurt had sent me than I did, but simply doing a favor for an old friend.

Soon thereafter, however, I received a phone call from a Hayden Moberley, who said he was the CIA representative in Indianapolis and could we have lunch together. I was very surprised to learn that the agency had a local agent, but at lunch at the Indianapolis Athletic Club the following week he explained his mission here. It seems that the CIA is not allowed to keep tabs on foreign nationals in this country, that being the prerogative of the FBI, so the only way he could get useful information about matters overseas was to question Americans who traveled there. He had arranged with the university in Bloomington to let him know when faculty members were traveling abroad, hoping to interview any who might be able to pick up anything of interest to the CIA in their travels. Would I be willing to meet with him whenever I was headed abroad, so that he could suggest what I might look for.

I felt somewhat sorry for him, suspecting he wished he were a real spy working undercover in some strange land, so as a patriotic American I was more than pleased to oblige, although I doubted that I would ever be of any help. In any case, I could look forward to a free lunch whenever I was getting ready to depart somewhere, and upon my return. One of the things he said I should be on the lookout for was any information about the state of health of any foreign leader. That seemed like a most unlikely possibility, but on a subsequent stopover in Karachi on my way to Afghanistan I found myself at a dinner in the home of the chief justice of the Pakistani supreme court, who introduced me to a Pakistani physician, noting that he was the country's foremost cardiologist. When I later overheard someone ask him where he had been recently, he said he had just come from a visit to the president in Islamabad. It took a time for a light to begin flickering in my brain, but I did manage to send a hastily scribbled letter to my secretary in our embassy's diplomatic pouch – a privilege of my State Department connection. I don't know what became of it all, but I had done my duty. Soon thereafter the CIA office in Indianapolis was moved to Cincinnati, and thus ended my career as a junior James Bond.

Later, however, I did acquire some useful intelligence information – and completely blew it. During one of my visits to my friend Bolf, he took me to his garden plot on the outskirts of Bratislava. It was on the edge of a narrow dirt road on which, he said, there had been a lot of traffic when he was tending his crops, mostly of cars full of high-ranking Russian officers. A road was being built just over the crest of the hill, and through the trees he had seen heavy-duty cable lines being laid in the road. He was sure it led to a Russian missile site. He insisted I go up and have a look, assuring me they wouldn't see us through the trees. I assured him that he was undoubtedly correct in his observations, and I really didn't need to be convinced through personal inspection. The last thing I needed was to be detained for questioning. I did, however, take a little peek, hoping the man attending an adjacent garden hadn't noticed my presence and reported it to the local constabulary, and was grateful that we immediately made our way back to the tram stop and home.

I fully intended to report the matter when I got home, for as Bolf explained, it was a violation of international law to have any such military equipment within a certain number of kilometers from any neutral country – and the Austrian border was just on the other side of the river. However, I needed to give a precise location. As we were leaving the village at the end of the tram line, Bolf had noted that a nearby house was the birthplace of the first Communist head of Czechoslovakia. I had neglected to ask the name of the village, and it was months before I finally was able to track down that information at our local library.

By the time I finally put together my report nearly a year had passed. Our senior senator, Dick Lugar, was scheduled to speak at the Indianapolis Rotary Club soon thereafter, and since he knew me, I decided to hand it to him there. As chairman of the Senate Foreign Relations Committee, he would know to whom to give it. He thanked me, and I later received a nice note from the CIA office in Cincinnati also thanking me but noting that the agency had been aware of the situation. As I said, I could never have been a spy.

When I again visited Bolf after the removal of the Iron Curtain all over Europe, gone at the border crossing between Vienna and Bratislava were the machine gun towers, barbed wire, baggage searches, and lengthy examination of passports. Americans no longer needed a visa, and passage on the bus into Czechslovakia was a breeze. Not so upon my departure, however.

I had attended the meeting of the newly-formed Rotary Club on my last evening there, the speaker at which was the Rotary district governor from Vienna, who kindly offered me a ride back to Vienna. At the border, we found ourselves in a line that had come to a complete halt. Determined to see what was holding us up, I walked several hundred yards to the front of the line, where construction had reduced traffic flow to a single lane past the checkpoint at the border, with the border guards apparently ignoring it.

As an oncoming pickup truck started working his way against our line of traffic, I spotted an opening between some freight trucks parked alongside the road, awaiting outgoing customs check. I moved in front of the pickup waving my arms like a proper traffic cop, directed the bewildered driver into the opening, and motioned the first car in our line to come ahead. Turning around just in time to see a huge oncoming freight truck heading for the gap I had created, I leaped into the blaze of his headlights and threw up the palm of my hand, to which he responded with a shuddering of his brakes. I then motioned our line through again, remaining in front of the truck until my own car arrived, jumped into it, and we roared off, leaving the rest to fend for themselves. The border guards seemed amused by the whole thing and waved us on.

62 – Extracurricular pursuits

My job also gave me the freedom to attend board meetings of the several organizations on whose boards of directors I served. By then I had already served on the board of International Students Inc. for some 30 years, and was on those of the Christian Medical Society, Medical Assistance Programs Inc. (now MAP International), the Paul Carlson Foundation, Bill Gothard's Institute in Basic Youth Conflicts, Campus Teams, the Iran Foundation, and CARE-MEDICO.

With one or two board meetings of each of these each year, some of which I managed to attend while living overseas, only because of the freedom of my job was I able to meet those responsibilities. By the time I retired from Indiana University I had also retired from most of them, but ISI had always been dear to our hearts, and only a few years ago did they retire me after more than 40 years. No organization should ever let a board member stay on that long! But I do miss the fellowship and the excitement of direct involvement in the work of these worthy organizations – and the friendship of some great physicians on the MAP board, such as C. Everett "Chick" Koop, who became the U.S. surgeon general during our respective board tenure

As I've noted previously, when I volunteered to take over the international student services on the Indianapolis campus of Indiana and Purdue University, I did so with the intention of spending only a year or so in the job, training someone to take my place so that I could become more involved in medically related pursuits. However, such was not to be the case. The university was unwilling to provide a position for an associate, and no obvious opportunities for involvement at the medical school presented themselves. I enjoyed the contacts with the foreign students, and the years passed so rapidly that I gave little thought to my initial resolve. By the sixth year, however, I began to reconsider the matter and decided to ask for a sabbatical leave in which to evaluate my options – should there be any.

Some years earlier I had developed a strong interest in the writings of C. S. Lewis, and in February 1985 I had become a part-owner in The Kilns, the Oxford home of C. S. Lewis and his brother Warnie until the death of the latter in 1973. The home had then been purchased by a university family, the Thirsks, who put it on the market ten years later. A California businessman and Lewis aficionado placed an option on the property, formed a limited partnership with himself as general partner, and sold shares at $5000 each to complete the purchase. With some 20 or so others we bought a share, and having decided to spend my sabbatical in England, occupying one of the vacant rooms at The Kilns was the logical choice of abode.

A young couple, Michael and Judith Apichella, had accepted an invitation from the general partner to be the caretakers of The Kilns. Michael was a free-lance writer and Judith was English, so both welcomed the opportunity to move to Oxford. They immediately became involved with the local and university community, as well as with a steady flow of American visitors anxious to see the home of the great Christian writer, theretofore closed to the public. The British pound had dropped to an all-time low early in 1985, bringing vast throngs of Americans to England, and the Apichellas recorded more than 300 visitors to The Kilns that summer. With all this entertaining and Judith recently having become pregnant with their first child, Pat and I felt that our presence should not add to their burden. Upon returning from a trip to Scotland in late July, we took a flat on Woodstock Road in Oxford, within walking distance of the center.

We had purchased a late model Saab – a welcome makeover of the earlier inverted bathtub design – and made the most of our freedom to travel throughout the English countryside. If it was raining when we awoke, we attended to the laundry, went to the bank, or whatever until the sun shone a few hours later, and then immediately headed off – usually into the nearby Cotswolds, that magnificent region west and northwest of Oxford. If the sun was shining upon arising, we had a hasty breakfast and quickly headed out, to enjoy as much of the day as possible before the next bout of rain. Covering an area roughly 30 miles east to west and 50 miles north to south, the Cotswolds comprises hundreds of hamlets and a number of major towns, linked by a dense network of highways and byways. I doubt that we missed a one of them that summer, putting more than 2000 miles on the odometer in just three months – an accomplishment surely worthy of inclusion in *Guinness World Records*.

An interest in collecting first editions of C. S. Lewis had begun some years earlier, but it now became an obsession with countless used bookstores to explore that summer – but I leave an accounting of those delights to a later chapter. Having a fine car for touring with four or five adults, we had the pleasure of entertaining such friends as Hal Guffey, president of

International Students, Inc., his wife Betsy, and their daughter Sondra, with whom we traveled to the north of Scotland, as well as John and Marge Meyer and Bob and Margaret Crosby from Indianapolis, who were with us for shorter jaunts. Visiting American friends living in England and our many British friends added much to the joy of this extended holiday – with little time devoted to serious consideration of what I would do upon my return to the university.

After three months of holidaying, Pat felt the need to return to her real estate business at the end of September. I stayed on, returning to a room at The Kilns now that the flood of tourists had subsided and Judith was more accustomed to handling her first pregnancy. I recall one memorable moment, on November 22nd, when I returned to the house late in the afternoon. Judith passed me as I was standing in the door of my room and asked, "Do you know what day this is?" "Thursday?" seemed an inappropriate response, so I expressed my ignorance with "No, what is it?" "This is the day on which C. S. Lewis died – at almost this exact moment – right there in your room!"

Although Michael and Judith had done a splendid job of managing The Kilns, despite the demands of her pregnancy, the general partner's ineptness in handling the purchase of the property had dismal consequences. The price of the property was only about £100,000 and at the time of closing, the pound had dropped to its lowest point in recent history – about $1.17. He could thus have met the entire cost from the proceeds of the sale of shares to limited partners, for had he informed us limited partners of the shortfall, we would have been more than pleased to lend him the little needed until he could sell a few more shares. Instead, however, he did not take us into his confidence, and used only half of the proceeds to make payment, retaining the rest of the funds to cover future expenses of repairs, utilities, etc.

Foolishly borrowing more than £30,000 from an Oxford bank to meet the remainder of the closing costs, he found himself with a rapidly rising monthly mortgage payment in dollars, for the pound had already bottomed out shortly before that and continued to rise steadily thereafter. Moreover, he had sent this young couple to England with no provision for their welfare, naively assuming that Michael would get a job to support the family and that they would thus be able to contribute to the cost of maintaining the house – failing to realize that an American cannot simply move to England and look for work under British immigration laws. By the time I arrived at The Kilns a few months later, they were already experiencing financial difficulties, without funds to buy the basic equipment to take care of the grounds, which had become terribly overgrown, or make simple repairs to the interior of the house.

Fortunately, another of the limited partners, a couple from California, arrived about the same time, and together we pitched in to buy tools and supplies needed to trim the hedges, repair the bathroom, and otherwise improve the situation. As the months went on the situation went from bad to worse, and eventually the general partner asked the Apichellas to move out so he could rent the entire place to students in order to meet the mortgage payments and other ongoing expenses. Eventually, he gave the entire property to the C. S. Lewis Foundation of Redlands, California, and under their management the house and grounds have been beautifully restored, and we are no longer involved with it.

Although Michael and Judith had a difficult time of it after being asked to leave, Michael managed to find employment of various kinds over the years, and God has blessed them with a wonderful, large family in the intervening years, eventually settling in the picturesque town of Bury St. Edmonds in England, where I have had the pleasure of visiting them from time to time. They hold no grudge, and I have used their story only to emphasize that about which Jesus warned his disciples in Luke 14:28-29: *For which of you, intending to build a tower, does not sit down first and count the cost, whether he has enough to finish it – lest, after he has laid the foundation, and is not able to finish, all who see it begin to mock him, saying, "This man began to build and was not able to finish."* Sadly, even in this day of supposed enlightenment, there are those who are so eager to begin something that they fail to count the cost.

63 -- Into "retirement"

I had had no contact with the university during my time in England, and I could conceive of no useful function I could further perform there. Shortly before leaving on sabbatical, I had learned of an unusual – and not well-publicized – retirement program available to senior Indiana University faculty members, which permitted retirement before the then mandatory age of 70.

When I sat down with Glenn Irwin, chancellor of the Indianapolis campus, to discuss my future, he noted that he was retiring under that program at the end of the academic year, and wondered if I might be interested in doing the same. I needed no further encouragement. Making the rounds of various undergraduate departments in the sciences, I filled the remainder of my time with assorted teaching engagements, and in August 1986 retired at the age of 60.

Stories abound of retired husbands who become the bane of their wives' existence. Mine found out very quickly that this was not to be true at 8153 Oakland Road, Indianapolis. Having officially departed (eagerly, I might add) from my office at the university on a Friday, I arose on Monday to a bright, new future. The morning was spent just reading the paper and contemplating the beauties of nature on that glorious summer day. By lunch-time I was so caught up in my reverie that I decided to surprise my dear wife upon her return from her real estate office with something to which I had never laid a finger – preparing dinner. Surely this would blow her out of her socks.

I have no recollection of what I prepared, but I awaited her arrival – and anticipated utter astonishment – seated opposite the entry from the garage and casually studying some piece of mail when she entered the room. Her words of greeting blew me out of *my* socks: "Hello, dear. What's for dinner?" I was so taken aback that I never thought to ask why she thought dinner was ready, but she later admitted that it was the delightful odor emanating from the kitchen. In any case, I had sealed my fate, for while she was a good cook, she never really enjoyed cooking. I had now become her personal chef – a position of which she has now been boasting to her friends for the past 20 years. I don't do windows, however.

At a marvelous retirement surprise party she put on for me some days later, one of the guests passed on a remark he had heard from a friend who had recently retired: "If I had known that retirement could be this much fun, I never would have gone to work in the first place." Indeed, such has proved to be the case. The incredible freedom to use the time God has given in any pursuit of one's choosing, without concern for earning a living, is a privilege normally granted only to some scions of wealthy parents. My goal has been to use this precious time wisely.

An early assignment came at the request of Kent Hotaling, a friend who works full-time with the National Prayer Breakfast fellowship. One of their other full-time associates had planned an extensive trip through Africa, meeting with leaders in several countries who had been involved with the fellowship, by way of encouragement to them. .

My enjoyable traveling companion, Chuck Wright, a former Presbyterian minister from Atlanta, met me in Rabat, Morocco, for the first leg of our trip. Our host was the American ambassador to Morocco, a close friend of Chuck, and I had my first taste of the luxury in which our ambassadors live. Gold-plated faucets in the bathroom of the VIP suite of the ambassador's residence yet! Our four-day visit with Tom Nasif was interrupted by a pressing engagement that took him away for two days, so we were able to take a two-day train trip to the ancient city of Fez, one of Morocco's great tourist attractions, stopping at a Christian orphanage along the way.

Passing through the airport in Cairo, where we sat up most of the night waiting for a delayed flight to Nairobi, we had just enough time in Nairobi to contact an old friend of mine, Sam Owens, with Campus Crusade for Christ in Kenya, and have lunch with him. This proved to be the impetus for a change in his affiliation, for Chuck was so impressed with him that he invited him to the next National Prayer Breakfast, where Doug Coe talked him into becoming a full-time associate of the fellowship. Sam has served faithfully in Nairobi ever since, establishing close friendships with the presidents and other leaders of countries in the region.

Our next stop was Lusaka, Zambia, where we met with a number of cabinet ministers of President Kenneth Kuanda, all outstanding Christian laymen active in their respective churches. These new contacts for me were to be the reason for an unexpected return to Zambia two years later.

From Lusaka we proceeded to Johannesburg – and some of the most interesting experiences I have ever enjoyed. After a restful night in one of the best hotels – at the price of a Motel 6 – we flew to Capetown, where our guide took us to Crossroads, the largest squatter settlement in South Africa. There we met with 12 black pastors, all of whom lived and had their churches within the settlement, and in the humble home of one of them we had dinner and spent the night. Never have I felt more welcomed!

This dear man had constructed a four-room dwelling from scraps of plywood, corrugated metal, and other castaway materials that was lovingly decorated inside, and he, his wife, and three daughters made us feel completely at home, sharing with us all they had. He was employed at a local factory, and served several churches 300 miles away in the settlement from which he had come, driving there once a month. He told us that his white boss at the factory was a fellow Christian who allowed him all the time he needed for this ministry, so that he never feared any consequences of a late return if something interfered with his journey.

Curious as to their past experience in entertaining white visitors in their home, I asked how many they had had. He told us that we were the first – and until only a few months earlier he would not have dared to invite anyone, lest the life of their guests be in danger from the criminal element in the settlement. However, these twelve pastors had at last successfully driven out these unwanted neighbors, threatening to shoot anyone who molested any of their flocks. We were to learn much of the other side of apartheid that never got into our news media.

From Capetown we flew to the capital, Pretoria, where we were hosted by General Chris Naude, chief of chaplains of the South African Defense Forces, who had arranged our side trip to Capetown and now had planned a spectacular tour of the front lines, where South Africa was protecting its borders against neighboring Angolan rebels. (He was later to become chaplain to the South African embassy in Washington. I've often wondered how many of the world's embassies have full-time chaplains-- certainly none of ours!) The next morning, by which time I had developed a cough and mild fever, we went to the airport, where we boarded a military Beechcraft Bonanza piloted by two South African Air Force majors.

After stopping overnight at a military rest camp on the Zambesi River in the extreme eastern tip of the country, we proceeded the next day for a lunch stop at another military base. We were given a tour of the hospital, where I elected to rest in bed while the others enjoyed lunch in the mess hall. Here we saw black and white troops thoroughly integrated—eating, sleeping, and working together. However reprehensible and unconscionable the rule of apartheid in South Africa, it was beginning to be clear that all was not entirely bad.

The next leg of our flight was extraordinary. We were headed for a front-line military base some 100 miles to the west. Passing over a large South African military airfield, we rapidly descended in tight circles from 4000 feet while an Air Force helicopter circled the base looking for any Angolan rebels who might have invaded their perimeter during the night with the intent of shooting down an incoming plane with a shoulder-to-air missile. Leveling out at 100 feet, we then sped hell-bent-for-leather to our destination, flying so low that there was little chance of anyone taking a shot at us. So exhilarating was the flight following that nice rest in the hospital that I was actually looking forward to our next stop, where we were royally entertained with a field demonstration of military fire power and a fascinating lecture by the commanding officer on the conduct of the war. The rebels were by now shelling the base only about once a week, and since the last round had fallen three days before, he assured us that we were in no danger. From there we flew to a base in Namibia for refueling, and thence back to Pretoria. All in all, it was a marvelous trip, one that I'm sure no other tourists were likely to enjoy.

Still a bit under the weather by the time we returned to the Naude home, I elected to let Chuck go on to Zimbabwe, where I would join him after a few days of recuperation. The Naudes were marvelous hosts, and I learned a good bit more about the situation in South Africa during my stay with them. It was clear that many more positive developments were already occurring in the campaign against apartheid than the foreign news media had been willing to reveal.

Harare being the last stop on our itinerary, Chuck and I decided to go our separate ways. I had been fortunate in being able to attend the weekly meeting of the Rotary Club upon reaching town, having found in the past that this was an invaluable way to meet key persons in unfamiliar cities. By the end of the day I had been put in touch with a number of persons who made my visit an unexpectedly pleasant one – including some visiting missionaries from Bulaweyo who had known my Indianapolis friend, Derek Wallace. Born in Scotland, Derek was the son of missionary parents who had spent most of their life in what was then Southern Rhodesia.

One of my Rotary acquaintances invited me to a round of golf the next day, and although I'm only an occasional golfer and hence a real duffer, this was another opportunity to add to the list of unusual places around the world where I've attempted the sport. Clubs were available for rent and balls were to be had from the caddies, who scrounged them from the rough and water holes. My caddy was most helpful in advising which club to use for each shot, politely addressing me as "sir" each time. However, when I made a particularly spectacular shot over a tree and onto the green at one hole, he loudly acclaimed, "*Good shot, bwana!*" It has been sad to see the decline of what was once a prosperous and exciting country, under the ruinous reign of the infamous Robert Mugabe, one of the worst of today's African leaders.

Thanks also to the National Prayer Breakfast fellowship, I have been blessed with a select group of friends who uphold me with their prayers whenever I travel. Brought together through the NPB, we meet every Thursday for breakfast to share what God is doing in our lives, to pray for each other, our families, friends with special needs, for our country, state and city – and just to enjoy good fellowship. Two of us have been in the group for more than thirty years, while others have moved away, and several have preceded us to our heavenly home.

For the past twenty years or so, we have met in an MCL cafeteria, one of a midwest chain whose president, then a member of the group, invited us to use one of their establishments when we vacated a downtown hotel whose dining room had became too noisy. When he retired and moved away less than two years later, he invited us to continue meeting there. Since it is not open for breakfast, we take turns bringing doughnuts or other pastries and choosing a subject for discussion, while the staff preparing for the lunch crowd keep our coffee cups full. The current president of the chain seems pleased to have his restaurant used as a house of prayer, so we continue to enjoy his largesse.

64 – The National Prayer Breakfast fellowship

My first exposure to the National Prayer breakfast fellowship – known simply as "the fellowship" among those involved – was in 1960. Having driven to Washington from Boston for my first meeting of the board of trustees of International Students, Inc., I arrived a bit late for the dinner given for board members, staff, and close friends of the organization. A seat had been saved for me at the end of the table, next to an imposing white-haired man who turned to me and introduced himself, with a slight Scandinavian accent, as Abraham Vereide. He immediately asked me what I did for a living, I told him I was on the faculty of the Tufts University School of Medicine in Boston, and asked him what he did. I don't recall his precise answer, which was given with a twinkle in his eye and not a clue as to its meaning, but he allowed no time for further inquiry.

"So, you're a medical school professor in Boston. How many medical schools are there in Boston?"

"Three." I replied. "Tufts, Harvard and Boston Universities."

"Do you have Christian friends who are at these other medical schools?"

"Yes, I have a few."

"Well, then, how would you like to organize a weekly luncheon to which you and your Christian medical friends could invite some of your non-Christian medical friends, just to meet together in the spirit of Jesus Christ? I have a lady friend in New Hampshire who will come down to help you get started. How about it?"

As I quickly learned, one could not easily avoid any request from this imposing giant of a man, the founder of the Prayer Breakfast movement. He tells his own story in his biography, *Modern Viking*, but this gives only a hint of the extent to which this man's vision has impacted men and women throughout the world, from the poorest to the most powerful – in government, business, education, or whatever. The National Prayer Breakfast, held every year on the first Thursday in February and attended by every president from Eisenhower onward, is only the tiniest tip of an iceberg of such proportions that few outside its inner circle have even the slightest knowledge of its enormous outreach and influence. Although I have been tangentially involved with the movement since that night in

Washington, and know many of those directly involved, including Abrahams's successor, Doug Coe, I never cease to marvel at the new things I learn about its activities. I could not begin to do justice to even a very superficial review of what the prayer breakfast movement has accomplished in the past 50 years throughout the world.

Let me cite just one example of what "the fellowship" has done. This meeting described in a recent *Washington Post* article took place following a National Prayer breakfast during the Reagan era at The Cedars, an impressive mansion owned by the fellowship on the banks of the Potomac in Arlington, Virginia:

"While none of the visiting heads of state met with Bush, Democratic Republic of Congo President Kabila and Rwandan President Kagame privately met for about an hour in the living room on the first floor of The Cedars. It was the first time the two warring leaders had met face to face. They sat on salmon-colored couches across from a marbled fireplace, their aides and bodyguards banished to another room. Kabila's father, the former president, had been murdered the month before. Rwanda had 30,000 soldiers within Congo's borders. Starvation and civil war had racked Congo for three years, leaving 2 million dead and an economy in ruins as rebels tried to gain control.

'It was an important meeting,' said Richard Sezibera, Rwanda's ambassador to the U.S. In the months that followed, members of the Fellowship reached out to both leaders, visiting them in Africa. The two men finally signed a peace accord in July in a deal brokered by the president of South Africa—a move that could be an important step toward peace.

'The fact that they met here probably saved hundreds of thousands of kids,' Coe said."

Needless to say, upon returning to Boston after that encounter with Abraham Vereide, I did contact some of my friends at the other two medical schools to discuss the possibility, and his New Hampshire friend did come down to help us get organized. I regret, however, that by the time the first luncheon was arranged, I had left for India – where I had my next contact with the movement. While visiting a friend in New Delhi, he introduced me to another American, Cliff Robinson, who was the fellowship's fulltime man in that part of the world.

Most of my involvement with fellowship has been nothing more than attending the National Prayer Breakfast almost every year, where I serve as an international host, assisting the many foreign attendees with their schedules. This, of course, has led to becoming acquainted with a wide variety of very interesting persons, many of whom I have later been able to visit in their own countries.

For the first 25 years or so, the main speaker at the breakfast was Billy Graham, but in later years the speakers have been prominent Christians from many walks of life. As I've noted, the president of the United States has always been present, with most of his cabinet, and a number of senators, congressman, and other government figures. The remaining attendees comprise over 3000 persons, almost one-third of whom are from other countries—a varied assortment of political, business, and professional leaders among others, who have been invited by the fellowship representatives in their respective geographical areas.

Other than the Africa trip previously described, my only other overseas venture directly associated with the fellowship was in 1986, when Pat and I used Pan Am Frequent Flyer mileage on what was to have been just a visit to missionary friends in Kenya. Before leaving, however, I phoned Doug Coe to see if there were any friends of the fellowship with whom I should make contact in those two countries. Noting that the "brothers" in East Africa were often visited by those of us here, he asked if I would consider stopping in West Africa, where there were some who were much more in need of encouragement – particularly in Ghana, where there had been a major revolution a few years earlier. Since Pan Am didn't fly to Ghana, it would be necessary to lay over in Lagos, Nigeria, and catch a Nigerian Airways flight to Accra.

Due to skyrocketing oil prices, Lagos had become one of the most expensive cities in the world – which, with my previous experience traveling on Nigerian Airways, made a stopover there less than appealing. And if that wasn't enough to put a damper on our trip, his request that I go to Accra was even less appealing.

65 – An unanticipated humanitarian adventure

Not only did Doug Coe maintain close friendships with an incredible number of leaders overseas, but he was very actively involved with many of the Washington diplomatic corps. Among these was a Muslim friend, the ambassador from Sudan, whom he had actually involved in a Bible study – and who had asked him if he could possibly arrange for one of Doug's American friends to be an impartial observer at a very important conference to be held in Khartoum just two weeks hence.

A major change had taken place in the Sudanese government, and for the past year the country had been under *shariah*—strict Islamic law. Christians and other non-Muslims in southern Sudan had complained bitterly that the law was being unfairly imposed on them (as it still is to this day), and the ambassador wanted Doug to send an impartial observer to this meeting – the "First International Conference on the Implementation of Shariah in Sudan" – and for that person to report back to him. Like his predecessor, Abraham Vereide, Doug Coe was one whose requests one found difficult to refuse, so I reluctantly agreed to these additions to our itinerary.

The first stop on Pan Am's daily flight from New York to Nairobi was Monrovia, Liberia, where we spent a delightful four days with new friends, Dr. David Van Reken, his wife Ruth, and their children – arranged by Dave's father, Everett, an old friend and longtime fellow-member of the Board of Directors of Medical Assistance Programs, Inc. Dave had gone to Liberia as pediatrician at ELWA, a large mission hospital near Monrovia, but at the request of the President Samuel Doe of Liberia had become pediatrician-in-chief at the John F. Kennedy Memorial Hospital, Liberia's foremost government hospital. Now, however, he was contemplating an invitation to join the department of pediatrics at the Indiana University Medical Center – which he did, and for many years now has been our neighbor in the house Pat sold them as the result of that visit.

Because of astronomical hotel prices in Lagos, I had arranged with a friend at the Sudan Interior Mission headquarters in New Jersey to stay in their mission guest house, a lovely place in which I had stayed some years before. Unknown to him, management of the guest house had been taken over by the churches in Lagos, who were now charging $100 a night for a room that was in such incredibly poor condition that we moved into a hotel the next day. (Pat still jokes about the toilet in our room – whose empty water tank was dangling off the wall, with the disconnected water supply pipe lying on the floor, and sleeping on her clothes rather than the filthy sheets, under a gray mosquito netting. "The worst place I've ever stayed!")

Thanks to contacts with local Christian friends of Doug Coe, however, we were able to make the most of our 3-day stay in Lagos. The most memorable event was joining about a dozen professional and business men in the early morning weekly prayer meeting in the chambers of J. A. Adefarasin, Chief Justice of the Supreme Court. I was reminded of Acts 10:7-8, where the Roman centurion in Caesarea, to whose house God sent Peter, is described as having "a devout soldier who was one of his attendants". Actively participating in the weekly prayer meeting was a Nigerian Army sergeant, the personal bodyguard of Justice Adefarasin.

Murtala Muhammed International Airport in Lagos was an impressive structure – at first glance. Built with oil money by a German firm, it was a lesser clone of Frankfurt's ultramodern airport, complete with moving walkways, "flipboards" showing the ever-changing flight schedules, etc.— none of which were working. Flights were posted on a chalkboard leaning against the high posts supporting the flipboard – and if one wanted to use the ladies restroom, she had to strip off the anticipated number of sheets of toilet paper from a roll on the handle of a mop leaning against the doorway, where a watchful attendant assured its not being stolen.

Needless to say, the flight to Accra had been postponed, but the passengers were required to remain in line at the entrance to the departure lounge – where through the window could be seen a bunch of workers lounging about while mechanics feverishly attempted some sort of repairs to the aircraft. After an hour or so of this, I disgustedly told Pat that we should just go back into the terminal and catch the next flight to Nairobi. "Patience!", she said, and eventually we boarded a flight to what proved to be the highlight of the entire trip.

Our arrival in Accra was at first more of the same – being driven all over the city looking for the mission guest house in which an American friend teaching at the medical school in Kumasi had arranged for us to stay. Everything abruptly changed from thereon, however, when we knocked on the door of a large house to which our taxi driver had been directed by a passerby.

Before we could say a word when we rang the bell and the door opened, we were greeted by a lovely Scottish lady who said, "You must be the Browns!" Isobel McKie and her husband Ira, veteran missionaries to Nigeria and Ghana, were to become our dear friends in the years that followed, and many pages could be devoted to relating all that took place in the four days we were privileged to spend with them and some others of the most remarkable Christians we have ever known – among them, John Agama, former head of the national police and Dr. Ofori-Atta, one of Ghana's most senior statesmen. Let me share just one very moving experience that made it clear why Pat was listening to God back there in Lagos when I was being swayed by nothing more than the inconvenience of a delayed flight.

Doug had sent me to Accra because he had had little contact with the several of the men who had attended the National Prayer Breakfast four years earlier, all of whom had suffered upon their return to Accra when the government was overthrown in a military coup. Among them was Dr. John Nabila. Senior advisor to the former president, he had been in prison for four years without a trial, suspected of having been part of a plot to assassinate the present head of state, Jerry Rawlings. As John Agama explained, the truth was that John Nabila had done just the opposite, having secretly exposed those who were part of the plot.

At dinner one of our evenings in Accra, someone commented that John Nabila was suffering from a back injury and had been admitted under guard to the university hospital. When they told me who he was and why he was in prison, I asked one of the medical doctors present, who was on the staff of the hospital, if it might be possible for me to visit John. Should anyone see a strange American visiting an important political prisoner, however, this might cast suspicion on whomever arranged the visit.

While at the Association of American Medical Colleges, I had been somewhat tangentially involved with the development of the medical school in Accra and its teaching hospital, and perhaps this might be used as a subterfuge for giving me a tour of the hospital. It sounded a bit risky, but since the next day was Sunday, the doctor thought that if he took me there early in the morning when he made patient rounds and few outsiders would be around, we could perhaps pull it off. At least it was worth a try.

He picked me up at 8:00 at the guest house, and took me directly to the surgical floor where John was in a private room opposite the nursing station, with an armed guard seated nearby with his head on a table – sound asleep. I was introduced as someone who helped develop the medical school and hospital, and the doctor would like to take me on rounds. The head nurse was delighted to have me, and we made a show of visiting all the patients in the ward. Returning to the nursing desk and making a pretext of going to the elevator while noting that the guard was still dozing, the doctor turned to the head nurse and said, "Oh, while we're here, I'd like to see how Dr. Nabila is doing." She obligingly unlocked the door to his room, and when I said, "I'll wait out here.", she said, "Oh, no! You can go in with him."

We quietly closed the door, and as John looked up in surprise to see a total stranger, I leaned over his bed and, in a choking voice, said, "Doug Coe sent me." Tears flowed all around, and when we had regained our composure, he reached for a notebook among some books by his bed, and thumbed through to a name and address hidden among its pages. "Quickly, copy this down!" He then explained that it was that of a relative in Chicago, who could give me the name and address of a former American embassy official in Accra, now back in Washington, who had known John when he was first arrested and had promised to try to help him. He had been able to convince the State Department to bring some pressure on Rawlings to release John, but apparently the negotiations had bogged down. Perhaps Doug Coe could contact this man and help bring more pressure to bear. We prayed briefly together, and the doctor suggested we beat a hasty retreat. He knocked quietly on the door for the nurse to unlock it, and we left. The guard was still asleep.

As soon as we returned to Indianapolis, I phoned the relative in Chicago, who gave me the name and address of Edward Perkins, who had been the political officer in our embassy in Accra when John was in office. I phoned him to tell him of my visit with John, and promptly forgot about the matter. Returning from a holiday several months later, I was given a telephone message from Mr. Perkins, taken by our daughter Wende. It was just, 'Tell your dad that John Nabila is free'. I immediately called the Chicago relative to see if he knew anything about it. Indeed he did. He had received only last week a Ghanaian newspaper sent to him by a friend working in the Middle East in which it was reported that John Nabila had been pardoned and released from prison.

66 – The Sudanese experience

After Accra, Nairobi could have been something of a letdown – but it was not. I had to head for Khartoum very soon after we arrived, but upon my return we had a full week of excitement. One of the contacts Doug had given me was the head of the American Express office, James Mageria. He kindly invited me to a weekly prayer breakfast with some of his business associates, in the course of which I asked him if he might be able to identify someone in Nairobi whom I had heard speak several years earlier at a Campus Crusade conference hosted by Bill Bright in their former headquarters in Arrowhead Springs, California. All I could remember was that the speaker was a high-ranking Kenyan police officer whom some friends had asked to take over the management of a large trucking company. When he asked why they would want someone like him with no experience in business, they told him it was because they knew he was a man of integrity – and that was all that mattered. They would teach him the business. Amused, James said, "Sure, I know him! It's me! In addition to the American Express office, we have a large trucking company here."

Our foremost objective in Nairobi was to see Bob and Karen Chapman, who were at a missions conference near Nairobi shortly before we arrived and would remain in the city before returning to their mission station in the north of the country. Bob had accompanied me to Ethiopia many years earlier when he was interning at Indianapolis's Methodist Hospital, and his mission board asked me to evaluate their medical work in that country. He, Karen and their children served for many years in Ethiopia, until the Communists took power there and drove out the missionaries, many of whom moved south into Kenya.

Nairobi was (and probably still is) a shopper's paradise, so Pat didn't mind staying behind while I was in Khartoum. The night flight on Kenya Airways to London was uneventful, but I was the only person to get off in Khartoum – not a favored tourist spot. The ambassador in Washington was to have arranged for my name to be on the list of delegates, but when I checked in at the registration desk, they couldn't find an Edwin Brown on the list. They did find another Brown, however – a journalist from London – and gave me an admission badge. I've always wondered if the other Brown ever showed up, and if so, whether he was turned away as an imposter when they saw his name already crossed off their list.

Wandering through the masses outside the great hall before the conference was to begin, I looked fruitlessly for a Western face with whom I might ally myself in taking a place inside. Instead, much to my surprise, I bumped into a Sudanese public health physician I had met at a medical conference in Senegal years earlier. He in turn introduced me to several local Indiana University alumni, and I was now part of the gang. They then introduced me to the president of the University of Southern Sudan, a physician who had trained in England and who invited me to sit with him. When he learned that Denis Burkitt, under whom he studied in England, was one of my closest friends, I had indeed arrived.

Doug had given me the name of another friend, Andrew Wieu, a Christian Sudanese leader, who much to my surprise was one of the first speakers at the conference. He was also the only one given time on the program to address the issue of unfair treatment of non-Muslims under *shariah* – a mere fifteen minutes or so in the two-day affair. Sitting among 3000 Muslims, many of them clergy as their various forms of attire indicated, was not a very comfortable experience, particularly when someone in the audience would suddenly shout, "Allah Akhbar!" and the entire audience would respond in kind. ("Allah the Great!" – the one wild last shout of the terrorists, according to the FBI, as they dove United flight 93 full throttle into the ground when Todd Beemer and the others tried to seize control of the plane.)

There was, as it turned out, another American at the conference – the guest of honor, Mohammed Ali. He had come directly from the New York hospital where he had been diagnosed with Parkinson's disease. At a dinner that night in his honor, I felt led to tell him how impressed I was that under those circumstances he would have traveled that far to fulfill an obligation. However much one may deplore his unfortunate choice of espousing Islam, he is certainly committed to his faith. Would that more Christians would emulate him in that regard.

Perhaps the single greatest advantage of having contacts in various fields around the world is the opportunity this affords for putting one person in touch with another whose work may be related and who may therefore have something to contribute to the other's work, either by way of direct assistance or advice or by reason of the second person's own contacts. I cannot think of any activity in which I've been engaged in which networking was not a major source of assistance – and at times a most unexpected source. This is especially true in Christian circles, where brothers and sisters in Christ are only too eager to "help out" when called upon, though they be total strangers to one another. The family of God on this earth today is but a presage of the glorious relationships we shall enjoy in heaven.

Twenty years ago our church in Indianapolis undertook a bold plan of planting one new church each year for the next twenty years. As of today, that number has grown far beyond that number. Our first two "plants" were in the Indianapolis area, but the third was in the Birmingham, England, suburb of Bromsgrove. The reason for the sudden move abroad was simply that a young British intern, Orrell Battersby, was completing a year at our church, and since his goal was to return to England to begin a new church in the Birmingham area, it seemed only appropriate that we should aid him in this undertaking.

As a member of the church planting committee, I was asked to be the liaison person with the new church, an assignment I gladly accepted. Visiting Orell and Christine about every six months, I was able to assess their accomplishments and their needs, and report this to our congregation. As the Bromsgrove congregation began to grow, not all of the area pastors were all that pleased to have another church in their midst – especially one not affiliated with a known denomination. One of these was the pastor of the local Baptist church, who was reported as having spoken out against this newcomer. It seemed to me, therefore, that I should call upon this man in an effort to try to smooth the troubled waters.

Orrell was not entirely sure that this would be a wise move, but we prayed about it and soon thereafter I called upon the man. He received me graciously, and as we chatted about various things, we soon learned we had a mutual interest in Afghanistan, being involved as a member of a local committee for Afghan relief. Orrell later reported a friendly relationship thereafter.

67 – Another African assignment – with embarrassing results

Some time after the African tour with Chuck Wright, I was introduced in Washington to a very interesting chap from South Africa. Until then, I had not heard of Michael Cassidy or African Enterprise. It is tempting to characterize him as a combination of Billy Graham and Mother Theresa, but that would not only be inaccurate but unfair to the impact this man has made on the African continent. For more than 40 years, this white South African has pursued his vision of evangelizing the continent on which he was born and has always lived.

Based in Pietermaritzburg, AE today comprises ten evangelistic teams of men and women of all races and denominations working out of Ethiopia, Ghana, Kenya, Malawi, Rwanda, Tanzania, Uganda, Congo, and Zimbabwe. Its stated mission is to "evangelize the cities of Africa through word and deed in partnership with the church". The Good News of the saving grace of Jesus Christ has been taken from Cape Town to Cairo, from Monrovia to Mombasa, with AE teams reaching out to thousands, many of them shattered by disaster—others simply seeking the love of God. Likewise, the teams have worked steadfastly in the area of reconciliation, and in recent years have helped heal the violence-torn areas of the continent, such as Rwanda and South Africa. Michael's greatest personal contribution has been his ministry to leadership, driven by the belief that leaders' minds changed for Christ will bless the lives of the people they lead. His most notable achievement in this area was the key role he played in convincing Prime Minister de Klerk of South Africa that he must free Nelson Mandela and bring apartheid to an end.

In my first meeting with him in his hotel in Washington, he told of the citywide evangelistic "blitz" conducted in one of the African capitals each year, when AE teams conducts over two thousand small meetings throughout the city in a single week, culminating in a citywide gathering on the final Saturday night. Each of the 75 or so evangelists on the team holds as many as half a dozen different meeting a day, from small groups in homes, visits to schools and factories, or lunches with city officials. When told that their next meeting was to be in Lusaka about six months hence, I told him of my recent contacts with a number of Christian government officials there and offered to be of service in any way in which I might be useful. I was not prepared, however, for the call when it came six months later. Phoning from Pietermaritzburg, he told me that he had just returned from a meeting with President Kenneth Kuanda of Zambia, who had offered to host a prayer breakfast to kick off the week-long campaign – just two weeks hence. Could I fly immediately to Lusaka and organize the prayer breakfast?

I lamely said that I would be pleased to do what I could, but did he understand that I had never had anything whatsoever to do with organizing the National Prayer Breakfast. Neither had he, nor with any prayer breakfast, and I had attended a good many – and I was his only suitable candidate. I booked a flight to London as quickly as I could, found a cheap flight to Lusaka in a London "bucket shop" – that euphemism for cut-rate travel agencies – and was on my way.

He had referred me to a German mission compound where I might stay and had given me the name of Stephen Tuck, a young Englishman from Birmingham who would assist me in every way. The breakfast was scheduled for the following Saturday—just six days hence, and to my horror I learned that no arrangements had been made for its location. I called immediately on the manager of the Intercontinental Hotel, Lusaka's finest, to see if they could possibly accommodate us. Fortunately, Lusaka is not a major tourist center and no other major functions of note were scheduled. He called in his catering manager, who told me he could accommodate up to 300 persons with an elaborate buffet breakfast – fresh fruit, eggs, bacon, sausages, sweet rolls, etc. at the astounding cost of only $3.00 per person. Michael had given me no budget, and I had not a clue as to where we would find 300 people, but at $3.00 a head I figured I could pay for the whole thing myself if necessary – so I booked for 300.

The next step was to print up invitations and get them distributed. The folks at the mission were marvelous, and by evening of my second day in Lusaka, they managed to turn them out on the most primitive of duplicating equipment and get them stuffed into envelopes. Stephen, my young British assistant, was incredible – a constant encourager, willing and able to undertake any task I assigned him. I had meanwhile contacted my erstwhile friend, Minister of Interior Sianga, and he volunteered to see that invitations were delivered to the top three persons in each of 30 some government ministries, which should produce about one-third of the needed participants. I had called upon the American ambassador, whom I had not met on my previous visit, just to let him know what I was up to, so when we needed a complete list of all the foreign embassies in Lusaka, his secretary kindly loaned me the official telephone directory with all the latest listings.

We addressed all the envelopes, and then divided them between us, to personally deliver each one to the respective embassy. My first call was at the American embassy to return the directory. As I entered, the ambassador was just leaving for some engagement. Seeing the stack of invitations in my hands, he said, "Here, let me see those. I'm having a dozen other ambassadors over for dinner to night and I"ll tell them they should come." He thumbed through the stack, removing the appropriately addressed ones, and I continued my rounds.

When I returned to the mission compound, Stephen reported that he had not only delivered his invitations but had got commitments from six ambassadors that they would be there. "How did you manage that?" "Oh, I just went up to the secretary and said I had an urgent message for the ambassador, so they ushered me in. I then told them the American ambassador would be there, and they would surely want to join him." Moreover, he had gone over to the headquarters of Nelson Mandela's African National Congress, the South African rebels who had taken refuge in Zambia, and invited a dozen of their leaders to the breakfast! The lad was unbelievable. From his maturity, I had assumed he was at least in his mid-twenties, but when I called upon his parents in England many months later, I was amazed to learn that Stephen was only 17.

For three days I had unsuccessfully attempted to get an appointment with the personal secretary to President Kaunda to confirm the place and time of the breakfast. Not until the afternoon before the breakfast did I get through to him, only to learn to my horror that the president had suddenly left that day for a meeting in Canada. In despair, I reported the news to the pastor who had distributed invitations to his fellow clergy and friends. He said not to worry. The vice-president was a friend of his and he would tell him that evening that his presence was required the next morning. The next blow was to learn from Minister Sianga that a prominent politician had died two days earlier, and it was likely that many of those he had invited would undoubtedly be going to the funeral the next morning, without time to attend the breakfast. In desperation I called the Salvation Army colonel whom I had met at the Rotary Club earlier in the week to see if he could round up some of his troops, which he graciously did that evening.

The time was at hand. Michael had arrived that day, and assured me that all would go well. We prayed about it, and the next morning he joined me in an anteroom to which the vice-president would be ushered. He was late, and for the next half hour I kept peering through the curtains at tables set for 300 people, and an enormous buffet spread that looked as if it would feed 500 – and scarcely 100 people in place. It was a nightmare – intensified by Michael's insistence that I join him and the vice-president at the head table.

Somehow I lived through it. When the American ambassador arrived, I left the head table to express my gratitude, and the Salvation Army colonel suggested I announce that all the leftover food would be distributed by his people to the orphanages in Lusaka. The hotel people were great, quietly drawing curtains across the room to remove from sight the 200 empty places. Michael was a brick, assuring me that I had done a great job and telling me about the gratifying meeting he had with President de Klerk of South Africa the previous week. The rest of the week went swimmingly, with some great meetings and a huge gathering for the final service. I was ready to go home.

Having begun my retirement with a major trip through Africa, I anticipated becoming more involved in that part of the world. I now had sufficient free time to travel, and it seemed desirable to expand the new contacts recently developed there. Yet the attraction was not strong enough to create a compelling desire to follow through on what seemed to be a logical expansion of my interests, and with no immediate further prompting from friends in Washington in the fellowship, I conveniently allowed myself to be drawn into unrelated pursuits.

For one thing, there were some responsibilities at home that required my attention, neglected during my time in England and the final throes of completing my assignments at the university. The most pressing of these was a house I had purchased to provide affordable accommodations for international students, all of whom had since graduated. With no further responsibility for such students, it was time to get rid of the house. Finding a buyer would require a considerable amount of repair and improvement, more as it turned out than I had contemplated, and being too frugal to let out the work to others, I chose to do it entirely by myself – a process that consumed nearly all my time for an entire year.

68 – A further introduction to Eastern Europe

Important changes were taking place abroad at that time, with the foundations of Communism beginning to show serious deterioration, and I began to develop a renewed interest in Eastern Europe as one after another of those countries showed signs of coming to life in a free world. In mid-1989 I had been asked by my pastor, Russ Blowers, if I would like to take his place in a proposed trip to Viet-Nam sponsored by World Vision. I gladly accepted the offer, but received word several weeks later from World Vision that the trip had been canceled and that the group would go to Romania instead, at a date yet to be decided. Witnessing on television the demise of the infamous Nicolai Ceausescu in Romania in late December, I was keen to be on my way, and when the proposed trip was still on hold a few weeks later, I decided to go on my own after hearing a report at a mission conference in England by Paul Negrut, pastor of Romania's largest Baptist church. At the same conference, I also learned that MAP International was preparing a container full of medical supplies desperately needed in Romania.

When I left for Bucharest I had not a single contact in that city. However, my friends at MAP had asked me to deliver the packing list for the container to the agency in Vienna whose representative in Bucharest would be handling the shipment when it arrived. At the Vienna office I was given the name of their man in Bucharest, and upon meeting him there I was immensely pleased to learn that he was working directly with the new minister of health – the most important man in the country with whom I might become acquainted. Thus on my first night in Bucharest I found myself with my new friend Jerry in the office of the Dr. Radu Dop – greatly impressed with a man of that stature who would spend a full two hours with an American tourist at that late hour. As our meeting drew to a close, he apologized that he could not lay on transportation at that late hour to take me on a tour of medical facilities the next day, but he would be happy to provide me with a guide and interpreter if I wished. Stepping to the phone, he made a hurried call, and then informed me that a young man named Bogdan would meet me at my hotel at 8:00 the next morning. Little did I dream to what ends that encounter would eventually lead.

Promptly at 8:00 a tall, handsome young man presented himself, speaking excellent English and eager to show me anything I wished to see. We hired a cab and by the end of the day had visited two major hospitals in the city, a rural health center some distance away, and had a whirlwind tour of

Bucharest. I asked Bogdan where he had obtained his excellent command of English, and was surprised to learn that he was self-taught, learning to read the language from every English language book and magazine he could lay his hands on, and spoken English from videotapes of American movies smuggled into the country by Romanians fortunate enough to have traveled abroad. I was even more surprised when he asked me where I was from, and then responded, "Oh, yes. You have the Pacers there, don't you?" Not being much of a sports fan, I had to stop for a moment to recall that the Pacers were our professional basketball team.

I had not allowed much time in Bucharest because of the limitations of the cheapest air fare I could find, so I promised Dr. Dop (who I now learned had called his sister that evening to ask if his nephew could take time off from university and squire a visiting American around town) that I would return soon. This I did two months later, stopping first in Austria to visit a doctor whom Jerry had recommended to me as one with a heart for Romania. Dr. Herbert Bronnenmeyer had bought several surplus buses from the Austrian postal service to help some of the Romanian churches bring people to their services. When I was about to board the train back to Vienna and thence to Bucharest, he suggested I wait a few hours and ride to Romania on one of these buses that would be coming by after being filled with relief supplies. It was an intriguing suggestion and one I shall always be grateful for having followed.

Traveling through the night, we reached the Romanian border about 6:00 a.m. We were but six passengers, the remainder of the bus being crammed full of all manner of medicine, clothing, and even a few pieces of furniture. When the Romanian border guard wanted to dismantle the lot looking for contraband, a feisty little German lady in our party asked him what he thought we were – a bunch of terrorists with a load of machine guns and hand grenades? Laughing, he threw up his hands and ordered the gatekeeper to let us through.

The city closest to the border was Oradea, and when I saw a hotel looming in the distance, and yearned for the comfort of a modern toilet facility, I suggested we stop in order to freshen up and have breakfast. It was a wise decision, and we went on our way gloriously refreshed. Our next stop was Cluj-Napoca, about 100 miles down the road. Delivery of some food and clothing was to be made to Vasile Suciu, pastor of a large church there, and when we arrived at his home I asked him how I might get in touch with two people in that city whose names Herb had given me. "What is your program? Are you going on with these people to Brasov?" I said I had no program, only that I was bound for Bucharest. "Then you are my guest for tonight, and tomorrow I will take you to our friends."

Hospitality to total strangers is a Romanian attribute – sharing whatever they have with their guests. Even the less well-to-do families usually have a hide-a-bed of sorts in their living room – which they will often use themselves, giving their own bedroom to a stranger. On one of my last trips to Bucharest, by which time Bogdan's grandmother had sold her home in Sibiu and moved into an apartment down the hall from his parents, she insisted on moving in with them so that I could have her apartment to myself.

Herb's other friend was Liviu Balas, a Baptist layman who, like Vasile, was to become one of my closest Romanian friends. For several years after the revolution he was the receiving agent for relief supplies sent by various American and European mission organizations, which he warehoused and personally distributed, to be sure that everything went to those who most needed it. Eventually he formed the first Romanian Christian relief agency, Ecce Homo, which he now operates, providing a multitude of services for the poor. On the last of many visits to Cluj, while sitting in Liviu's modest office, I asked him how I could be of service to him. "I've never *done* anything for you, my friend." "What do you mean, you've 'never done anything' for me? You have always visited me whenever you came to Romania!" I was deeply moved by that, for I had never really appreciated what the simple act of encouragement can mean to those who devote their lives to serving others under difficult circumstances.

After two days with Vasile I flew to Bucharest, where Radu laid out a program for me, including a flight to Suceava in the northeast part of the country, where I was able to visit a number of medical facilities, including a 1000-bed hospital. Like those in Bucharest, all were in a deplorable state, having suffered dreadfully under Ceausescu's dictatorship. Such medical equipment as they had was at least 25 years old and in a terrible state of repair, and medical supplies were in very short supply. Yet the country had many well-trained physicians and surgeons who somehow made do with such shortages. A typical health center serving some 5000 people would have two full-time physicians, the sum total of whose equipment consisted of one stethoscope each, a shared blood pressure apparatus, and an ancient scale for weighing patients.

There was no provision for doing even the most basic laboratory tests, and only odds and ends of drugs. Everywhere I went, the medical staff would plead for help in obtaining used equipment from the West, and adequate supplies of drugs. Although well-meaning persons in America and Western Europe were bringing in sizeable quantities of drugs, I saw most of these being trashed either because they were outdated, or the trade names were unrecognizable and there were no up-to-date pharmacopoeias by which the drugs could be identified by their generic names. I assured these hard-pressed medical colleagues that I would do what I could to help rectify the situation.

Upon returning to Bucharest, I took an overnight holiday trip to Constanta on the Black Sea coast, flying there and back. For a penny-pinching traveler of Scottish descent, I was in my glory. Under Ceausescu, everything in Romania was subsidized by the government, and insufficient time had as yet elapsed to effect the inevitable price increases. When I hailed a taxi that morning in Bucharest, I exchanged enough dollars with the driver to pay for my round-trip air fare, taxi to and from the airport in Constanta, dinner, a hotel room, and breakfast the next morning – all paid for with the currency received in exchange for the $20 bill I had given the driver the day before!

With the demise of Ceausescu, the artificial economy of what was a prosperous, productive nation prior to the Communist takeover swiftly began to unravel. The ruthless dictator had exported the best of everything the country produced to raise cash for his wild, self-centered schemes, resulting in shortages of everything. As I was to learn in future trips, the situation was to get worse before it got better, with skyrocketing inflation. For visitors with hard currency, however, Romania was to remain a buyer's paradise for several more years. For many Romanians, the country today is in some respects worse off economically than it was 15 years ago, when a bloody revolution gave promise of much better things to come.

69 – Our family acquires another extension

Throughout the 1990s I was able to travel frequently through Eastern Europe, thanks to frequent flyer mileage accumulated during the previous ten years. TWA (how I miss them!) had a particularly attractive award at the 50,000 mile level – a free first class ticket anywhere they flew, with a coupon that allowed a ticket purchased at any economy class to be exchanged for a first class ticket. On six consecutive trips to Romania I enjoyed the theretofore forbidden luxury of first class, with three free tickets and another three first class flights on economy tickets costing an average of about $350 each. With a first class ticket selling for $5,500, I thus received first class travel that would otherwise have cost $33,000 for slightly over $1000. Today, 50,000 frequent flyer miles gets one a single economy fare ticket to Europe. The Lord provides in marvelous ways.

Although TWA flew only as far as Vienna, stopovers in London were permitted, giving many opportunities to visit friends in England, and onward train travel to Romania for one-tenth the cost of a Vienna-Bucharest ticket could be had by taking a one-hour bus ride from Vienna to Bratislava, Czechoslovakia, and catching the East Berlin-Bucharest train. This not only afforded the pleasure of visiting old friends in Bratislava, but for a time also stopping off in Budapest to spend time with my brother Paul and his wife Ruth when they were doing an 18-month mission stint there, and meeting with Hungarian friends I had come to know through the National Prayer Breakfast.

I returned in October that first year, bringing much excess baggage filled with drugs and other needed items. I had by now established a firm relationship with Bogdan Lazaraoe, who with his father met me at the airport and took me to their apartment, which henceforth was to be my home whenever in Bucharest. World Vision had asked me to join a group of a dozen of their supporters, all doctors and nurses, whom they were sending on an extended tour of the country, culminating in attendance at the first meeting of the new Christian Medical Association of Romania in Cluj. I therefore volunteered to precede the group by a week, during which I would work out the details of their itinerary, and Bogdan volunteered to take off the entire month from university to be our guide and interpreter.

The most pitiable sights were those in hospital wards devoted to the care of infants and young children with AIDS – a legacy of one of Ceausescu's hare-brained schemes abetted by a bizarre medical practice. Most of the early cases had occurred in and around the port of Constanta, where much of the country's banked blood supply had come from ship's crews on shore leave and from local riffraff. These, presumably, were the sources from which the HIV infection had entered the country.

Ceausescu was obsessed with the notion that Romania could increase its productivity by increasing its population. Abortion was outlawed, and women younger than 45 were expected to have at least five children. Women were rounded up at their jobs and taken to clinics each month for pregnancy testing, and financial incentives were offered for having more children. The resulting overproduction forced many families to place children in state institutions – the infamous Romanian "orphanages". Those considered to be too frail to warrant proper care were neglected, whereas the normal infants were given injections of blood in the vain hope that this would improve their growth. Thus did Romania come to have the highest incidence of pediatric HIV/AIDS cases in Europe – and with the repeal of the antiabortion law Romania now has the highest abortion rate in the world.

On my third visit in 1990, I bought an old Mercedes sedan, which Bogdan's father, Ioan, registered in his name and lovingly cared for it in my absence. During the next ten years I was privileged to tour the length and breadth of Romania, several times with Pat, driven by Ioan and with Bogdan as interpreter, since Ioan spoke very little English.

Everywhere we saw many examples of how God was working through his people, not only to bring the message of the Gospel through the thousands of churches that have been established since the revolution, but in meeting the needs of the poor in many different ways. Large numbers of children in the government orphanages have been moved into Christian orphanages, and many of these children have been placed in Romanian Christian families. Many of the churches have started small businesses that either serve the poor directly or generate the funs to serve them. The government has welcomed Christian teachers into its schools, and many of the larger churches have started their own schools. In Oradea, Dr. Paul Negrut, the Baptist pastor who first encouraged me to go to Romania when we spent an evening together at that mission conference in England in February 1990, now heads the Christian university he founded after the revolution.

On one occasion, through God-ordained circumstances too complex to detail here, we met a remarkable young man, Silviu Rogobete, at the university in Timosoara. We were able to give him some small but much-needed financial assistance, and I later visited him in London, where he was a student at the London School of Theology. He returned to Timosoara, where he became an important force in evangelical theology, as well as establishing the Department of Political Science at the West University of Timosoara, a major university with 25,000 students – and just this year was appointed Romania's consul general in Capetown, South Africa.

Three years prior to my going to Romania, Pat and I were blessed with a wonderful addition to our family – a lovely Chinese girl from Taiwan, Shu-Chun Liou, whom Ted married in 1987. With Carrie (as we know her) came her family living in California – mother Wu-Mei; brother Al with wife Judy and son Dan; brother Louis with wife Lily and sons Richard and Jeffrey; and still in Taiwan, brother Lennie and her extended family who welcomed Pat and me into their family when we later visited there with Ted and Carrie.

Now, as the result of Bogdan Lazaroae having walked into our lives in 1990 and becoming like a son to us over the years, we were further blessed with his family -- father Ioan, mother Doina, grandmother Nina, sister Ioanna and uncle Radu, who have likewise welcomed us into their family.

In 1991, an Indiana University medical student, Susie Householder, asked me to arrange for her a two-month externship at the Children's Hospital in Bucharest during her following senior year. She and Bogdan fell in love, were eventually married in Indianapolis, and moved to Washington, D.C., after Bogdan obtained an MBA at the University of Rochester, New York. Sadly, after seven years of marriage and two lovely little boys, they were divorced in 2003.

My early involvement in Romania included the acquisition of used medical equipment, and many thousands of surgical instruments purchased at giveaway prices, as well as large quantities of medical textbooks and journals obtained by donation to my one-man IRS-approved charitable organization, International Medical Assistance, Inc. In more recent years the emphasis has been on supplying glucose meters and test strips needed by diabetic patients to manage their disease. Working with my friend, Dan Rizea, who sells medical supplies to physicians and hospitals throughout the country, he is able to make these much-needed items available at low cost to patients who could not otherwise afford them.

70 – A change of focus

More recently, my interest in that part of the world had been drawn to other Balkan countries – Serbia, Croatia, Bosnia-Herzogovina, Kosovo, and Macedonia, all once part of the erstwhile Jugoslavia. Much of that interest was stimulated by Dr. Peter Kuzmic, founder and rector of the Evangelical Theological Seminary in Osijek, Croatia. I first met Peter when he was spending more of his time in America than in Croatia, as the Distinguished Professor of Missions and Eastern European Studies at Gordon-Conwell Theological Seminary in Massachusetts. More recently, however, he and his family had moved back to Osijek, and it has been my privilege to travel with him throughout much of the region, visiting government leaders with whom he has developed close friendships, many of whom have attended the National Prayer Breakfast.

In 1999, during the Allied bombing in Kosovo I was asked by a friend, Dale Collie, if I had any contacts in Macedonia. Dale, who had long collected used clothing for Indianapolis's Lighthouse Mission, of which he was director, had greatly expanded that program of the mission by sending many containers of clothing to Ukraine. Now seeking to further expand this ministry, he asked our local airline, American Trans Air, to take 20,000 pounds of clothing and other supplies to Macedonia in their empty Lockheed L-1011 jumbo jet chartered by the UN to pick up Kosovar refugees there for transport to the U.S. They were willing to donate the space, but before loading the goods they needed documentation from a government-approved agency in Macedonia to assure the acceptance of the shipment – and the plane was to leave in just five days.

I did have a contact of sorts but neither knew his name nor whether he knew anyone who could provide such documentation. I had passed through Skopje from Belgrade a year earlier enroute to Thessaloniki, Greece, to visit my nephew, Alan Brown, a church-planting missionary there. He had given me the name of a missionary friend in Skopje in case I needed any assistance there, so I phoned Alan, who had only an email address of his friend, Mike Jurkovich. Hoping he read his email frequently, I fired off a message late that night. Early the next morning I had a reply, with the phone number of someone who might be able to help. I phoned that person, told her my problem, and was immediately assured that she could take care of the matter. She was just leaving her office but would stay on while I phoned Dale to give him her number. He immediately phoned her, found out what she needed to know about the shipment, faxed her the details, she faxed back the necessary documents, and by the next day ATA had loaded the goods – all this accomplished through the marvels of today's ease of communication by phone and the Internet.

Dale then asked me if I would like to join him and several others on the flight, including a TV journalist and his cameraman from one of our local stations. With passport always at the ready, I was on my way – and, as I was to learn from Pat when I phoned to report our safe arrival, the front page of the *Indianapolis Star* the next day bore a large photograph showing me about to board, with the name of the plane showing high above my head—"Big Ed". Friends who had often called me Big Ed were duly impressed when I appeared to be boarding my personal aircraft . (I hasten to note that "big" refers to my height, not my weight.) I learned from the captain that the crew had tired of flying a plane identified only by the large FAA ID number, E-78234 painted on its tail, and had recently christened it thus, expanding the "E" to "Ed" and persuading the company to paint the name on its nose.

The most significant benefit derived from this junket has been the friendship of Marija Vuletic, her husband Sasha, and their beautiful little Tamara – and more recently, little Luke. Marija is the representative of Samaritan's Purse in Macedonia, on whose behalf she was able to accept the shipment, and Sasha is pastor of a Pentecostal Church in Skopje, and a leader in the evangelical community. Both are graduates of Peter's seminary in Croatia, and representative of the hundreds of graduates now ministering in more than 40 countries, many in the Balkans.

Like many of the former Communist countries – and all but Slovenia in the former Jugoslavia – Macedonia struggles with political problems that have seriously hampered its economic development. Less than one percent of Macedonians are evangelical Christians, vastly outnumbered by the majority who are members of the Orthodox Church and a large Muslim minority. Yet the late President Boris Trajkovski, who died in a plane crash in February 2004, was a committed Christian and Methodist lay preacher who was elected by a substantial margin, and the evangelical churches are having a substantial impact in reaching out in love to the needy throughout the country. Another new friend, Tadeusz Jarcev, a member of Sasha's church, is a policeman who had served as the president's personal bodyguard, but thankfully was not with him on that flight.

Travel in the countries of the former Soviet bloc has had its interesting moments. In Romania, for example, Pat and I were on an extensive tour of the country, with Bogdan as our interpreter and his father, who spoke virtually no English, as our driver. Gasoline was in short supply, and where available one could wait for hours because of the long lines. Stopping in the southern city of Craiova, where the police chief was a friend of Bogdan's father, we had lunch while the chief sent one of his squad cars to look for gas for us. Parked near the police station and waiting for the car to return, I was amusing myself by panning my video camera around the neighborhood – including the police station on the corner. I was abruptly interrupted by three men in plain clothes coming from the other direction, one of whom announced that I was under arrest for filming a police station. Holding on to each of my arms, they were about to escort me to the station when Bogdan, who was watching from across the street, shouted something to his father, who was standing on the far corner talking to the chief. The chief then shouted to the three men – one of whom we learned was the deputy chief – and I was quickly released.

Returning from his mission, the policeman in the squad car informed the chief that there was no gasoline to be had for miles around. A brief discussion with Bogdan's father ensued, and he motioned to us to get in the car. We followed the police car to a secluded neighborhood where the officer proceeded to siphon several gallons from his own tank, and we were on our way.

Although I've incurred an impressive record of traffic violations driving in Europe over the past forty-some years – many of them in Romania, where traffic laws are loosely interpreted by the police – I've been arrested only once since the episode just described. The charge, however, was the same – forbidden photography. Photography of anything that might be off limits – such as Muslim women or certain buildings – has always been done surreptitiously, but in this instance I was completely innocent. I had been staying in an apartment in Osijek, Croatia, during an extended visit with Peter, across the street from a military cantonment – which I could have easily snapped from my bedroom had it been of any photographic interest whatsoever, which it was not. Standing across the street one morning with my back against the wall of the cantonment, I took a picture of my apartment building. It had recently been rebuilt after being totally destroyed a few years earlier, having been directly in the path of Serbian shells fired from across the river into the cantonment.

Although there was no way in which I could have photographed the cantonment while that close to its wall, a young soldier down the street shouted at me, came running up, and proceeded to usher me at gunpoint to his guard post. Fortunately, his sergeant spoke English, and when I presented my Indiana driver's license in lieu of the passport he demanded (which I always leave safely hidden in my room when in any foreign city, lest it be lifted by a pickpocket), he let me go my way after I assured him I had taken no pictures of his establishment.

The Serb shelling of Osijek had occurred during the Serbo-Croatian war, when Serb artillery batteries surrounded the city on three sides. Getting off the train on my first visit to the seminary in 1997 I observed what appeared to be a great deal of construction going on outside the station and down the street, as indicated by what I thought were bags of cement piled in front of every building and long wooden planks leaning over the doorways of hotels, restaurants, and other public building. I soon realized that these were sandbags, covering the windows of the basements, to which the occupants fled during the shelling, which was occurring about every other day. Fortunately, this was apparently an off day, for people were on the streets and showing no evident concern. Wooden planks, which also graced the doorway of the church next to the seminary, allowed exit and entry to the buildings, while absorbing the impact of shells that landed in the streets.

Although the shelling went on for over a year, the seminary was miraculously spared, and a few years later while spending those several weeks with Peter, I noticed that every building on either side of the seminary and on both sides of the street opposite bore many scars. Except for the city of Vukovar, 36 kilometers southeast of Osijek, which was virtually destroyed by Serb artillery, Croatia shows few signs of the bloody conflict that raged across the region a decade ago. Bosnia and Kosovo are steadily rebuilding, and even Sarajevo, which took a terrible pounding from Serb artillery and Serb snipers in the surrounding hills, has replaced much of the damage with new construction.

71 – New friends in Serb-occupied Bosnia-Herzogovina

The most important transition, however, has been the exciting growth of the evangelical church throughout the region. I frequently receive email from pastor friends in the area, telling of the marvelous way in which the Holy Spirit is changing the hearts of many, bringing reconciliation between Serb and Croat, Muslim and Orthodox, Catholic and Protestant. It has been thrilling to worship with many of these dear people who have suffered so much, and to see the dedication of foreign Christian relief workers, like Anti and Ulla Tepponen, Finnish missionaries living in Tuzla, Bosnia-Herzogovina, where Anti has overseen the rebuilding of many homes in Serb-controlled areas to the north that were destroyed in the war.

It was during that first visit to Osijek that I met Anti, Ulla, and their two children. The seminary had printed a large quantity of Scripture portions in Serbo-Croatian for distribution in Bosnia by the Tepponens, so I was invited to accompany the driver who was to make the delivery. Crossing the Sava River separating Croatia from Bosnia south of Osijek required the use of a ferry, the bridge having been destroyed during the war in the early '90s. The daylight crossing was only mildly nerve-racking – the return crossing after dark was a nightmare. Unfortunately, ours was the first vehicle on board, consigned to the extreme forward position on the off-loading ramp which slanted downward – with no restraining barrier between our van and the river and only the van's parking brake to keep us from rolling forward into the rushing current. The driver appeared oblivious to the obvious danger, dozing comfortably in his seat the entire crossing, whereas I, cold though the night air was, chose to stand outside where I could grip the rail should the brake give way, plunging the van into the river.

My next visit to Tuzla occurred a year or two later, when I promised Kish Swift, a member of my adult Sunday School class and Pat's former real estate client, that I would visit her daughter Jennifer, a helicopter pilot at the U. S. Army base in Tuzla, the next time I passed by the area. "Passing by", as it turned out, involved taking an overnight train from Bucharest to Belgrade, remaining two days in Belgrade to catch the occasional bus into Serb-occupied Bosnia, and transferring to a local bus north of Tuzla.

In Belgrade I had visited a prominent Serbian dissident who had phoned a friend in Tuzla, asking him to take me in and look after me while in Bosnia, but upon arrival at his office I was dismayed to learn that he had been called away, leaving me stranded in downtown Tuzla. A hasty phone call to Anti and Ulla saved the day, however, and I enjoyed their warm hospitality the entire weekend. After spending all day Saturday visiting Jennifer at the Army base, I was taken on Sunday afternoon by Anti into the Serb-controlled area, where his vehicle with UN markings allowed us free passage.

Our mission was to locate the home of an elderly Catholic couple I had met in a refugee camp near Osijek the year before and report back to their son in Germany, who hoped to recover it eventually from its Serb occupiers if it hadn't been destroyed. Their story was typical of thousands of Bosnians forced from their homes by Serbian forces. They had just finished dinner one evening when Serbian soldiers burst into the house, told them to pack a few belongings, and summarily forced them to leave. By walking and sometimes getting a ride from sympathetic truck drivers, they had eventually made their way to the refugee camp, where they had now lived for more than a year. I had left some money with one of the older students at the seminary in Osijek who had taken me to the camp and promised to look after their needs from time to time. With the help of an American Army lieutenant in Frankfurt, Germany, whose name and email address I had obtained from a list of AOL subscribers in that city, I had later been able to track down the son.

With the help of a detailed U. S. Army map of the area, supplied by Jennifer, we were able to locate not only the village but even the street we were looking for, and then cruised slowly down the street looking for the house number. Unfortunately, it was a sunny Sunday afternoon, and three tough-looking Serbian men were lounging in front of the house. When our slow-moving vehicle caught their attention, Anti gunned the engine and headed for the main highway with the comment, "I don't like the looks of those chetniks. They could easily have grabbed a gun and taken a shot at us." (Chetniks were members of the Serbian nationalist guerrilla force formed during WW II to resist the German invaders, earning a reputation for being ruthless killers.) At least we were able to determine that the house appeared to be unscathed by the fighting that had gone on there, unlike entire villages we had passed earlier that had been totally demolished.

Regrettably, I didn't have the opportunity to visit that area the next time I came to Tuzla two years later, in order to learn if the couple had regained their home. I was traveling with Peter Kuzmic on that visit, paying calls on the mayors of Tuzla and Mostar, whom we had met at the National Prayer Breakfast in Washington the year before. Selim Beslagic, the heroic Muslim mayor of Tuzla, had in 1991 stood up to the Serbian forces that were threatening to pound the city with artillery as they had done earlier in Vukovar, Croatia. During his term as mayor, Mr. Beslagic was able to deflect the tide of ethnic nationalism that swept through former Yugoslavia during the 1991 conflict, rallying both Muslims and Christians in a bold front that convinced the Serbian commander to bypass the city. Tuzla thus came through the war virtually unscathed.

Meeting with him in his office, we learned that he was to receive an honorary doctorate from Northwestern University for his peace-keeping role that summer. Unable to accept his invitation to be present at that ceremony, Peter asked me to represent him, and in June I had the privilege of being with him and his family at the Northwestern graduation ceremonies in Evanston, Illinois.

72 – Thrilling developments in China

Following the premature death of my younger brother Dave some years ago, his wife Carole felt drawn to a term of service in China as an English teacher under the auspices of one of the several American organizations who have sent Christians to that great country in recent years as English teachers. With English having become the international language of education and commerce, the demand for English teachers is enormous. In early 2004 Pat and I arranged to visit her during her mid-winter break. The timing proved to be remarkable for two reasons.

First, I had received an invitation to join at that same time a small study group of an organization in Indianapolis, Overseas Council International, whose mission is to aid in the development of Christian leadership in the non-Western world. The program included visits to seminaries in Kunming and Wuhan and a newly developed department of theological studies in a Beijing university, as well as visits with some house church leaders.

Second, I had just finished reading a very challenging book, *Jesus in Beijing*, by David Aikman, a journalist and former Beijing bureau chief for *TIME* magazine whom I had met some years earlier. The book traces the history of Christianity in China, from the 7th century, when Nestorian Christian missionaries came to what is today the city of Xian, to the phenomenal growth of Christianity in recent years in the largest country in world. Despite continued persecution, imprisonment, and even torture and death from Communist authorities in some parts of the country, the church of Jesus Christ is growing at the phenomenal rate of more than 30,000 Christians every day, on average, with an estimated total of as many as 100 million believers. As Aikman says, if this growth continues at the same rate (and there is every indication that it is continuing to do so), China will be a Christian nation within twenty years – not that everyone will be a follower of Jesus Christ, but as has happened in Korea, Christians will play an important role in every area of society – business, higher education, the arts, science, politics, and so on.

Just as Korea has become the greatest missionary-sending country in the world, so are committed Chinese Christians going out in large numbers to carry the life-saving Good News to Muslims, Hindus, Buddhists, and others in the neighboring countries. All over China men and women are being intensively trained in the language and customs of the countries to which they will go, fully expecting that they will be persecuted and many will die for their faith – and included in their training are such practical matters as how to jump from a second-story window without breaking a leg, how to pick handcuffs and jail cell doors, and even how to witness for their faith while being led to their execution!

As I read those statistics, my mind went back fifty years to my first visit to Hong Kong. Christian friends in England had put me in touch with a number of Christian organizations in that city, among which was the Far East Broadcasting Company, pioneers in broadcasting the Gospel message to those in closed countries, such as China. One of their staff was a retired British Army officer, Colonel Fox-Holmes, whose job was to read every newspaper report and listen to every broadcast coming out of the mainland, hoping to learn something of the fate of the church in China.

With the overthrow of Chiang Kai-shek's government by the Communists in 1949, in a little more than a year some ten thousand Protestant and Catholic foreign missionaries were forced to leave China. In the ensuing years there was much speculation about the state of the church under Communism, and in the absence of any contact with the believers who had been left behind, by 1965 there were some who accepted the possibility that the church has been wiped out. Colonel Fox-Holmes job was to try to determine what had actually happened.

On my next visit to Hong Kong within the year, I learned of a dramatic development that had taken place some months earlier. An escapee from the Communist state who had successfully made it to Hong Kong by swimming through heavily guarded waters separating Hong Kong island from the mainland reported that the church had gone underground, with small groups of believers meeting in homes, and moving from home to home to escape detection. Like Mark Twain, who once reported that "rumors of my death have been greatly exaggerated", the church was alive and well.

Pam Burris, leader of the Overseas Council group, had kindly supplied us with their itinerary and invited us to touch base with them at any point in which our paths might cross – and on the morning after our arrival in Beijing we were joined by Carole on a flight to Kunming. Pat and I had not been in China since a very brief visit almost 20 years ago, and we were amazed to see the extent of its development – from the ultramodern airport, the broad highways into the city, and magnificent new buildings everywhere, Beijing was a sight to behold – and as we were to learn, so were the other major cities of that exciting country. Even more surprising was the freedom extended to tourists compared to the restrictions of twenty years ago – free to travel anywhere by any means without restriction, with the utmost courtesy extended by all with whom we came in contact. So broad is the effort to accommodate tourists that in Beijing and other large cities, the signs on major streets are in both Chinese and English, as are those on most commercial buildings.

We joined the seven members of the Overseas Council group at Kunming airport (the site of Claire Chennault's Flying Tigers base in World War II), our flight from Beijing arriving at the same time as theirs from Hong Kong. Following dinner in the beautiful Sakura hotel where we were all to stay, Pam invited us to her room where we met a beautiful young woman, Deborah, who through an interpreter told something of her work as we sat or stood in that crowded hotel room. Not until the end of the evening did I learn who she was – none other than Sister Ding, as she is known to the Chinese Christians, to whom David Aikman had devoted ten pages. This 42-year-old mother of a 12-year-old boy is the foremost female leader in the house church movement, spiritual leader of an estimated 28 million Christian women! I had my copy of *Jesus in Beijing* with me in the event we should meet anyone mentioned therein, and surprised her when I opened to page 98, showed her the picture David had taken of her three years earlier, and then told her to keep the book. Scarcely 24 hours in China, and we had the incomparable privilege of being with one of its choicest saints.

The following day we visited Yunnan Bible Seminary, where some 50 young men are being trained to go forth and minister to the remote tribes of northwest China. While there are hundreds of "underground" seminaries in China, this one, although thoroughly evangelical, is one of the few recognized by the government, but operates on an extremely limited budget because it is forbidden to receive financial support from the outside.

Kunming is also the site of Project Grace, an umbrella group that provides organizational cover for about twenty foreign Christian organizations from America, Holland, Scandinavia, and Britain. Because they are involved in medicine, agriculture, education, AIDS prevention, and leprosy work, these Christians are well received by the government and are making a substantial contribution.

Christian "tentmakers" are found throughout China, many in the field of business – Christian businessmen who lend their expertise either as teachers or consultants, or by establishing businesses. One such enterprise is New Day Creations in the small town of Qingyundian about 15 miles southeast of Beijing, a small factory founded by Byron and Karen Brenneman, a young couple from New York City. Employing several dozen local artists, sculptors, and other artisans, the factory produces beautiful molded figures of many different kinds which have been much in demand by both Chinese and foreign tourists. The heart of their work, however, is the New Day Foster Home across the street from the factory, where Karen, the Brenneman's teenage daughters, some local volunteers, and a staff of nurses, nannies, and other employees care for some 20 infants and very young children with correctable physical problems, who come from local Children's Welfare Institutes. From donations of supporters and local doctors and hospitals who offer their services at reduced rates or gratis, New Day Foster Home is able to provide all of these children with the care they need, giving them a better chance at a healthy life and adoption. Our few hours there with these faithful servant leaders and their totally charming charges was the highlight of our trip.

Back in Beijing after stops in Kunming and Xian, Pat, Carole and I were again invited to Pam's hotel room there to meet another house church leader and his wife. Introduced only as "Uncle Liang", this 52-year-old leader of some 10 million Christians in Henan Province has, like so many of the house church leaders, spent much of his adult Christian life in prison. It was in Henan Province that the great British missionary, Hudson Taylor, founded the China Inland Mission, and today, despite the incredible persecution of the Cultural Revolution not long ago, Uncle Liang told us that the vast majority of villages and even some of the smaller towns in the province are almost completely Christian. Sadly, it is also in Henan Province that harassment, persecution, and imprisonment are still among the strongest in China – and just two years after we met him he was again arrested and sentenced to seven more years in prison..

Having given my copy of *Jesus in Beijing* to Sister Ding, it was not until our return to Indianapolis that I re-read another copy and learned to my surprise that Uncle Liang was none other than Zhang Rongliang, considered to be the most influential male Christian house church leader today in China. What an incredible privilege had been ours – to have spent several hours with both the leading female and male house church leaders in that great country!

73 – Romania revisited – with God's marvelous provision

In June 2005 I decided it was time to visit old friends in Romania, having not been there for the past 2-3 years. With my accumulated frequent flyer miles, I was able to stop off in England to spend a week with friends there before proceeding to Bucharest.

Although it has been my privilege to visit England frequently over the years, it has been a particularly joyful experience in recent years when my base in London has been the home of Howard and Nora Norrish, whom we had known in Saudi Arabia. As the head of the Muslim ministry of the great British mission organization, Operation Mobilization, they serve the needs of OM's teams in every predominately Muslim country in North Africa, the Middle East, and the former Soviet Union. – and always have exciting reports of the amazing way in which God is working today among Muslims.

With other friends throughout England, the use of a car is essential, but in recent years I found it more and more difficult to rent one because of my age. The Norrishes have come to the rescue by introducing me to an offshoot of OM, Icthus Motors Mission, which operates a fleet of donated cars and makes them available to visiting missionaries. Although I certainly don't qualify as such, Icthus Motors has generously loaned me a car on my last three visits, in return for which I am able to show appreciation with a substantial donation to the ministry. I am likewise grateful to many other friends like the Lloyds in Oxford, the Johnsons in Banbury, the Apichellas in Bury St. Edmunds, and the Collins in Lincoln who have opened their homes to me in recent years.

On to Bucharest, where from the Dan Rizea's comfortable home near the train station I had planned to go by train throughout the country during the next two weeks. The first week went very well, with travel through the southern tier of the country, primarily to do an errand for Barbara Crawford, a friend in the Washington, D.C. area, and neighbor of Bogdan. She had asked me if I might try to find a way to help a group of Catholic nuns from Slovakia and other countries who were establishing a hospice for the poor in Timosoara, and had run into problems importing needed donated supplies from America due to new Customs restrictions imposed by the Romanian Ministry of Health.

Certain that Bogdan's uncle, Radu Dop, would be of help in this regard, I had made prior arrangements to meet with Sister Superior Jeana and representatives of Caritas, the Catholic relief agency with whom they were working. She proved to be a charming lady, and the very impressive hospice, whose construction was well under way, will be an outstanding contribution to the poor of that area.

With all the needed information I returned to Bucharest after visiting friends in Timosoara and Arad. Before setting out the following week for the northwest part of the country, I spent a delightful weekend with Dan and Daniela Rizea in their weekend retreat in the Carpathian mountains north of Bucharest. This also gave me opportunity to visit a young doctor friend, Gloria Petrisor, in Brasov, whom I had provided with some medical equipment years earlier. Following lunch in the beautiful mountain setting of Poiana Brasov, just a few miles from and high above the city, she was walking me back to the bus station when I suddenly developed a very uncomfortable pressure in mid-chest. Just a bit of gas, I thought, but when it again occurred back in Predeal while walking from the bus station to the Rizea apartment, I was not so sure. But it soon passed, and we drove back to Bucharest the next day.

When it occurred a third time while walking to the train station to depart for Cluj, I decided it was time to face the music. Dan had mentioned in passing that Radu Dop had opened the first private hospital in Bucharest – a state-of-the-art medical facility funded by Dutch investors. I therefore phoned Radu to tell him of my symptoms. Twenty minutes later I was in his ICU, with his cardiologist informing me that I had experienced my first heart attack and that I needed to head for home at the earliest opportunity for angiography to determine the extent of coronary artery occlusion. Unfortunately, Air France was unwilling to change my return reservation, saying that no free seats were available, so I moved from the ICU to a private room across the hall to spend a comfortable week awaiting my flight. What was curious, however, was that I seemed to be the only patient on the floor. I thought Dan had said that the hospital had been opened two years ago, but when I questioned Radu about the paucity of patients, he explained that it had opened only two *days* ago!

With a full complement of staff, including three nurses to look after me, a TV in my room, and a telephone at my bedside on which I checked in with Pat a couple of times each day, I was well cared for – and was able to use the computer at the nurses' station to check my email regularly and even to bid on some books on eBay. On the second day I phoned Miriam Lazar, who had been my interpreter in Timosoara, to ask for the number of the offending Ministry of Health directive, so I could pass that on to Radu.

"Good morning, this is Ed in Bucharest."

"HOW ARE YOU? We heard you had a heart attack – and all the nuns are praying for you!"

"How did you know *that*?"

"Sister Jeana told me."

"How did *she* know that?

"Barbara Crawford called her from Washington, D.C."

From Pat I had already learned that she had phoned Bogdan about it, and he in turn had told Barbara. A brand new state-of-the-art hospital, and all my friends, including nine nuns, praying for me – how could it get any better than that?

Pat had also informed our cardiologist friend, Bill Storer, of my situation, and was instructed to have me phone him as soon as I arrived home. I was been given two syringes containing the anticoagulant that had been administered twice a day in hospital, to be used during the long flight, and Air France provided superb wheelchair and other service at Charles de Gaulle airport in Paris during the change of planes.

Arriving in Indianapolis that evening, I immediately phoned Bill, who told me to come at 8:00 the next morning to the Heart Center of Indiana, which he headed. Early the next morning Pat drove me there, and three hours later I was the proud owner of a stent in my right coronary artery, which was shown to have 95 percent blockage – and a few weeks later I was back playing tennis.

74 -- A hobby that grew like Topsy

One of the joys of retirement has been the freedom to devote as much time as desired to a hobby that went far beyond the very limited bounds I originally envisaged thirty years ago – collecting the works of C. S. Lewis. Not only was I able to amass the most extensive private collection known, comprising first editions, manuscripts, letters, and other ephemera of the twentieth century's greatest Christian writer, but it has been the means of giving far more to missions and other Christian ministries than could ever have come from our limited retirement funds. Only the Lewis holdings at the Wade Center at Wheaton College exceed it in scope, due to its founder, Dr. Clyde Kilby, having known both C. S. Lewis and his brother Warnie, and having received much material from the Lewis estate. I am particularly grateful that the collection is now at Taylor University, of which our daughter Wende is an alumna.

We had hoped to donate the collection to the university, but when it became apparent that our retirement funds would be insufficient to warrant divesting ourselves of an asset in which so much had been invested, the university generously found a donor who provided the funds for it. That was about seven years ago, and we have since been richly blessed in being honored by Taylor University as I continue to be involved with what it proudly named *The Edwin W. Brown Collection*.

The most remarkable thing about the collection, however, is not its scope but the amazing way in which the hand of God manifested itself in so many different ways throughout the process of assembling it. My purpose in undertaking it was simply to enjoy an interesting hobby; God's purpose was to honor his faithful servant, C. S. Lewis, by making him better known through a very special collection of his works available to all.

The many tales of these God-directed experiences are to be found in *In Pursuit of C. S. Lewis: Adventures in Collecting His Works*, published in June 2006 -- a highly-acclaimed tome which I shamelessly promote, available through major book distributors but preferably ordered directly from me at (317) 257-7454 or ewbindy@aol.com. With apologies to those who have read it and are now making their way through this, my second (and probably last) book, allow me to whet your appetite for this earlier volume with some its highlights.

My interest in Clive Staples Lewis, or "Jack" as he was known to family, colleagues, and friends, goes back to my college days, when I first read *The Screwtape Letters*, the work that made him best known to readers in the English-speaking world. (He acquired the nickname Jack, when at the age of four or thereabouts he announced one morning to the family that his name was "Jacksie", soon thereafter shortened to Jack, and refused thereafter to answer to any other.) It was not until 1972, however, that I began reading him in earnest. While living that summer in the north of England, I found many of his books in paperback in the bookstore of the University of Durham, and took them with me to Switzerland for reading during the winter. My reason for beginning to collect his first editions, however, goes back to our passing through London for the first time, on our way home from India nine years earlier.

A guided tour of London took us to some famous pubs, frequented by great literary figures of the past, and I became enamored of these marvelous establishments, with their dark wood decor, walls often covered with green felt, brass fittings, stained glass windows, all producing a unique ambience. Many pubs, especially in the larger cities, are nothing but smoke-filled drinking places, but the *real* ones are wonderful neighborhood social clubs. In many smaller English communities they may be the only place other than the parish church where neighbors can gather, and, sadly, the parish church is second choice for many.

When we moved to Indianapolis from Washington, D.C. in 1966, we bought an old brick-and-stone English tudor-style home on Meridian Street that simply cried out for a pub as decor for the basement recreation room. But it couldn't be a mere replica like Union Jack's or those other commercial establishments with their reproduction pub mirrors and signs. Only the real thing would do, so on subsequent trips to Europe and the Middle East, I began assembling my pub.

In London's flea markets and low-end shops were to be found a marvelous assortment of bits and pieces of genuine old pub hardware, the result of the efforts of the breweries (who own most of the British pubs) to modernize their establishments. My check-in luggage at Heathrow *en route* home soon began bulging with brass fittings, decorated beer pump handles, old pewter mugs, old bottles, and other pub paraphernalia. Carrying on board an antique advertising mirror with its ¼" glass was a particular challenge – asking permission to board first so I could stow it away, rushing to the rear of the plane to be wrapped in blankets and placed on the piles of trash bags inevitably found in the closets of TWA flights from London, and then standing in front of the curtains to inform other passengers that "this one is full but the closet on the other side of the galley is empty."

Although I was able to find an antique English back-bar among a container of goods arriving in an Indianapolis at a wholesale antique establishment, there was little chance of anyone importing a 12-foot long bar. However, when I lucked upon a beautifully crafted, ancient grocery store counter in a barn in southern Indiana, I hauled it home on a trailer, worked on it for over a year to remove layers of white paint, and finished off my pub with a magnificent walnut-stained piece of furniture, complete with brass rail. Well, almost finished it off..... All it lacked was a hundred-year-old brass cash register – and after searching fruitlessly for years in England, at last I found one at an antique show in Indianapolis. Manufactured by National Cash Register in Dayton, Ohio, with its tabs in pounds, shillings, and pence, it had been exported to England at the turn of the century and now found its way back home.

My pub thus became a reality, with its walls covered in green felt, and its ancient brassware gleaming amidst the rich dark brown of the woodwork. But it lacked an essential feature – a name. The names of British pubs reflect the rich history, mythology, and other elements of the erstwhile British Empire – the Duke of Wellington, the Bear and Ragged Staff, Jack the Ripper, the Cheshire Cheese, George and Dragon – to name but a few of a seemingly endless variety. With my library now graced by a proper British pub, an appropriate sign was in order.

On the next stopover in England I visited Oxford for the first time, and there my quest ended. I had never heard of the *Eagle and Child* until I wandered into it one evening, and to my surprise saw a small wooden plaque on the wall:

C. S. Lewis, his brother, W. H. Lewis, J. R. R. Tolkien, Charles Williams, and other friends met every Tuesday morning between the years 1939-1962 in the back room of this their favourite pub. These men, popularly known as the "Inklings", met here to drink beer and to discuss, among other things, the books they were writing.

I learned from Mr. Reading, the publican (the manager of a brewery-owned pub, as are most of the British pubs), that the sign during Lewis's time had been replaced by a smaller one of different design when the brewery renovated the building some years earlier. The old sign had been given to the man who had been Lewis's secretary for a short time before Lewis's death – which is how I first met Walter Hooper, editor of most of the many posthumously-published works of Lewis, and a close friend these many years since. I took a picture of Walter's sign and gave it to a London artist specializing in the reproduction of old pub signs.

These meetings of the Inklings have been memorialized in at least two works of fiction by Oxford authors, one having been featured in the popular British television series, *Inspector Morse*:

In the back bar of the Eagle and Child in St. Giles', the two men sat and drank their beer, and Lewis found himself reading and reading again the writing on the wooden plaque on the wall behind Morse's head. And strangely enough it was Sergeant Lewis's mind, after (for him) a rather liberal intake of alcohol, which was waxing the more imaginative as he pictured a series of fundamental emendations to this received text: "CHIEF INSPECTOR MORSE, with his friend and colleague Sergeant Lewis, sat in this back room one Thursday, in order to solve...."

The only Lewis works in my library thus far were paperbacks -- a rather tacky accumulation vis-a-vis the many attractively bound old tomes. With most Lewis titles then being published only in paperback, it would be necessary to seek out the earlier printings – but if one were going to that length, why not enjoy the distinction of having the very first printing? Little did I realize the implications of that decision.

About that time we were scheduled to join two good friends, Hal and Betsy Guffey, on an extensive tour of the Middle East, visiting associates of International Students, Inc., of which Hal was president and on whose Board of Trustees I served. Pat and I decided to meet them in London, stopping *en route* in Dublin, having never before visited Ireland. There I began my first search for Lewis first editions, assuming, however, that Catholic Ireland would not likely be a repository of books by a Protestant writer of religious works. In a sense I was correct, finding only two common titles in the dozen or so bookshops visited—but my reasoning was based on a distinctly false premise. When asked if he might have any Lewis first editions, the proprietor of the first shop visited replied, "I'm sorry to say that I don't—he's so popular that they go out as fast as I get them in."

I did find one of his more common titles, but not until taking a day off and going up to Belfast did I strike gold. What the locals called "the troubles" had turned the city into an armed camp, with British soldiers patrolling the streets and pedestrians being screened and searched at frequent checkpoints in the downtown area. Consulting the yellow pages, I phoned Emerald Isle Books, the nearest antiquarian book dealer, to inquire about the availability of Lewis first editions, and was invited to come to the house because the shop was closed. This proved to be the beginning of a close friendship with Jack and Jean Gamble, whose shop was, in fact, nonexistent as the result of being blown up by IRA thugs only two days earlier. Two men had come to the house on the pretext of wanting an appraisal on a rare book of Irish history, one of whom had taken Jack to the shop at gun point in order to plant a huge bomb while the other held Jean and the children hostage. The purpose of the bombing was to destroy a British police post next door, but all that was accomplished was the destruction of some 50,000 books and a now condemned building.

Despite interruptions by police, newsmen, and his attorney, Jack graciously showed me through the house, in which books lined the shelves of almost every room. Two hours of browsing produced a dozen or so Lewis first editions, and my collection was well underway by the time Jack drove me to the train for the return to Dublin. Over the years he has provided me with some of my finest acquisitions, and Pat and I have enjoyed their hospitality on each of our further visits to Northern Ireland.

On one such visit I had the unexpected privilege of having lunch with an American hero, former astronaut Jim Irwin. Jack told me one day that an accountant friend of his had mentioned that Jim was in town and had accepted an invitation to meet for lunch in the accountant's office with a few of his friends. When Jack noted that he had an American visitor, I was also invited to share their table.

Jim was seriously affected in two very different ways as the result of his walks on the moon on two Apollo missions – his heart was subjected to severe strain on the Apollo 15 mission, and his experience in space brought him closer to God than he had ever been, leading to his founding of the Christian ministry, High Flight. Although he was deemed to have fully recovered from the assault on his heart, he had his first heart attack only six months later – and although he lived for another twenty years, he died of a heart attack at the age of 61.

75 – Serendipity, thy name is golden

Even thirty years ago, first editions of Lewis's works were in considerable demand, and well-preserved copies of the more popular titles were already scarce. I began buying every first edition I could lay my hands on, but soon learned that condition is all important in the book collecting world – and the price differential between a fine copy in like dust jacket can be many-fold that of an identical copy without the jacket. A superb copy of *The Lion, the Witch, and the Wardrobe* in a fine dust jacket, for example, today sells for as much as $18,000, whereas an equally fine copy of the book alone can be had for about 90 percent less.

One soon learns which titles are the most difficult to find and which are more common. In the early days, browsing through bookstores was the only way in which I could find books, but in becoming known to various dealers I would sometimes be contacted by them when they had something of special note. It was thus that I gained ownership of one of the very few Lewis manuscripts ever to come on the market (indeed, one of but a few manuscripts of his published works that still exist) – and whose existence was unknown until it fell into the hands of an obscure London dealer shortly before I acquired it.

Somewhere around 1930, Lewis wrote the draft of a short story in what we would today call a "composition book" – a note-book in heavy board covers, comprising 150 or so pages. It was a rather strange story about a man who had been born blind, but through surgery in adulthood regained his sight. He becomes obsessed with knowing what "light" is, and drives his poor wife up the wall with questions when she tries her best to answer him, not grasping that light is not something one sees but is that by which objects can be seen. He concludes that people are keeping something from him and that he really doesn't see very well. In his quest to find light, while out on a walk one day he finds an artist painting at the edge of a stone quarry. When the latter comments that there's some great light down in the quarry, the man leans over to look, and falls to his death. (I said it was a rather strange story!)

After Lewis's death in 1963, Walter Hooper was given responsibility by the estate to go through all of Lewis's paper, at which time he came across this short story, as well as the first 72 pages of a much longer story. In 1977 he published both of these in *The Dark Tower and Other Stories*, giving the title, *The Man Born Blind*, to the short one. The original is written on seven right-hand pages in the note-book, but on the left side opposite page four Lewis has rewritten one of the paragraphs, and on the next three blank pages has further revised that paragraph. Not knowing what to make of this, Walter simply made mention of it in the preface, and published only the seven pages as originally written.

Unknown to Walter and anyone else, Lewis soon thereafter redrafted the entire story, and presumably sent the final version, written on four sheets of lined paper, to an unknown magazine publisher – as evidenced by the notation in the upper right corner: "From C. S. Lewis, Magdalen College, Oxford". The story was not published, nor was the manuscript returned, showing up nearly fifty years later among some papers acquired by an obscure London secondhand book dealer. He sold it to another dealer, who in turn sold it to the dealer from whom I purchased it after he offered it to me by phone.

What is most remarkable about the acquisition of this manuscript is that it is directly related to the only other Lewis manuscript to come on the market during my collecting days, acquired only a few years later and from a very different source. Although this one also had not been published, it was the subject of a lengthy academic treatise by a Canadian scholar: *C. S. Lewis's "Great War" with Owen Barfield,* by Lionel Adey. Its Latin title, neatly printed by Lewis on the first page of the same type of black note-book he used for the first draft of the *Light* manuscript, is *CLIVI HAMILTONIS SUMMAE METAPHYSICES CONTRA ANTHROPOSOPHOS LIBRI II*, "Clive Hamilton" being the same pseudonym he used for his first two published works – his given first name and his mother's maiden name. Begun in November 1928, the manuscript is the culmination of the "Great War" between Lewis and his friend, Owen Barfield. In his autobiography, *Surprised by Joy,* Lewis notes: "Barfield's conversion to Anthroposophy (*1923*) marked the beginning of what I can only describe as the Great War between him and me. It was never, thank God, a quarrel, though it could have become one in a moment if he had used to me anything like the violence I allowed myself to him. But it was almost an incessant disputation, sometimes by letter and sometimes face to face, which lasted for years. And this Great War was one of the turning points of my life."

After three pages of index, Lewis filled the next sixty-eight pages with his arguments against anthroposophy and mailed the note-book to Barfield in London. Barfield made cursory notes throughout the text, and then on page 71 wrote the title of his reply – *REPLIZIT ANTHROPOSOPHOS BARFIELDUS* – followed by thirty-six pages of response to specific sections of Lewis's arguments. He mailed the note-book back to Lewis, who then responded with twelve pages of further argument. The discourse ends at that point, but laid into the note-book when I acquired it from Owen were fifteen neatly handwritten sheets of additional argument later sent to him by Lewis. When I asked him about this, Owen said that he just tired of the written exchange and didn't bother to return the book to Jack – who himself tired of waiting for it and sent the additional fifteen pages.

Sometime during this same period in the late 1920s Jack wrote the first draft of the short story, to which he gave the title *Light* in the final version sent for publication. In the introduction to the excellent book, *Light on C. S. Lewis*, edited by Jocelyn Gibb two years after Lewis's death, Owen Barfield wrote in the introduction:

"And it was about the same time, or a little later, that he further expressed his own position in the form of a short story about a man born blind, who recovered his sight by an operation. The result was disastrous for the protagonist, because he insisted upon trying to see *the mysterious thing he had heard people calling 'light'; whereas you do not see light itself, but only the objects it illumines. Light is what you see* by. *As far as I know, this was never published."*

Although I had read *Light on C. S. Lewis* years before acquiring both these manuscripts, I did not recall this comment by Barfield, and it was not until several years later that I learned that Lewis had written the short story largely as a further argument in their Great War. That revelation came from a most unlikely source – an American missionary doctor in Kathmandu, Nepal, by way of the pastor of a church in northern New Jersey! Both men were ardent Lewis scholars, and when the pastor, Jerry Daniels, heard that I had acquired the *Light* manuscript, he wrote to ask if he might have a copy to send to his friend, Dr. Steven Thorson, in Nepal, who was writing a thesis on the Great War. Steve later visited me while on furlough from Nepal, telling me of the connection between these two manuscripts. What an amazing "coincidence" that the only two Lewis manuscripts to have come on the market during my collecting days should have been so closely related. But there have been many such instances in which such precious Lewis items have come into my hands, confirming in retrospect God's direction in all of it -- too many to include in this account of my life, but many to be found in *In Pursuit of C. S. Lewis.*

Why are so few manuscripts of so prolific a writer no longer in existence? The answer lies in the legendary Lewis frugality. When a manuscript was returned after being published, he viewed it only as a source of "scratch paper", tearing the sheets in half and using the blank sides for notes. When the notes were of no further use, they were consigned to what he called the "wpb" (waste paper basket) – but even then some would find further use. Folding a discarded note into a "stick" long enough to reach through the grate of the gas heater in his study, he would light the paper with an ordinary match and use the stick to light the fire.

Only one such scrap of paper from one of his manuscripts is known to have survived, retrieved as a souvenir by a teenage girl who worked at the Lewis home during the war. She was June Flewett, daughter of a prominent professor of Latin in London, and came to be dearly loved by the Lewis brothers, who carried on a friendship with her the remainder of their lives. Today she is Lady Freud, living in London with her husband, Sir Clement Freud, grandson of Sigmund Freud and a prominent former member of Parliament. Through an autograph dealer cousin of Lady Freud I acquired some years ago that scrap of paper, folded and burned along one edge, with penciled notes on the reverse—the sole remnant of the manuscript of *Beyond Personality*. Studying the penciled notes upon my return from England, I was astonished to find that they were the initial notes for his next book, *Christian Behaviour*, the text appearing in the opening paragraph of the book in slightly modified form.

Consider the sequence of events resulting in the survival of what is undoubtedly the most significant and only fragment of that manuscript because of the penciled notes on the back: ….a page ripped in two, used, discarded, used again for a very different purpose, again discarded, consigned to the trash, retrieved as a souvenir by a teenage girl who "happened" to choose that particular scrap as a souvenir and kept it for 50 years with no knowledge of the significance of the penciled notes – and now a trophy displayed in the Taylor University library, to be shared with all. The odds of this incredible sequence defy calculation

76 – And the beat goes on….

Such serendipity in finding a hidden treasure in the purchase of another treasure was mine on another occasion. For years I had sought a copy of his first book, *Spirits in Bondage*, and when one finally turned up in London in 1985, I happily bought it, although disappointed that the original owner had defaced it by writing his name and address at the top of the title page. Hopefully, I would eventually be able to replace it with a virgin copy. That was the summer we were living in Oxford, toward the end of which time I was reading *They Stand Together*, the collection of letters to his boyhood friend in Belfast, Arthur Greeves, In one of these he notes having visited his uncle in Scotland. In a footnote the editor, Walter Hooper, notes the name of the uncle and that he lived in Helensburgh. A light flashed in my memory bank, and I rushed to the bookshelf, frantically opening my copy of *Spirits in Bondage*. Yes, the inscribed name and address of that thoughtless person was none other than that of his uncle Richard. What was first regarded as a defacement suddenly became a thing of beauty, not only adding greatly to the monetary value of the book but even more to the pleasure of having a copy that belonged to a family member. I know of only one other such copy of that very rare book – one given to his father and now in the Wade Center at Wheaton College.

In the almost 20 years since, I have known of only half a dozen or so other copies of the first edition of *Spirits in Bondage* that have come on the market. A copy was offered to me about ten years ago at what then seemed too high a price, and being content with the one I had, I turned it down. It is now in the Lilly Library of rare books at Indiana University in Bloomington, who purchased it for a fraction of its present value. Live and learn!

Like any collectible, be it coins, stamps, or whatever, condition is of prime importance. With Lewis first editions going back some eighty years, and with many of them having been printed during World War II, when quality paper and binding material were usually unavailable, much of the search had been to improve existing copies. Books without dust jackets needed them, and those with jackets needed better ones. By the time the collection went to Taylor seven years ago, I had accumulated multiple copies of every Lewis title, only the finest of which was in the collection. Thus left with more than two hundred Lewis first editions, I let it be known through a couple of websites devoted to him and his works that I had Lewis first editions for sale.

More recently I have added Lewis letters to those acquired years ago. Lewis received prodigious numbers of letters from colleagues, friends, and admirers, and as busy as he was with his academic responsibilities, speaking engagements, and writing books and pamphlets, he never failed to answer a letter. However, few appear on the market today, most having been contributed by their owners to the Bodleian Library at Oxford University, as well as to the Marian Wade Center at Wheaton College by students who had written to Lewis while taking courses from its founder, Dr. Clyde Kilby.

I had the privilege of meeting Dr. Kilby after he had retired from the Wade Center, and it was due to his kindness that I acquired the finest prize of all – the complete collection of the 44 original drawings by Pauline Baynes for the second of the Narnia books, *Prince Caspian*. Soon after publication of each of the other six Narnia titles, the publisher returned her drawings to her, but somehow those for *Prince Caspian* went astray, and not until 30 years later were they discovered in a file drawer of another publisher, to whom they had been sent for publication of the paperback edition. The finder dutifully returned them to Pauline, who then contacted Dr. Kilby to ask if he might know of someone who would like to buy them. He generously referred her to me, and thus did I not only acquire this treasure but a lasting friendship as well with this talented artist.

With relatively little time now needed to pursue this hobby, I began devoting some of my spare time to a very different venture. Having been aware of the need for the rapid and easy diagnosis of anemia, one of the most common medical conditions seen in the Third World, I undertook improving the prototype of a small piece of laboratory equipment developed by a Texan friend, Dr. Kendall Smith – a microhematocrit minicentrifuge. By spinning at 12,000 rpm a tiny glass tube filled with blood from a finger prick, the percentage of packed red cells (the hematocrit) could be instantly read from a scale printed alongside the tube on the rotor.

The key component was a unique 3" plastic rotor, designed in Germany for the great Bayer Corporation's Diagnostics Division, and used in their fine little machine about the size of a common brick, which sold for about $800. Kendall had obtained the rotor from Bayer's parts department and attached it to a small 6 volt DC motor mounted in a plastic box, the whole assembly, less the rotor, costing less than $10 – very crude in appearance, but it worked. Over time I was able to improve upon the design to the point that it could be run on internal rechargeable batteries or by an external AC/DC adaptor connected to any AC voltage, and looked as if it had been factory-produced rather than made in my basement. For situations in which no external power was available to recharge the batteries, I found a simple solar charger for that purpose.

I sent a number of these to various friends in mission hospitals in Africa and elsewhere, but eventually Bayer increased the price of the rotor so much that it became impractical to produce the machine at an affordable price. I met with the plant manager at their factory in Ireland, who thought he could get the price down, but Bayer's head office refused his request for a much lower price he had calculated. Soon thereafter, when Bayer ceased production of their machine for lack of sales, I asked them if I could buy the five different rotor components directly from their suppliers, in order to assemble the rotors myself. The negotiations took some time, but eventually I was able to get the parts from Ireland, Germany, and Austria.

Although getting the word out to small mission clinics that most need the device has been somewhat frustrating, the Lord has provided an unforeseen – and very unusual – market for the device to help support the project. An eBay listing has led to orders from veterinarians who make house calls and from owners of anemic cats who use it to test their cats at home and thus avoid frequent visits to the veterinarian! Thus far I have had orders from cat owners as far away as Italy and Germany.

Profits from sales of the many surplus Lewis first editions remaining after my basic collection went to Taylor University have enabled us to enjoy a considerable increase in giving to Christian ministries. Collecting the works of the foremost Christian writer of the twentieth century has been a fascinating hobby, and the investment of time and financial resources has been wonderfully rewarding, as God honors his promises to those who recognize that everything we have – our lives, our possessions, our hope, our dreams – belongs to him. We are only stewards of what he has given us, and our responsibility is to manage it all as he directs us. But conducting even a part-time business such as this consumes far too many hours in front of a computer, sending and receiving email, so I am rapidly winding it down, It is time to move on.

77 – Quo vadis?

In his great work, *Quo Vadis*, Nobel Laureate Henryk Sienkiewicz has Peter asking Jesus, *"Quo vadis, Domine?"* – "Where are you going, Lord?" *My* question at this juncture is, "Where are you taking me, Lord?" In my past eighty years God has demonstrated over and over the wonder of his grace, just as he bestows abundantly on all who recognize that we have all been born with a sinful nature, the only cure for which is surrendering ourselves to Jesus Christ and letting him guide us in all we do.

As Billy Graham has said when asked in recent years when he planned to retire, "I don't see anything in the Bible about retirement.". My own concept of retirement for a follower of Jesus Christ is simply the end of a salaried job. Beyond that, one continues to devote the equivalent of a working day to productive labor with the privilege of spreading those "working hours" throughout the day and evening and over the weekend, as circumstances dictate and one's physical condition permits. Like a regular job, time may be taken for relaxation and refreshment, including pure vacationing – but allowing the latter to become a prominent feature of "retirement" seems to me to be hardly pleasing to our Lord.

These "golden years" are the time for reflection, and while one can and should look back at one's errors and omissions and wonder how he might have done better, it is not the time for self-flagellation. Surely I have done great disservice to my wife and children through my frequent and often extended absences, especially to my children in their early years, and I pray that they have forgiven me. But one can't go back, so my overwhelming desire is to see children, grandchildren, other family members and friends who have not yet turned their lives over to Jesus Christ do so.

My greatest hope is for them to recognize their need for a personal relationship with him as the only assurance of spending eternity with the God who loves them so much that he gave his only son as a sacrifice for the sinful nature with which all of us are born. Sadly, most of us are too preoccupied with making a living, raising a family, or whatever else we're doing to spend any time thinking about what will happen to us when this present life is over. Even more disturbing is the fact that so many of us have been deceived in believing that we will merit entrance to heaven if we lead moral lives, treat others with respect, help those in need, and generally do our best to be good persons.

Unfortunately, that isn't how it works. The owner's manual that God gives us – the Bible – makes it abundantly clear that there is absolutely nothing we can do by way of "good works" to earn our salvation. It is a free gift, paid in full by his son 2000 years ago. But a gift is only of value to the one who accepts it.

Our loving God turns no one away. He leaves the choice to us. We can choose to spend eternity with him, or we can choose to be forever separated from him. As C. S. Lewis succinctly put it, "There are only two kinds of people in the end: those who say to God, 'Thy will be done', and those to whom God says, '*Thy* will be done.' " My fervent prayer is that those I love who have not yet made such a choice will choose Jesus Christ.

Pat and I have been richly blessed with a family extending into Europe and Asia. Number one son Ted, still living in California, has pursued a highly successful career in computer science which has taken and continues to take him all over the world, while his wife Carrie works in the San Francisco assessor's office. Number two son Jack and his wife Jan have recently resettled in Dallas where he is happily engaged in a new career of developing medical software after many years of service in emergency medicine in Indiana and Kansas. Their older son Matt carries on the family tradition as a medical student, daughter Liz is a third grade teacher, and younger son Andy is completing an MBA, all of them still in Kansas.

Our daughter Wende, who began her career as a fourth grade teacher, now works with students having special needs on a one-to-one basis at Heritage Christian School in Indianapolis, where youngest child Stephen is in high school. Older daughter Kiersten has completed her studies in food management at Indiana's Ball State University, while her younger sister Kayla has begun studies at Purdue University. Jeff, husband and father, is a valued employee of Eli Lilly and Company, responsible for printed packaging materials.

We thus have one contingent of the family still with us in Indiana, but the remainder are widely scattered, with brother Dick and his wife Jean, together in New York with their large family – daughters Bonnie and Molly, and sons Rick and Scott with their wives Jackie and Debby. Brother Paul and his wife Ruth are in North Carolina, with son Steve and his wife Mary in Connecticut; son Alan and his wife Whitney in Thessaloniki, Greece, as missionaries; and son Bruce and his wife Sandra in Florida. Brother Dave's widow, Carole, is in Oregon with son Benjamin and his wife Angela, while daughter Sarah lives in North Carolina.

Despite the distances that separate us, we have always managed to keep closely together in love and with family reunions that brought everyone – or nearly everyone – together from time to time, as well as frequent visits with one another. We have borne each other's suffering in the loss of family members and shared the joys of each other's accomplishments. We have experienced the importance of family, and are deeply disturbed by all that is going on in our society that leads to disintegration of family.

I am deeply grateful for the privilege of living on an earth that is still rich with beauty despite all that has been done which mars that beauty – but earth is not my home. Thanks to his monumental work, *Heaven*, my favorite living author and friend, Randy Alcorn, has me eager to go home. However, despite the best medical opinion many years ago that forecast an abbreviated life span, and more recent diagnoses of equally threatening disorders, I find myself free of any seriously disabling symptoms, suggesting that my Lord and Savior Jesus Christ may be leading in some new direction for the ninth decade of life. The past two decades since official retirement have included too much precious time devoted to often trivial pursuits. It seems time for a change.

www.ingramcontent.com/pod-product-compliance
Lightning Source LLC
Chambersburg PA
CBHW031236290426
44109CB00012B/316